Rudd v. Abbott

"POWER TRIP"

RUDD

v.

ABBOTT

"POLITICAL ANIMAL"

TWO CLASSIC QUARTERLY ESSAYS BY

DAVID MARR

Black Inc.

Published by Black Inc.,
an imprint of Schwartz Media Pty Ltd
37–39 Langridge Street
Collingwood VIC 3066 Australia
email: enquiries@blackincbooks.com
http://www.blackincbooks.com

A Cataloguing-in-Publication entry is available from
the National Library of Australia

ISBN: 9781863956338 (pbk.)

Printed in Australia by Griffin Press. The paper this book is printed on
is certified against the Forest Stewardship Council® Standards. Griffin
Press holds FSC chain of custody certification SGS-COC-005088.
FSC promotes environmentally responsible, socially beneficial and
economically viable management of the world's forests.

Contents

POWER TRIP

*The Political Journey of
Kevin Rudd*

Wonderful, Wonderful

"Those Chinese fuckers are trying to rat-fuck us," declared Kevin Rudd. As snow fell on Copenhagen – on its palaces and squats, on police and their dogs, on protesters rugged up against the fierce cold and on the big, bland Bella Center where the largest gathering of world leaders in history sulked and plotted – the prime minister of Australia faced the collapse of old dreams. This was the little boy fascinated by China, the kid who longed to be a diplomat, the man who believed a better world might be built through international agreement, and a prime minister struggling to meet "one of the greatest moral, economic and environmental challenges of our age." Life had brought him, inevitably it seemed, to this icy Scandinavian city a few days before Christmas 2009 and he blamed the Chinese for wrecking it all.

The Copenhagen that mattered began on 17 December and lasted forty hours. Rudd slept for one of them. He wasn't shy. He relished working with the big boys. Almost to the very end he was a player in the meetings that mattered. He began the last long haul working with Gordon Brown to try to persuade low-lying states like Kiribati and the Maldives to let the world warm a little more than 1.5 degrees. Mid-morning saw him deliver his set speech to the full plenary in the big hall. It was superior Rudd – pared down, not too much jargon, only a little mawkish about Gracie:

> Before I left Australia, I was presented with a book of handwritten letters from a group of six-year-olds. One of the letters is from Gracie. Gracie is six. "Hi," she wrote. "My name is Gracie. How old are you?" Gracie continues, "I am writing to you because I want you all to be strong in Copenhagen. Please listen to us as it is our future."
> I fear that at this conference, we are on the verge of letting little Gracie down.

Australians with sharp ears might have picked the trademark boast that Rudd had done his homework: "If you examine, as I have done, the 102 square bracketed areas of disagreement that lie in the existing text before us …"

After Queen Margrethe's state dinner at the Christiansborg Palace – Rudd so monopolised Princess

Mary's attentions that the British prime minister on her other side was left staring at his plate – he joined Nicolas Sarkozy, Angela Merkel, Brown and another twenty world leaders in freewheeling and futile efforts to find agreement. At 3 a.m. they left the haggling to their environment ministers. By this time delegates were sleeping on sofas all over the Bella Center. Rudd had an hour's kip in an armchair, all he felt he needed to keep going.

Barack Obama jetted into the city that morning and joined the talks. The United States was offering little in the way of emissions cuts but wanted what the president called accountability. "Without any accountability, any agreement would be empty words on a page," Obama told the delegates. Absent was Wen Jiabao. The snub was deliberate. Rudd believed the Chinese were intent on sabotaging any deal that involved binding obligations and international monitoring.

Tired and exasperated, surrounded by a knot of Australian officials and press, Rudd began to rage against the Chinese. He needed sleep. His anger was real, but his language seemed forced, deliberately foul. In this mood, he'd been talking about countries "rat-fucking" each other for days. Was a deal still possible, asked one of the Australians. "Depends whether those rat-fucking Chinese want to fuck us."

Obama postponed his departure a few hours. At nightfall on an already endless day, the leaders of the twenty-six nations met again, with Wen Jiabao once more pointedly absent. The *Guardian*'s Mark Lynas reported the Chinese blocking every initiative:

> "Why can't we even mention our own targets?" demanded a furious Angela Merkel. Australia's prime minister, Kevin Rudd, was annoyed enough to bang his microphone.

The bones of the Copenhagen Accord were decided that evening in a meeting between the US, China, India, Brazil and South Africa. Rudd was not there. The leaders agreed to vague targets, no monitoring and more gatherings down the track. This bare deal was sent on to Rudd's group of leaders. Meanwhile Obama briefed the US press and flew out on *Air Force One*. When Rudd emerged an hour later, he had to be told the world already knew the outcome. Addressing reporters with barely the energy to take notes, he declared bravely: "We prevailed. Some will be disappointed by the amount of progress. The alternative was, frankly, catastrophic collapse of these negotiations."

His efforts at Copenhagen are Rudd's answer to those who accuse him of being a bureaucrat at heart, an incrementalist, a leader unable to dream. He sees Copenhagen as proof that he's willing to go out on a limb, spend political capital and court trouble at home for a great cause. And Rudd insists Copenhagen was not a failure. He is one of an unusual species: the diplomat turned leader. Though his time in the foreign service was a brief seven years, they've marked him for life. For the diplomat, negotiations have never failed so long as there's a prospect, however vague, of agreement somewhere down the track. For someone who thinks as he does, it can be just as important to keep everyone at the table, to keep talks going, to keep hopes alive, as it is to bring great issues to a head. The rhetoric of success Rudd used in these exhausted hours wasn't all spin. It was authentic Rudd.

That he was still on his feet seemed a miracle. This least athletic of men has deep emotional and physical resilience. His climate-change minister, Penny Wong, was dead on her feet. Rudd seemed unaware of this. He was taken aside and urged to get her out of there, to get her to her hotel. Wong found a shower somewhere and stayed on for the last session. Later that morning Copenhagen came to a formal end, with the parties merely "noting" the vague deal brokered by Obama and Wen Jiabao.

Rudd's bond with the people began to fray after Copenhagen. Having picked him as a leader long before he became his party's choice, Australians had held Rudd in extraordinary affection for years. Never had the polls shown a prime minister so popular for so long. But after this debacle the mood shifted. Malcolm Turnbull had fallen. His place as leader of the Opposition was taken by a Tory head-kicker unembarrassed to embrace the denialists' cause. The old consensus on climate change, which Rudd had identified himself with so closely, began to melt away. In April 2010 when he abandoned his emissions trading scheme until the far reaches of a second term, the people and the polls turned on him savagely. His leadership was in question. Rudd had sold himself to the Australian people as a new kind of leader: a man of intellect and values out to reshape the future. If he isn't that, people are asking, what is he? And who is he? Rudd seems to have been with us forever yet still be a newcomer, indeed a stranger, in the Lodge. Millions of words have been written about him since he emerged from the Labor pack half-a-dozen years ago, but Rudd remains hidden in full view.

If Australia saw him through Canberra's eyes, he would be done for. Though he has led until now a formidably disciplined first-term government – few leaks, only one minister lost – negotiated the global banking crisis of 2008 with exemplary skill, pulled off the great symbolic coup of the Apology and routed two Opposition leaders, the capital is tired of him. He's seen in that little world of power as a weird guy and a failing prime minister. He puzzles his caucus, frustrates his ministers and irritates the press. The *Australian* has turned on him with a determination often as comic as it's brutal. He is accused of running a chaotic office and bullying public servants. A habit of making endless speeches at big public events has earned the man – known at various times in his career as Dr Death, Pixie, Harry Potter and Heavy Kevvie – a new nickname: the Castro of the South Pacific.

When his approval rating began to dip sharply in the polls in early 2010, commentators wondered if he might be the first prime minister since Scullin back in the Depression to lose power after only a single term. There was speculation that he was in a very delicate position: essentially friendless in the party and ripe for decapitation by Julia Gillard even before the looming elections. The impossible was being touted despite the debts owed by the party to only the third man in sixty years to bring Labor from Opposition to government. But the strange patterns of the man's political career left him oddly vulnerable.

He is not Labor's leader because he reshaped the party around him as Gough Whitlam did. Nor was he a favourite son like Bob Hawke. Nor did he wrest the leadership after long internal warfare as Paul

Keating did. Rudd leads no faction in the party and has won few friends in caucus. His rise to power was a peculiar triumph over his own party's opposition – indeed, derision – achieved by appealing directly to the Australian people. Rudd's dominance in the party is first and foremost about the polls.

Leaders aren't there to be liked. Being an arsehole is no bar to high office. They always disappoint. The public understands this. And people know the climb to power can be bloody. Such things are forgiven if it all proves worthwhile. But of Rudd it has to be said that there is a large number of people who, having worked with him as a diplomat, public servant, shadow minister, leader of the Opposition or lately as prime minister, loathe the man. Between the verdicts of the public and those who come to know him face to face, there is a curiously wide gulf. It's narrowing fast. Mark Latham once told him that he only held his position in the party "because of his media profile and public standing among people who have never actually met him." That's characteristically cruel, but it points to the fundamental question about Rudd that remains unanswered: who is he?

Colleagues from his time as the key back-room boy in Wayne Goss's reforming government have an old joke they trot out whenever they meet to talk about those days of high hopes and disappointment.

They don't remember Rudd kindly. The joke: he is a creature from outer space. The proof? Who but an android would say so often, "I am only human."

Eumundi Lost

On 14 December 1968, Bert Rudd drove his white Rambler down to Brisbane for an afternoon of indoor bowls followed by a dinner at the Buffalo Temple in Fortitude Valley. He drank beer and whiskey at both. Driving home alone to the farm where 120 cows would be waiting to be milked in the morning, he hit a telegraph pole near Caboolture. The impact ruptured his spleen. He was taken to Royal Brisbane Hospital where he died of septicaemia eight weeks later.

His son Kevin was eleven. For a long time, he wouldn't tell the story of the bad years that followed his father's death. That he'd grown up a dreamy barefoot kid on a dairy farm was no secret, but what happened then was something friends and colleagues knew little or nothing about. They didn't ask questions. They sensed his childhood was a no-go zone. Rudd was forty-five and beginning his run for the leadership of the Labor Party before he began talking of the events that still drive his plain, conservative politics. That long silence says much about Rudd's pride. Until it became necessary to speak about those hard years, he thought them better forgotten. He wanted to be known for what he had become and what he had achieved rather than the mess his family found itself in when he was a boy. He couldn't claim the Rudds had suffered a uniquely terrible tragedy. Others had it much worse. So secret was the family's past that when the dire circumstances of his early years provoked a political hullabaloo before the elections of 2007, there were cousins in the hills round Nambour who had never heard of the hardship Marge Rudd and the kids endured after Bert's death.

Nambour was a place of secrets and high expectations, where respectable families didn't complain, worked hard and got on with things. Sugar, milk and government were the business of a town dominated, as it had been for the best part of a century, by the chimney of the sugar mill and the Methodist church – first weatherboard and then brick – on Maud Street. "The drive to create strong civic, commercial and educational institutions flowed strongly through the Nambour burghers' blood and spirit," argued Professor Michael Wesley in *Griffith Review*. "Sober men with stubborn jaws" set the rules the town still lived by. New people were pouring in, but the old families ran the place:

This fostered the flipside of Nambour's dynamism – the steady stream of people who left. Many who left had absorbed the town's gifts – its cheerful optimism, strong traditions of schooling excellence, public health facilities – but also felt stifled by its proprieties, snobbishness and low horizons.

Rudd's mother Margaret (Marge) De Vere was a well-spoken, fussy, hard-working, teetotal Catholic who trained as a nurse during the War. Her father had taken up farming after first drinking the profits of the Commercial Hotel in Currie Street. The politics of the family were conservative but mixed. Her brothers were solid Country Party: Eddie was Nambour's mayor for years and the other Kevin in the family was chairman of Gympie Shire. Small-town politics was in the blood. Her children would grow up with close family connections to the political machine that ran Queensland. But her own politics were even more conservative: Labor until the great Split of 1954, after which she cast her vote for the Catholic Church-backed Democratic Labor Party for forty years.

Bert Rudd was a blow-in from New South Wales who came to the district with a mate after the War. The Rudds – no relation to "Steele Rudd," creator of Dad and Dave – were from way down the heap:

Protestant fettlers and rural labourers from around Wagga. Convict stock. Bert and Marge met at a dance and married in the Catholic Church in 1948. Bert didn't convert. He remained, like so many in the district, a keen member of the Buffalo Lodge. A first son, Malcolm, was born swiftly in 1949; a daughter, Loree, followed in 1950; another son, Gregory, came a few years later; and baby Kevin appeared in September 1957. By the most perfect coincidence Labor lost power that week to the Country Party in Queensland. Rudd would be intimately involved in the party's return to office thirty-two years later.

The Rudds were living in a neat little house on a low rise outside the village of Eumundi. Bert was share-farming for Aubrey Low, the milk and butter Czar of the district. Kevin was sickly and lived in the protective embrace of his mother. An operation at the age of three to correct his badly bowed legs left him having to learn to walk again. Sometime between the age of five and seven he was struck down by rheumatic fever and he found himself once again in hospital and recuperating at home for long stretches. That the fever had affected his heart was not discovered for half-a-dozen years. The damaged heart was on a list of dark Rudd secrets that would only emerge in a Liberal Party smear campaign before the 2007 poll. Did he have the ticker?

The boy was a fussy little dreamer. He had a horse and wandered barefoot to the local primary school, but nothing much was expected of him round the farm: "I was the last in the litter and most of the hard work was done by those who came before me," he told Julia Baird on ABC radio. His sister, Loree, remembers him lost in his own world: "When he was young, he preferred to design castles out of the cow feed in the huge feed-box at the centre of the dairy rather than actually run diligently with the stuff to feed-boxes between cow rotations." His brother Greg complained of sharing a room with a little brother who nagged him about being messy. "Is it so hard," the child would ask, "to pick up those socks and put them in that drawer?" Rudd remembers as a small boy being woken before dawn by his knocka-bout father to be taken on the Anzac Day march: "I always remember in the dim, very early morning light, hearing the gentle clink of medals." Bert still clung to the idea that little Kevin would grow up to be a farmer. "Have you made up your mind?" he asked his ten-year-old one day as they stared down the road. "Is it going to be beef or is it going to be dairy?"

Marge had other plans. She had him learning the piano, turning up at the Eumundi School of Arts in fancy dress – a Chinaman one day and Rubens' Blue

Boy another – and taking ballroom dancing classes. As prime minister he confessed: "I grew up in a Queensland where it was perfectly acceptable for a ten-year-old boy to dance the 'Pride of Erin' for recreation." Into her child's dream world she dropped a book on archaeology. Of the handful of details about his early life Rudd has always been happy to give – the carefree years on the farm, loving parents, an old horse – this is curiously potent: a book about the ancient world with one chapter on China that brought its emperors and armies, temples and palaces to life.

Marge Rudd raised her children Catholic. She took them to mass every Sunday and catechism every second Saturday. "Mum would bellow out the window of the farmhouse across the flats, 'It's time for catechism,'" Rudd told his biographer Robert Macklin. "She had a habit of being able to round you up pretty quickly and get you in there." She and the children said the rosary together in her bedroom on Sunday nights as Bert watched *Disneyland*.

Her faith was strong and individual. She did not go to confession, assuring the priests she made a clean breast of her sins directly to God. She was not sectarian. The moral lessons she taught her children were drawn as often as not from the good example of Protestant worthies of the district. Hers was an "old-style Queensland rural Catholic Country Women's Association" faith, her son would say: "If you saw someone in distress you couldn't be indifferent to that, you had to do something about it." The church's teaching on social justice did not interest her. Rudd did not absorb at her knee the words of Leo XIII's *Rerum Novarum* on the failings of brute capitalism. She wasn't one to bother with Papal encyclicals.

Her God could be cruel. Marge Rudd's favourite passage of the Bible has the Lord tending his vines with secateurs:

Every branch in me that beareth not fruit he taketh away: and every branch that beareth fruit, he purgeth it, that it may bring forth more fruit ... if a man abide not in me, he is cast forth as a branch, and is withered; and men gather them, and cast them into the fire, and they are burned.

Perhaps in this teaching of destruction and renewal she was able to accommodate the calamity that befell the family in the summer of 1968 when her husband crashed the new Rambler outside Caboolture. Her youngest boy had lately turned eleven and she had stayed behind in Eumundi to watch him perform at the Christmas party of the kids' ballroom dancing class in the School of Arts. News of the crash came through to the farmhouse in the early hours of the morning. Most of the next eight weeks she spent at her husband's bedside in Royal Brisbane Hospital. Her youngest boy shuttled back and forth as Bert slowly died. "There were great concerns about the calibre of the surgeons who were operating on him toward the end," Rudd told *Sixty Minutes*' Ellen Fanning nearly thirty years later. He was convinced it was not the crash but the wretched state of Queensland's hospitals that killed his father.

Eumundi has come a long way since then. The dairy farms have gone. Kids wear shoes to school. The Berkelouw brothers have opened one of their swish bookshops on Eumundi Memorial Drive. But all these years later the town is still divided over the fate of the Rudds after Bert's death. The parties have now gone to ground. One of farmer Low's daughters, Jill McCone, had her Sydney solicitors warn me off: I was to cease trying to contact their client. They told me in Eumundi, where Low is remembered as an old drunk who wove down the roads in big American cars, "You'll never get to the truth around here."

Bert Rudd was a sharefarmer. The house came with the job. That Marge Rudd and her children had to leave after his death is not really in dispute. Even so, the departure was humiliating for the mother and child. The boy would later say that being thrown off the farm – the Narnia of his childhood – caused him more anguish than his father's death. He called it *eviction* and told the *Women's Weekly* it came swift and hard:

> Within two or three weeks of Dad's funeral, we were told we had to go … I can remember the terrible discussion between my mother and the fellow who owned the land. That was really tough for Mum – my two brothers were away at school and she had me and my sister, Loree, to care for, but Mum handled herself well and off we went.

But according to McCone, the Rudds' departure was slow and considerate, not the work of a ruthless landlord but the natural order of things in the bush. She told the *Sun-Herald*'s Kerry-Anne Walsh:

Margaret would always have known at some point, inevitably, an incoming farmer would have to occupy the farmhouse. But provisions were put in place by our father for Margaret. He explained to her she could remain on the farm, at no cost whatsoever, until such time as the new farmer arrived … to continuously say he was evicted immediately after his dad's funeral is quite an unbelievable statement. Not only does he blame our father for the so-called eviction, he subsequently mentions having to sleep rough in a car.

Rudd responded furiously when the *Sun-Herald* alerted him in early March 2007 to its scoop. He took it he was being accused of lying and set out, in the words of the *Sydney Morning Herald*'s Alan Ramsey, to kill the story: "And when I say kill, I mean kill. Not deferred, or gutted, or rewritten to suit the Labor leader. Gone altogether. Kaput. Never published."

After a number of abusive calls from Rudd's staff, the paper's editor, Simon Dulhunty, gave him a week's reprieve and sent a journalist north to Eumundi. News next weekend that the story was going ahead reached the leader of the Opposition as he was lunching at the house of the *Daily Telegraph* columnist Piers Akerman. His staff rang and abused Dulhunty. Then Rudd rang and many harsh things were said – e.g. "You're kicking my dead mother in the guts" – in a call that lasted at least half an hour. Dulhunty told Ramsey:

Rudd kept insisting the story shouldn't run. He hung up, but called back again, asserting that to publish would be "a serious mistake," it wasn't right, it was "an assault" on his character. "Cut to the core, Simon," he said. "This is nothing about anyone else, it's not the story of a family's interpretation of events, this is an assault on my character. Cut to the core."

When the shouting died down, Rudd dictated a dignified reply to the Lows' claims that appeared next day in the paper. It was all he had ever needed to say in the first place:

Mr Low got on well with my father and I understand was well respected in the wider community – but he was a tough, very tough businessman, as my mother discovered in her dealings with him after my father's death. I understand that the Low family will want to honour their father's story and the good things I am sure that he did for the wider community, but when it comes to his business dealings with my mum after my dad's death, it is exactly as I have described. Others from the time have exactly the same recollection.

Rudd had made a hash of things. His determination to micro-manage the story left the public with exactly the impression he was desperate to avoid: of being caught peddling a fake hard-luck yarn to win public sympathy. Two truths emerge from this spat. He has a glass jaw. And the loss of his childhood paradise on the edge of Eumundi is a wound that has never healed.

The Rudds were suddenly poor, with only the charity of their De Vere relatives to fall back on – "I didn't find that a terribly dignifying experience," said Rudd – so his mother found a job in a nursing home at Scarborough on the Redcliffe peninsula outside Brisbane. The boy was farmed out to neighbours to finish the term at Eumundi primary, then followed her south. After a brief stint at a local De La Salle school, the little boy turned up halfway through 1969 as a boarder at Marist College Ashgrove in the Brisbane hills. He was a charity case: the school met the bills because Marge Rudd was known as a good Catholic. At about this time, she moved into the Mater Hospital in Brisbane to begin a year's retraining as a nurse.

Ashgrove marked Rudd. He emerged with an icy hatred of the school. "It was tough, harsh, unforgiving, institutional Catholicism of the old school," he told Julia Baird. "I didn't like it." Was there physical abuse, she asked. "Some of the Brothers whacked kids and some were actually quite kind, but it was still the culture, I think it's fair to say – and others would agree with me – which condoned violence." Not all the Brothers were quite in control of themselves. Old boys talk of Brothers beating children for no clear reason in a paroxysm of rage. They seemed to pick on the weak and the lonely. Nor were threats of sexual abuse entirely absent. "Some of the Brothers had a dubious affection for their young charges," Cosima Marriner reported in the *Sydney Morning Herald*. "Former students can still remember the Brother who would always volunteer for shower duty."

The day began at Ashgrove with mass at six. But the other religion of the school was rugby. Everyone had to play. There was cricket in summer and long cross-country runs which left Rudd trailing far behind. He tried to keep up but couldn't. A medical examination revealed his damaged heart. At the age of twelve, his status as a sickly child was confirmed. He was invisible to his classmates. Though he showed some promise at the piano, his schoolwork was mediocre. Each night this prissy kid who had lost his father and was separated from his mother found himself living, in the words of his brother Greg, "in a dorm with fifty guys farting and their smelly socks." Plus the Brothers on patrol.

Holidays were difficult. Now that his mother was training at the Mater, they had no home base and the boy was conscious of being passed "from pillar to post" as they moved between friends and De Vere relatives: "You've always got to be polite and you know you're not quite part of who you're staying with, you're only there temporarily." On perhaps two or three occasions there was nowhere for them to stay. Marge pulled the VW Beetle over to the side of the road and they slept in the car. The boy thought to himself: "It doesn't get much crooker than this."

He escaped Ashgrove after two years. His mother, having finished her training, found a job in Nambour at the Selangor Private Hospital, bought a fibro cottage round the corner and brought her boy home in the winter of 1971. Rudd has never since encouraged Ashgrove to claim him as its own. "I prefer not to remember those days," he told a Brisbane lawyer in the 1990s. "I received my education at Nambour High." Over the course of that lunch he left this distinguished Ashgrove old boy "in no doubt that he detested the joint." In 2009 Rudd sent on DVD an official message of staggering rudeness to mark the opening of a new science block named after his old headmaster. Sitting in front of a few shelves of Hansard and an Australian flag, Rudd mangled the man's name, reminded Ashgrove's old boys more than once that he was prime minister and subjected them to a brief stump speech about Labor's contribution to science education across the nation. His scorn was colossal.

The move to Nambour High in September 1971 was not an immediate success. This jumble of classrooms on the low side of Coronation Avenue was the boy's fourth school in three years. He arrived there a little fearful of what might befall him as he once again finessed his way around a strange playground. But back home under his mother's protective care, he soon found his feet. He was always his mother's son.

That was the year Gough Whitlam visited China. The boy was glued to the set, mesmerised by the sight of the Labor leader being feted in Beijing. Even at the age of thirteen he sensed he was watching a great man at an extraordinary moment: "What leadership!" Rudd was sixteen when Whitlam returned to Beijing as prime minister. Again he was transfixed. "I watched with wide eyes on the flickering tube Gough and Margaret embark on their triumphal march to China in 1973. I read every word about who Gough met and what was said at his meeting with Zhou Enlai and Mao Zedong." This was not the enthusiasm of a Labor neophyte. Rudd had yet to make contact with the family that would transform his politics. Whitlam's adventures in China meant something more fundamental than that:

> As a kid growing up in the Queensland country under the occasionally benign, but more often malign, Bjelke-Petersen dictatorship of the 1970s, it was Gough who opened this person's eyes to the world beyond, by which I mean not just

beyond the Tweed – radical though that was at the time as the Tweed, in those days, constituted our very own Mason–Dixon Line – but the region beyond our shores …

By this time the gears had meshed. When school resumed the following year – 1974, his last at Nambour – the teachers discovered a boy implacably determined to succeed. "I have never met a mind like Kevin Rudd's in forty years of teaching," recalls Fae Barber. "He was cherubic, sitting in the front row just waiting to absorb knowledge. To this day, I love and admire him." And he counts her one of the great influences on his life. He immersed himself in his work. He read. He questioned. He imaginatively entered the worlds Barber took him to: literature and ancient history. "I remember teaching him about Caesar's troubles with Pompey the Great, and young Kevin was *angered* by Pompey's poor behaviour."

This was more than mere swotting. He was determined to rebuild himself from the ground up. This would be a new Kevin Rudd, not the vulnerable kid who had suffered what he called "a deep sense of loss of dignity" since the family was thrown off the farm. Not the boy who had been shocked by the violence of Ashgrove. With steely determination he would rise above the wrongs of these past years and make a big life for himself. The aim was to become unassailable. And he began to see this determination to remake himself as having a larger purpose. "I just got determined to make sure that I could look after myself in life," he told Julia Baird. "And do something about what I saw to be wrong things happening in the world."

Babe in the Woods

Rudd found Labor almost by accident. Among his few friends at Nambour High were the Callander girls. They remember him as an awkward kid. "When he was up on his feet and talking, he was most comfortable in his own skin," says Fiona Callander (now Neucom). "But he was not a confident person in a social situation. He was not the life and soul of the party." They brought him home to their pineapple farm where he met their father, Bob. Twenty-five years later in his maiden speech Rudd would acknowledge that "Bob Callander ... introduced me to the Australian Labor Party."

This prince of the newsroom had decided at the age of forty to abandon his career at the Sydney *Sun* and grow pineapples. So entirely unlikely and so doomed was this venture that for years journalists at Fairfax were warned to watch out when turning forty "not to do a Callander." Dashing, fashionable and larger than life, he had reported from London and the Middle East, was right there on the Darwin tarmac when the KGB tried to hustle Mrs Petrov onto her plane, and had risen almost to the top of one of Sydney's big afternoon papers. He was also a friend to young talent. Peter Barron, who went on to greatness in Kerry Packer's empire, was a Callander protégé. So was the young Kerry O'Brien.

The decision to give all this away was largely dictated by his doctors. After some nasty bouts of pancreatitis, Callander had given up the grog and was anxious to break with the hard-drinking culture of the press that was killing his friends. On the wagon and looking for fresh adventures, he took his family north to Woombye on the outskirts of Nambour and watched his first pineapples rot in the floods of 1972. The great consolation of that year was the election of his hero Gough Whitlam. Callander's daughter Kerry says: "Politics is what made him tick."

Callander was the first Labor man Rudd was ever aware of meeting. He was a raconteur and the boy lapped up his stories. "Kevin was an absolute babe in the woods, but Dad could see his potential," recalls Fiona Neucom. "Dad would bait him in a joking way to open his mind. He didn't like to see a brain go to waste, and anyone with a brain like Kevin's voting for the National Party would really be going to waste."

With the Callanders he went to his first political meeting: Bjelke-Petersen addressing a packed

Nambour Town Hall in the Queensland campaign of 1974. The Callanders didn't stand for the national anthem. Rudd did. He was a good boy. He was at the Callanders' to watch television on election night and see Labor reduced to a cricket team in the state parliament. But it was so exciting to be there with Bob: he knew the people up on the screen.

At some point that year Rudd had begun dropping in on Young Labor meetings at the Nambour Cane Growers' Hall on Lowe Street. The first speaker to address them was that old fossil Senator George Georges. The boy did not join the party. There was a small kerfuffle at school when he conducted a voter survey in the playground. Support for Labor was running at a dispiriting 28 per cent. Later press stories of him clashing with authorities over his new political beliefs are exaggerated. He told me he was only ever asked to remove a Young Labor sticker from his clipboard. "He never did anything to get into trouble at school," says Barber. "He was the one with the halo."

Nambour's service clubs, a legacy of the town's ethos of self-improvement, were to prove more important to the boy in this formative last year at school than Young Labor. To the Jaycees, the Lions and Rotary, he delivered his set piece: "Australia – The Democracy." The Nambour *Chronicle* reported an early version of this work in progress:

Kevin said the present apathy on the part of many voters, and the "donkey" vote, could only be overcome by the dissemination of a workable knowledge of the subject of government in such a form as to be comprehendable to the man in the street. He called attention to the fact that no compulsory provisions exist for a student to obtain even an elementary knowledge of this subject at school. He advocated that the subject of government be introduced to school curricula, which would entail an examination of the policies of major parties and the structure of government.

Marge Rudd drove him more than a thousand miles that year to speak. Eliminated in May from the Lions Club's "Youth of the Year Quest" in Brisbane, he then triumphed in the Jaycees' "Youth Speaks for Australia" competition, winning watches, sets of encyclopaedias, a pile of books on ancient history for the school library and praise from the *Chronicle*: "Once again it's well done Kevin." After the local finals in tiny Biloela and the state finals at Clifton, he flew over to Perth a few weeks after his seventeenth birthday and lost. How did he respond to defeat? "He'd studied Caesar's troubles in the Gallic wars," says Fae Barber laconically. "It stood him in good stead."

What was he going to do once he triumphed – an outcome rightly taken for granted – in his final exams? Perhaps the stage: he had become a keen young actor and the vice-president of Beryl Muspratt's Young People's Theatre of Nambour. In his last year at school he was cast as rather pompous grown-ups in two or three shows, including *Salad Days*, in which he played the Minister of Pleasures and Pastimes, the nark who tries to shut down the magic piano. He learnt everyone's part. Acting and mimicry are Rudd's uncelebrated talents. But he knew he wasn't good enough to go on the stage. The idea was easily and early rejected.

Perhaps the law: so entirely had he immersed himself in the study of *A Man for All Seasons* – Robert Bolt's morality play about the martyrdom of Sir Thomas More at the hands of Henry VIII – that he thought he might become a lawyer and was accepted by the Law School of the University of Queensland. This was not an option he rejected out of hand.

Perhaps diplomacy: towards the end of this cocky kid's time at school, he wrote asking Whitlam how he might become a diplomat. In a reply signed by the man himself – "I held it up to the light each morning to make sure of that" – Whitlam recommended he go to university and study foreign languages. Rudd's mother found the letter. "Consternation broke out in the household ... the thought of her son receiving correspondence from Australia's Socialist-in-Chief was a little too much to bear."

Perhaps politics: as early as his final year at school, Rudd began to have glimmerings of political ambition. In these heady years, young Australians fell in love with Labor because Whitlam promised to renew their nation's stale society. Young Rudd's infatuation had another cause. He saw Labor as a gateway to the world: the party that sustained Callander on his foreign adventures and allowed Whitlam his triumphs in China. The boy's political ambitions were vague, indeed barely formed, but they lay beneath all the others. He would have to be something else first and see what political opportunities opened up to him.

He ended 1974 the Dux of Nambour High but decided to postpone university for a year to consider his options. He was only just seventeen. Some months passed before he left town. He worked for a while at Bartholomew's Music Centre on the corner of Queen and Howard streets teaching piano and organ. He toured with Muspratt's company to a students' festival of creative arts and sciences in Canberra. Not perhaps until mid-1975 did he put Nambour behind him and head first to Brisbane – sorting books in the university library and pulling beers at the Paddington Hotel – and then to Sydney. He lived in share houses and grew his blond hair long. If he drank, it was only a little. Drugs were not part of this journey. He told Julia Baird: "I used to have very conservative views about that sort of stuff."

He had spent that last year at school as a swaggering atheist. It hadn't proved convincing. His gap year was a time of religious introspection. He hung round Sydney's Protestant churches hoping to come to a clearer view of Christianity. There he found a faith even less sectarian and less submissive to priests than his mother's. The existence of God was central; the importance of denominations marginal. He could not countenance Papal infallibility nor accept the magisterium of the church, the binding authority of the bishops to teach. The result was a very Rudd compromise reached, perhaps, to cause the least pain all round: he would neither break with Rome nor accept its discipline. He would worship where it suited him. That meant the Uniting Church. He said: "Through that process I came to an adult view of faith."

The last months of 1975 were one of the most turbulent political periods in the history of the country, but young Rudd was taking no part in Labor's struggle. Nor was he galvanised into political activity by turning eighteen and knowing the next election would see him cast his first vote. He was at work on 11 November when he heard Whitlam had been sacked:

"I was mopping a floor in the emergency department of the Canterbury Hospital in Sydney where I was employed as a wards man, and I leant on my mop and said: 'That … is … mind-boggling.'" Then you picked up the mop? "Oh well, I was on duty."

By year's end he had decided he wasn't a lawyer, wasn't an atheist and wanted – at least for now – to be a diplomat. The boy Frankenstein of Nambour planned yet another transformation of himself: he would make his way towards that career by studying Chinese. Why Chinese, he was asked years later by the ABC journalist Catherine McGrath. Without hesitation he replied: "To escape."

Rudd is lucky. He works at his luck and knows how to use it, but the raw luck of the man at nearly every stage of his life is astonishing. In his first couple of days at the Australian National University's Burgmann College he found Thérèse Rein. She told the *Women's Weekly*:

We met at a Christian friendship meeting and we started talking on the way back from this meeting. We sat down and had a chat for about an hour and a half, and I liked him. I liked his humour, self-deprecating humour, I liked his integrity, I liked his heart, his compassion if you like, and he's very bright.

She told him: "I think you're the first Kevin I've ever met." He thought the remark "marvellously snotty." The girl was way out of his league: a private-school child from Victoria, daughter of an aeronautical engineer, Anglican. They had important things in common. She too was reaching a resolution about her own beliefs: "I personally committed to Christ." They both knew something of suffering. She told him about her paraplegic father who worked all his life as an engineer while confined to a wheelchair. He confided to her stories the public wouldn't hear for another twenty-five years: "He told me about growing up in Eumundi, losing his father, leaving the farm, his mum training as a nurse, and I thought, he's known suffering in his childhood too." And they talked politics. Rein told Kate Legge of the *Australian*:

> He dissected the fledgling Fraser government, laying forth his vision for the future. "And I said to him, 'Well, I think you should go into federal parliament. I think the nation needs people like you.'"

They fought over many big issues in their years at university, but there was no difference over this: he would one day go into politics. Rein told his biographer Robert Macklin that she waited for this, "From the very first meeting."

Rudd is aware there is a pattern here: a young man who has lost his father as a child setting out to become a political leader. He's done a little reading about this phenomenon, without delving deeply into the lessons it might hold: "I'm not good at reflective questions." Churchill, Eden, Callaghan and Blair are only the latest names on the long list of British prime ministers who were young when their fathers died. Recent names from the American list are Clinton and Obama. The pattern is not so clear in Australia but, counting those whose fathers were for some reason unable to be fathers, we have Andrew Fisher (father incapacitated), Joseph Cook (dead), Joe Lyons (useless), Earle Page (ruined), Ben Chifley (estranged) and poor Billy McMahon, whose mother and father had both shuffled off by the time he was eighteen.

The BBC journalist Jeremy Paxman has drawn on a number of studies to examine what these leaders often have in common:

> A childhood deprived of affection, unusual sensitivity, an outstanding mentor, extreme self-discipline, an overdeveloped religious sense, aggression and timidity, overdependence on the love of others, all featured in many of their lives.

That fits Rudd not quite like a glove, but well enough. He would be more a loner than the pattern suggests. Once he was clear of school and university he would have no mentors other than his mother and his wife. But the rest is there in some measure: the energy, the astonishing emotional resilience Paxman also notes, and the suggestion that he, like other leaders with such dislocated childhoods, sought to patch himself together by pursuing power.

Rudd found power at the university in another quarter altogether. He led a group of evangelicals called the Navigators, intent – or so it seemed to other students – on imposing a puritan rule on Burgmann, a campus college. The Navigators were particularly worried about liquor – Rudd is remembered as a serial complainer about booze being sold in the college bar – rock music and fornication. Philip Hurst, an international lawyer who was then a fellow student at Burgmann, remembers Fresher Rudd vividly: "He would walk down the corridor and in his wake like ducklings after a mother duck were his Christian acolytes." Hurst adds: "It was simply power."

Rudd didn't lift a finger for Labor in the high political excitement of Malcolm Fraser's early years. He didn't march in the streets against Whitlam's nemesis, the governor-general Sir John Kerr, or man the booths in the election campaigns of 1977 and 1980.

The wild politics of the campus held no fascination for him. He told me:

> I just thought university politics was a bit silly, to be quite honest. It didn't strike me as being really about real things and I went to university to study and to learn things. I read the student newspaper and read what they were fighting about. It shocked me that they were fighting about castles in the air as opposed to real things. So it never really captured my imagination.

Instead he studied Chinese. His homework was impeccable. He always asked the pertinent question. Fellow students remember him as painfully correct, a bit of a sociopath, almost invisible. But his tutor Pierre Ryckmans (nom de plume: Simon Leys) thought young Rudd a cut above his fellows. "His courtesy, articulateness, impeccable manners and cleanliness (in contrast to the more bohemian and shabby looks of most of his classmates and of his teacher!) always made me assume he came from a rather privileged background, private schools etc.," he told the *Australian Financial Review*'s Lenore Taylor. Rudd spent his fourth year working on the language in Taiwan and returned to ANU to write what was then thought a rather eccentric thesis on the mainland human-rights dissident Wei Jingsheng.

His first-class honours degree opened the door to the Department of Foreign Affairs in January 1981. Later that year, as they were about to leave for a first posting in Stockholm, Rudd and Rein married. She was twenty-three and he was twenty-four. The wedding was in St John's, the old church near the War Memorial where Canberra's powerful pray. Rudd had signed up with his wife's elastic Establishment Anglican flock.

And at last he joined the Labor Party. He was driven to this by fresh hopes, old principles and his new career. His hopes had been stirred by the 1980 election. "Between my Chinese-language classes sitting out there in the student quadrangle in college … I seem to remember the poll indicated that Bill Hayden might actually just get there." Labor clawed back seats but fell far short of victory. But now Rudd felt it was important to take a stand.

> We'd been illegitimately tossed out of office, I was now out of university and now into a working life and my principles on this had not changed and so I decided to formally align …
>
> I was, at that stage, principally taken by Australia's place in the region and in the world. It struck me as a vastly changing world in the frankly

post-domino era of south-east and east Asia. Remember 1981 is only six years after the fall of Saigon. So you're looking therefore at a whole new unfolding world ...

Was he thinking of a future political career when he took this step? "As a possibility, yes. As any sort of formal resolution, no."

Sugar Country

The land is green, the sea is blue. Coal ships are strung along the horizon. But on this brief hop from Townsville to Mackay only the security guards are gazing out the window. Everyone else on the prime minister's plane has his or her head stuck in a ring binder. Rudd's toy-town version of America's mighty *Air Force One* is a neat jet emblazoned with the familiar but incongruous word *Royal.* As a concession to the needs, or perhaps the addictions, of his staff, mobile phones are only turned off at the very last minute, almost as the plane is leaving the ground. These young men and women look oddly naked without phones to their ears. And they *are* young: in their twenties and early thirties. The work never stops. There is no chiacking. Serving the prime minister may offer them profound satisfaction, but you don't read it on their faces. They make a sombre band.

Rudd was up north handing out large licks of money to hospitals a week or so before his showdown with the premiers in April. His daily routine was this: give early morning radio interviews by phone, visit hospital, give news conference, disappear with staff to attend to matters of state, emerge for coffee or sandwich with local newspaper editors, then fly to next town. Cameras and press trail after him. Everywhere he goes, citizens ask to have their photographs taken with him. Usually one of the security guards takes the snap. Whatever dark techniques they have been taught to protect Rudd's life remain, thank God, a secret. What we did see everywhere on display in North Queensland was their skill with cameras: digital, disposable, SLR and phone.

"They can't be *too* sick," an administrator at the Townsville Hospital confided. Patients the prime minister visits have to be up for the ride, presentable and not at death's door. After all, the footage is destined for the evening news. Yet finding four television cameras, half-a-dozen local journalists, two or three hospital administrators and Kevin Rudd at your bedside is an alarming experience. He asks chipper questions about the disease/condition/operation being endured. He's personable. Not insincere. Then he launches into a little stump speech: "We're here to deliver ... seventy million bucks. It's a big investment, but I think it's worth it ... It's not just here – we're rolling it out across the country ..."

Half an hour later we're in the air. Trim air-force stewards, their hair in neat buns, serve chicken and avocado baguettes with a refreshing glass of water. Rudd wanders out of his room for a cake cutting: one of his staff is leaving after a couple of years on the trail. The celebrations are modest. Rudd is pale, precise and a little puffy. His hair is ghost grey and his eyes are sharp. Standing in the cabin eating a tiny slice of chocolate cake, he has the slightly distracted air of someone who has woken from an afternoon nap. We fall into conversation: about his school days, the Callanders and his time as the right-hand man to Wayne Goss. Did I realise, he asks, that we'd just flown over Mundingburra?

That was the seat in Townsville's suburbs that brought Goss down, a sad end to an extraordinary era. Goss had broken the Nationals' grip on Queensland, come to power with such high hopes and won a second big victory at the polls before his government was carried off on a tide of disappointment, antagonism and weariness. Rudd was at Goss's side almost from beginning to end. There are veterans of the administration who claim Rudd must take a share of the blame for the Goss collapse. They are not without admiration for Rudd's achievements but remember him as an arsehole, mechanical, cold, a cunt, unbelievably arrogant and an absolute prick to deal with.

Watch out, they say, history is repeating itself. What happened in Brisbane then is happening in Canberra now.

Rudd's brief diplomatic career had taken him to Beijing after Stockholm. In both posts he impressed his superiors enormously. They gave top marks to this earnest, clever, hard-working man with an urgent need to get things done. He was deft with the powerful people around him, working to be seen by them in a positive light. They thought him a decent man. At this level – Rudd was first secretary in China – diplomacy is not about policy but process. He was very good at process. His mastery of the language was exemplary. Beijing did not leave him with a sentimental affection for China. He was wary and would grow more so as China rose to power once more in the affairs of the world.

Though marked for big things in the department, he seemed a little impatient when he returned to Australia in 1986. His thirtieth birthday found him sitting at a desk in Canberra. By this time, the Rudds had two children: Jessica and Nicholas. It's often said that Rudd is a man always looking to move on. The department had begun to offer diplomats "leave in the public interest" to work with business and political leaders. The short-lived scheme was rather a disaster: no one ever came back. In 1988, Rudd was given a year's leave to be chief of staff to the new leader of the Opposition in Queensland, Wayne Goss. The two men were peas in a pod. They hit it off at their first meeting.

People round Goss were a little taken aback when Rudd appeared in Brisbane in the winter of 1988. "He was bright," says a Labor figure who worked in Rudd's orbit for the next seven years. "But he was nerdy and out of his comfort zone dealing with the sort of personalities you deal with every day in politics. He appeared to have no experience of them at all. But he worked hard at fitting in. We began to hear him cultivating ockerisms. He started to swear in conversation or when he was arguing a point. He wanted to be part of the mob."

Rudd had little impact at first. Directing the overall campaign to restore Labor to government was Wayne Swan, thirty-eight, academic, writer, federal Labor staffer and a former head prefect of Nambour High. He'd been three years ahead of Rudd. They'd not known each other at school. In everyone's mind except Rudd's, Swan was the next generation's Queenslander most likely to succeed in federal politics.

"I identified the top forty companies in Queensland and I obtained their annual reports," Rudd told Lenore Taylor. "I identified their CEOs and directors and I tracked them down. I organised meetings between myself and Wayne [Goss] and all of those people, as well as with all the peak industry bodies in the state." This much-celebrated tactic was straight out of the diplomatic textbook, one he would use time and again in his climb to power. "You need access to operate," the veteran diplomat Richard Woolcott told me. "Good access means you can operate well. If they play chess, you play chess. If they play tennis, play tennis." Rudd, as it happens, plays neither.

The Goss victory in December 1989 ended thirty-two years of National Party government in Queensland. Labor had a sweeping mandate for change, but Goss intended moving cautiously. He told Craig McGregor he had two objectives: "First, to run a traditional Labor government and drive important reforms; and second, to deliver a long-term, stable government. Taking the public with us." His aim was to entrench Labor as the natural government of Queensland. "The last thing we want to be is working-class heroes for three years and mugs for the rest of our lives."

Goss and Rudd drew close. Some say they played to each other's weaknesses. Both are intelligent, driven, cautious and rigorous. Both made heavy demands on their staff. Both cut ill-prepared advisers to shreds. Yet Goss earned the loyalty of those working for him. Rudd didn't. "He was Goss without the humanity," says one of the inner circle. Camaraderie is not his style. He doesn't have the great leader's ability to know when to put the kind hand on the shoulder. But the clarity and energy he brought to government after years of sloth and confusion under Bjelke-Petersen were a revelation. In the middle of 1990 Goss rang Woolcott to ask that Rudd's leave be extended. The premier said: "I've become rather dependent on him."

Rudd became the pre-eminent figure in the government machine the following winter, when Goss set up a Cabinet Office with him at its head. Though designed to work as similar offices did in New South Wales and Victoria – screening submissions from ministers as they moved through to the Cabinet – Rudd had other ideas. As he now boasts in his official CV, he saw himself "driving the Government's reform program as Director General of the Cabinet Office, the central policy agency of the Queensland Government." Hitherto, everyone had passed his desk on the way into Goss's office. Now he cut a door from his new office into the premier's room so he could still keep an eye on things. One of his colleagues from the time says, "We used to call it the cat-flap."

From this point the accusations began that Rudd was usurping the role of ministers and their departments. His staff of bright young advisers grew from about half-a-dozen until over eighty of them occupied two storeys on George Street. One of those kids for a time was Noel Pearson, co-opted from his legal studies in 1991 to work on the land-rights legislation Rudd had taken out of the hands of the minister for Aboriginal affairs, Anne Warner. Rudd was Pearson's first real boss:

> Notwithstanding the acrimony of our parting ... it was not possible to work with Rudd without being impressed by him. I detested what I considered to be his mealy political trimming when dealing with issues that had been on Labor's policy platform during the long winter of National rule in Queensland. But even in the depths of my detestation, I have never been able to deny a grudging regard for Rudd. After all the expletives and bile would come: "Yes, but this man is formidable."

Pearson also remembers him as a daring negotiator. "I recall witnessing a 33-year-old Rudd deal with industry and civic leaders and lobbyists with breathtaking verve and skill." He did have some foibles which old hands noticed early on. He loved to keep people waiting. He was too keen to show he knew more than anyone else in the room about whatever was on the table. Often he did. Deft argument wasn't his only weapon. "You would find to your horror that your secretary has booked him in for an hour to discuss the teaching of Mandarin in high schools," recalls one interstate official. "It's the fifth time you've seen him on the subject. He's absolutely dogged. He gains results by persistence and erosion, by wearing you down."

Rudd had never managed anything in his life. However hard he worked – and he never ceased working – there was an element of chaos and frustration about his office. Material poured in, but not much came out the other end. Rudd's ambition to micro-manage change exceeded his capacity and that of his army of young advisers. Toes were trodden on, noses put out of joint. Public servants were bullied and harassed for information because the office wasn't coping. That aggression was passed down the line. Few had the guts to challenge him. Good work emerged from the Cabinet Office, but it was always hard-won. "The arteries of government were clogged," one old Goss staffer told me. "This was a good system with some very good people, but it was built around a single choke point: Rudd."

Sometime in 1992, Kevin Rudd was seen hanging round the branches in the seat of Griffith. Though it was held by one of Keating's Cabinet ministers, Ben "Gentleman" Humphreys, contenders were already manoeuvring for the succession, which was thought to be a couple of elections away. At this time there was in the air an idea that the successful Goss team might transfer en bloc to Canberra. Swan had pre-selection for the seat of Lilley, north of the river. But it came as a surprise – particularly to the Left faction of the party – that Rudd had his eye on the old water-front seat of Griffith to the south.

That stretch of the city has had its ups and downs. Traditionally, it took in David Malouf's childhood stamping ground of South Brisbane:

> Edmondstone Street even then was "mixed." Beginning at Melbourne Street, not far from the Bridge, and skirting the south side of Musgrave Park – a dark, uneven place, once an aboriginal burial ground but later redeemed and laid out with Moreton Bay figs of enormous girth and a twelve-foot checker board – it consisted chiefly of old-fashioned, many-roomed houses from the days when this was the most fashionable area south of the river; but there were factories as well ...

Rudd had known some of this territory from his childhood: the Mater Hospital was in Griffith. Beyond the hospital were prosperous Liberal suburbs.

Labor's strength lay along the river, where the branches were dominated by a small faction known officially as Labor Unity and derisively as the Old Guard. Humphreys was Old Guard through and through. Rudd joined the faction to win the seat, even though it placed him way to the Right of the party and at odds with the dominant AWU faction of the Goss government. He still faced the prospect of a bruising battle to be the party's candidate until 1994, when a redistribution so depleted the Left's forces in Griffith that Rudd became, without rough and tumble, the heir apparent. In October that year Alan Ramsey wrote: "That was all quietly fixed a long time ago."

Rudd's purpose was to become prime minister. Right from the start it was only ever about that. He stood down from his old job and became a mere adviser on commonwealth–state relations in the Office of Cabinet. But he was still part of the inner circle preparing for the state elections in July 1995. Goss seemed assured of victory until a few months from the ballot, when support began to melt away. The polls dipped. Focus groups turned feral: talk of protest votes gave way to talk of booting Goss out. A tetchy campaign saw the government lose nine seats but cling on – for the time being at least – with the help of a single independent.

What had gone wrong? The Right swore Goss had done too much, the Left too little. The Right blamed change fatigue. The Left argued the Goss crowd – and Rudd in particular – had disappointed the high hopes of those who swept Labor to power. Craig McGregor wrote: "On the fateful night in 1989 when Labor at last won government in Queensland, and the relics of Bjelke-Petersen's regime were swept away, Goss told his ecstatic supporters: 'Take a cold shower.' In a way, they've been taking it ever since."

Bad mistakes had been made. Rudd wasn't responsible for the most damaging of them: the decision to renege on old assurances and build a tollway to the Gold Coast. That alone cost Goss five seats. Rudd was remembered for shutting down government services – so many of them so wasteful – in little regional towns. And he had made a particular contribution to the disaffection of the Queensland public service, which had come to loathe all the government stood for. By the time of the poll, Goss had lost the teachers, the nurses, the bureaucrats and the regions. Rudd also had a part in the government's underlying problems of style: the perception out there that Goss and his team always knew best.

Rudd says he has no regrets for the control he exercised, the time he took, the enemies he made, the bureaucrats he frustrated, the staffers he exhausted.

He told me: "I know of nobody who's ever occupied a position – either being the chief of staff or a head of a central agency in the public service, state or federal, in this jurisdiction or abroad – who doesn't have those sorts of criticisms levelled at them." That's leadership. Wreckage is to be expected. People are upset when their advice is rejected, their performance criticised, their hopes thwarted. There are no lessons for his career to be drawn from these criticisms. "They are structural to any person who occupies those positions. I say that, by the way, with no sort of idealistic view of any sort of perfection of my role in times past."

Though Rudd sloughs off criticism of his bureaucratic style, he is extremely sensitive to accusations that the policies he was driving were without heart. As he sees it, Goss was preoccupied with the big structural changes necessary to clean up the mess left by the Nationals. That was the principal task of the government's first term. To that end Rudd was deeply involved in ending National Party boondoggles across the state: shutting railways, schools, government offices and hospitals. This policy was deeply resented – not least by the Left of the Labor Party – and would be counted against him in time. Rudd claims he was also pursuing policies to make Queensland a more decent place. The aim was to turn Louisiana into

California, but cautiously. Rudd's mantra was: all policy must be evidence-based. But how good were his political instincts? Nil, according to one colleague from those years: "He has a computer-like mind that can analyse all 12,000 policy options, but he chooses by comparing and contrasting, by elimination. Not by instinct." He remains in awe of the way Rudd taught himself to be a formidable bureaucrat but puzzles over his lack of *feel*. "Does that instinct come from liking and trusting people?" he wonders. "He doesn't have that."

Another of the puzzling aspects of Rudd's years with Goss was his reluctance to put powerful forces offside. He is remembered as a little too willing to take backward steps, too slow to call the bluff of interests long used to getting their way and, in particular, too easily intimidated by business. Perhaps this was almost inevitable in a government of men and women who had grown up in the monoculture of the Bjelke-Petersen era. From the safety of another state, one of Labor's emeritus leaders wonders if there is something particularly Queensland about Rudd: a fugitive sense that the other side is legitimate and Labor the interlopers?

Rudd's blond, serious head was now appearing at the flyscreen doors of Griffith. The thought of this nerd trying to win the hearts and minds of the electorate provoked mirth in party ranks. Not for the last time, he was underestimated. At the age of thirty-eight, Rudd set out to conquer a new skill: campaigning. He did so with all his endless energy and mastery of detail. He taught himself the task almost perfectly. But there was no disguising the fact that he was a most unusual candidate. At a roast and fundraiser at Brisbane's Sheraton Hotel – the cream of Rudd's contact book was there and CUB donated the booze – the deputy prime minister, Kim Beazley, told a little story. When Gareth Evans was elected to the Senate, his colleagues at Melbourne University gave him, said Beazley, a couple of suitcases to carry his ego to Canberra. "You might like to think about that, Kevin."

Perhaps what happened next was karma. Complaints about the conduct of the poll in the state seat of Mundingburra led first to an inquiry and then to a by-election. Opinion polls had Labor heading for a narrow victory there until Paul Keating called the 1996 federal election. Mundingburra was lost. A few days later, Goss finally folded.

Rudd's own situation was precarious. The redistribution that delivered him federal pre-selection made Griffith much harder for Labor to hold. And as Goss said: "Queenslanders are sitting on their verandas with baseball bats just waiting for Keating to come."

Thérèse Rein joined her husband on the beat. The Rudds rallied from Nambour. By polling day in March 1996, they had knocked on most of the 32,000 doors of Holland Park, Norman Park, Coorparoo, Gumdale, Tingalpa, Camp Hill, Balmoral, Morningside, Hawthorne and Bulimba. But it didn't work. Eleven of Labor's thirteen seats in Queensland were wiped out. Swan lost Lilley. Pauline Hanson won Oxley. Rudd didn't win Griffith. Keating lost government.

Rudd was shattered. The hostility of his electorate could be measured with pinpoint accuracy. He was utterly unused to losing. Out of the wreckage of his childhood had come an extraordinary narrative of success. Everyone's expectations had been exceeded, except his own. Now he had lost. He believes commentators never grasp how terrible this is. It's left him, he says, with deep sympathy even for his opponents when they face the people and lose. Schadenfreude was freely expressed by his critics: they hoped he might now be a little humbler, might start to listen. That appears not to have been the lesson he drew from this engagement with democracy. The secret of Rudd's success has always been his astonishing emotional resilience. He moped and raged for a while after March 1996, then put himself back in harness.

He had no job. He and Rein decided it was time he returned to his old department, in the hierarchy of which he had continued to rise while absent on leave. They were looking for a minister in Beijing and consul-general in Shanghai. His return was in train when Philip Flood, the new secretary Howard appointed to the department, let it be known that Rudd's career had been "too colourful" and that he was to take voluntary redundancy. Rudd knew that he couldn't be sacked in this way but with an old adversary, Alexander Downer, now minister, he could see himself languishing forever in obscure posts. He took redundancy and became a freelance adviser to business on dealing with China. His principal client was KPMG.

"He had no trouble working a long day," recalls Stephen Lonie, the then managing partner of the firm in Queensland. "He was intensely driven." Rudd made introductions rather than doing deals. He helped corporations in trouble. His presence wasn't always welcomed. He trod on the toes of the KPMG partners in Hong Kong. But he was rated capable, a success. It was always clear he was going to pursue politics. "The game is on again," he told Lonie sometime in 1998. "I'm getting out the van. If I win, it's over. If I lose, I'll be back again."

He knocked on doors. He railed against aircraft noise and the prospect of John Howard's GST. He and Lindsay Tanner in silly hats rode a tandem bike through the city to promote the Opposition's bicycle policy. The turning political tide saw Labor win back six of its old seats in Queensland and Kim Beazley nearly win office from Howard. Swan regained Lilley. Hanson lost Oxley. Rudd became the member for Griffith and turned up in Canberra in November to take his seat and immediately deliver his maiden speech. His mother was in the gallery.

More often than not, going through the entrails of these speeches is a waste of time. Not so in Rudd's case. Most of what matters in his politics is sketched here:

> When my father was accidentally killed and my mother, like thousands of others, was left to rely on the bleak charity of the time to raise a family, it made a young person think. It made me think that a decent social-security system designed to protect the weak was no bad thing. It made me think that the provision of decent public housing to the poor was the right thing to do. When I saw people unnecessarily die in the appallingly under-funded Queensland hospital system of the 1960s and 1970s, it made me think that the provision of a decent universal health system should be one of the first responsibilities of the state.

The key word is decent. Nothing radical is proposed. The vision is personal and conservative. His ambitions for government were old-fashioned: to pursue the public good at home and abroad. Government must be made a better machine for regulating markets and caring for those who cannot look after themselves. Australia must secure the respect of its neighbours and be active in world forums. Though these appear to be modest aims – a clarion call for fine-tuning – Rudd sees himself on a transformative mission. To think otherwise is to misunderstand him entirely. He won't acknowledge any incongruity between his policy and his political ambitions. Both are big. Perhaps the two can't be disentangled in his mind. The first words of that first speech Rudd gave in parliament were, "Politics is about power."

Sunrise

Hundreds of us were trapped for two and a half hours without interval in a rowdy piece of community theatre called *Waiting for Kevin*. Everyone was shouting. No one could be heard. Beautiful young party workers – children the last time Canberra changed hands – posed in "Kevin 07" T-shirts. Cameras flashed like firecrackers. Up on the big screens Kerry O'Brien was tolling through the count like an old priest saying mass. No one was listening. A little after 7 p.m. Queensland time, the premier, Anna Bligh, appeared from the party's headquarters upstairs and walked through the melee confiding to those in her path: "Kevin Rudd is the prime minister of Australia."

But there was no sign of Kevin. As the scythe of democracy cut across Australia, the decibels kept rising in that long room under Brisbane's Suncorp Stadium. The rough dignity of John Howard's concession speech was met with cat-calls and booing. Only the sight of Maxine McKew hushed the crowd for a few moments at a time. Her battle for the seat of Bennelong was the nearest the night had to a cliff-hanger. She won, she lost and she seemed to be winning again. Over her left shoulder could be glimpsed the old party strategist Bob Hogg, struggling to hide his triumph as his partner trounced the man who had dominated Australian politics for a dozen years.

Men with wires in their ears appeared from nowhere, generic rock and roll pumped out of the speakers and Rudd was among us, a pale, neatly dressed man with a tight smile. His eyes were invisible. The room responded with a mighty roar as he and his family climbed onto the platform: "Kevin. Kevin. Kevin." Thérèse Rein was ecstatic. The pride of the children in the face of this ovation was heart-stopping. Then Rudd killed the party.

"OK, guys," he said, holding up his hands like a slightly weary teacher to shush the rowdy enthusiasm. "A short time ago, Mr Howard called me to offer his congratulations ..." Such courtesies are obligatory, of course, but Rudd went on and on about the virtues of his fallen opponent. The revellers waited him out: waited to burst back into life; waited for the moment when Rudd's face would break into a smile of triumph; waited for him to lead the celebrations. That never happened. The rhetoric was leaden:

Today Australia has looked to the future. Today the Australian people have decided that we as a nation will move forward to plan for the future, to prepare for the future, to embrace the future and together, as Australians, to unite and write a new page in our nation's history to make this great country of ours, Australia, even greater.

He seemed neither to welcome nor need acclaim. He wasn't basking in the verdict of the ballot box or the delight of his audience. God knows what emotions were coursing through him on the platform – vindication, relief or perhaps exhaustion, after having fought his way towards this moment for at least twenty years – but he was losing the crowd. Rein could tell: her face fell as he ploughed on.

Tomorrow, and I say this to the team, we roll up our sleeves, we're ready for hard work. We're ready for the long haul. You can have a strong cup of tea if you want in the meantime; even an Iced Vo Vo on the way through, for the celebrations should stop there. We have a job of work to do. It's time, friends, for us, together as a nation, to bind together to write this new page in our great nation's history. I thank the nation.

The klieg lights went out. The cameras packed up. The screens fell silent. That was about it for the party. Sober revellers wandered out into a warm Brisbane night. The peculiarities of the event were passed off as a joke: that's Kevin! But at victory celebrations across the nation there were those who, however jubilant to see the back of Howard, asked themselves: what have we here?

"Leadership," Rudd told me, "is always a lonely race. Anyone honest about their reflections on that reaches the same conclusion." Through hard and lonely work he won the leadership of his party. "I've always just been a person who believes in rowing his own race, that is, doing what you believe to be the right thing, doing it with vigour, doing it with conviction and doing it with determination." True enough. Bob Carr remembers the years, the determination and the work Rudd put into climbing to the top: "He nagged the party into it, kept insisting. He willed himself there. He couldn't be overlooked. He was always in your diary or at your door."

Rudd's arrival in Canberra in 1998 hadn't set caucus alight. He didn't hide his ambitions. "There was only one job he was really interested in, and that was being prime minister," says the Labor strategist Bruce Hawker. To be shooting so high so soon marked him as a bit of a prat. Beazley was no fan. He was not given a place on the front bench. Rudd's position was, indeed, lonely: the Brisbane Old Guard was a faction of two and he made few friends in Labor ranks. Where, they wondered, did he fit?

Mark Latham put him on the list of "more careerists, more technocrats, more plodders" who turned up on the Labor side of parliament at that time. The new man wasn't tribal Labor nor did he revel in Labor history. He didn't join those in the party – mainly from New South Wales – who worship the ground the US Democrats walk on. One of the few political heroes Rudd mentioned in these years was Keir Hardie, the Christian socialist who founded the party in Britain:

> He was a man who thought rolling up to church on Sunday without engaging the resources of the state to improve the lot of his fellow man was a recipe for hypocrisy.

What his puzzled new companions in caucus missed was the peculiarly personal nature of Rudd's political faith: a commitment to politics growing not out of history, work or ideological conviction but out of the public and private hell of his childhood.

With customary zeal, Rudd began networking. He courted journalists and would, in time, cheerfully admit to being a "media tart." He wrote high-falutin' stuff about China for newspapers and worked the press gallery. In the long political silence of the Christmas break, he was infallibly working, travelling, always ready to be interviewed. "This rather strange, isolated will o' the wisp would bob up every now and again, knock on the door and come in," recalls Alan Ramsey. "When you rang him, he was always away. He'd never answer but ring back from somewhere in the world a day or so later." Winter is think-tank season in Australia and Rudd never missed the annual gatherings convened by the Centre for Independent Studies, the Australian American Leadership Dialogue – he had been a member since it began in 1993 – and the Australian Davos Connection. "He would be there from the first drinks to the last lunch, whether contributing to a session or not," remarked a wry fellow-attendee. "He would be there cultivating these business people." Perhaps here is an explanation for 2020, the great conference he called on becoming prime minister. The mass of ideas it generated have got nowhere, but they probably weren't the point: it was an opportunity on a huge scale for Rudd to network.

Another figure would have earned the admiration of caucus for throwing himself so energetically into the business of being known. But something about this man jarred with his colleagues. They thought him too dogged, too cool, too academic. That he had such impossible ambitions made his efforts seem absurd. Once again Rudd was being underestimated. As he had taught himself to be a bureaucrat and a candidate, he would teach himself to be a politician. And he wouldn't trust his future to caucus: he would make his own mark. That's where Channel Seven's *Sunrise* comes into the Rudd story. One of Rudd's former staffers told me: "It was an operation to cook caucus from the outside."

With the muddy Brisbane River over his shoulder, a rather woebegone Rudd appeared on the show for the first time in February 2001. "He needed work," admits Hawker, who knew Rudd from the days of helping on Goss's election campaigns and suggested him to the show's producers. "He did need to become a much more direct communicator." Just as woeful was the sparring partner Rudd produced: his parliamentary prayer-breakfast mate, the Liberal politician Ross Cameron. The show was a dog and the politicians were dull. The future of the whole enterprise was uncertain. Cameron asked his flatmate Joe Hockey to stand in for him once or twice and the producers wanted the cheerful minister for small business to stay. Hockey told me: "Rudd went in a flat panic to Cameron to say that if he didn't make way for me, the segment was going to be lost." Cameron made way. A new producer arrived and David Koch became one of the show's presenters. Hockey and Rudd went on to be "The Big Guns of Politics" for the next six years as *Sunrise* turned into one of the most watched shows on Australian television.

"It was retail politics," says Hockey. "It introduced us to an audience that wasn't interested in politics. The audience loved the fact that we looked like mates. They accepted that Kevin was the straight-laced one on the team. He found on *Sunrise* a constituency that supported him: mums with kids. They liked him. They accepted this terribly careful guy because it was part of the routine. They didn't switch off. They liked us – mums under forty-five with a couple of kids, doing the double drop-off, working a couple of days a week to pay the huge mortgage. The show talked about its target being, I think, Mary from Ipswich. Howard treated these people with indifference and it was a great failing."

The *Tampa* election of 2001 saw Labor lose ground, Rudd increase his majority – the placards in Griffith read "Keep Kevin" – and Kim Beazley relinquish the leadership of the Opposition. The new leader, Simon Crean, tribal Labor to the fingertips, made Rudd the party's spokesman for foreign affairs. He would spend the next five years jousting with his unpromising contemporary in the Department of Foreign Affairs, Alexander Downer. It was always personal.

Crean performed poorly. As the invasion of Iraq loomed, Rudd was left to finesse the policy contradictions of a deeply divided Opposition. It didn't help that his advice to Crean was wrong: Rudd insisted the UN would decide on the invasion and that weapons of mass destruction would be found. As confused as Labor's position was, the debates of 2002 gave Rudd unprecedented public exposure. Television cameras followed him to New York, Jakarta, Zimbabwe and the Afghan border. Labor voted against the war when it came, but many in the party blamed Rudd for Labor's opposition to the war not being sharper, sooner. Crean seemed unlikely to survive.

Even at this early point, Rudd saw himself as a contender. He had essentially no support in caucus and little backing from the public. His name cropped up in Newspolls for the first time in late 2002 and April 2003, but he appeared to be in a hopeless position, with only 4 or 5 per cent naming him as their choice to lead Labor. That put him in the pack with Latham and Swan. This is the moment – after the invasion of Iraq and those early Newspolls, with a challenge to Crean in the air – when Rudd began to flesh out the story of his life for the first time.

On 18 April the *Age* carried Michael Gordon's fine profile of "the standout performer on the Crean front bench." It was a mixed blessing. The hostility of caucus to Rudd was vividly presented:

> "It's like he's got a grand flaw," said one who bears him no ill will. "He has all these tremendous attributes … but the flaw is his inability to read how people are reacting to him. His response is to adopt a boss–underling approach, which among equals tends to build resentment."

But the public read – and remembered – Rudd talking of Bert's death, the eviction from Eumundi, something of the turmoil of the years that followed and the nadir reached the night he slept rough in the VW with his sister and mother:

> People ask: how did I end up in the Labor Party, having grown up in a conservative political environment? If I trace it back, I just remember sleeping in the car that night and thinking, "This is crook. This should not happen to anyone."

Rudd's media assault in 2003 worked beautifully. In a little over six months, support for his candidacy rose fourfold to more than 20 per cent. Maxine

McKew gave Rudd a lavish spread in the *Bulletin* that allowed him to display his intellectual charm and leadership potential while reassuring readers about his reputation as a God-botherer. He declared: "I'm a Jeffersonian separatist." McKew remarked that this man had "more votes in the community than in caucus." That, in a nutshell, was the problem Rudd would face for the next hard-fought years. *Sunrise* and the profiles had lifted him out of the ruck. Swan was never a leadership contender after this. The two men who had been sharing a house in Canberra fell out badly. But the higher public profile didn't help Rudd win support where he needed it: in the parliamentary party.

Beazley moved too soon against Crean. At that mid-year attempt, Rudd voted for Beazley but not before letting it be known in the press gallery that he had seriously considered making a run himself. When a besieged Crean eventually decided on 28 November to resign, Rudd considered it his turn. Though pollsters had Beazley as the overwhelming choice of the public to lead the Opposition once more, Rudd was favoured over the only other contender, Mark Latham. A McNair Ingenuity poll in the *Sunday Telegraph* ranked support for the contenders as Beazley 47 per cent, Rudd 24 per cent and Latham 18 per cent. A Morgan poll published days later had the same message of hope for Rudd but slightly different figures: Beazley 38 per cent, Rudd 21 per cent and Latham 17.5 per cent. The pollster found:

> Those who preferred Mr Rudd liked the style of his politics and thought he was a better choice than other potential candidates for the position.
>
> "I like the sound of his politics. Latham's too divisive, Beazley's had his turn, I don't know about Swan."
>
> "Beazley's going backwards. He's already had a go."
>
> "He's young, intelligent, articulate. He handles his portfolio well."
>
> "He speaks well and presents himself well."
>
> "New blood, new ideas."

Yet Rudd could muster only eleven votes in caucus. Had he stood he would have been routed. He never put up his hand. Latham narrowly beat Beazley. A senior Labor figure tried without success to comfort a very unhappy Rudd: "I know you're shattered, but Latham is someone Labor has to get out of its system. If you'd won, he'd be shadowing you. Now it's him. Then he will be out of the way."

From this defeat, Rudd drew the lesson that it was time to court caucus as assiduously as he had been courting the public. So began a three-year campaign to convince his colleagues that he was next in line. Rudd went about this in a way that was typically disciplined and systematic, absolutely appropriate and faintly absurd. Spreadsheets were prepared containing everything that mattered about every one of them, down to their children's names and wives' birthdays. He began to hang about awkwardly in the bars where his colleagues drank. He let them talk. He practised the art of listening. It was camaraderie by numbers. He flew all over the place, popping up unexpectedly at Labor events around the country. "He would be there just to be there," says one party official in Sydney. "At a retirement dinner for a union secretary, Rudd would turn up, not to speak, not to be in the official party, not even to be acknowledged by the chair – but just to be there."

Latham loathed and distrusted the man he called "Heavy Kevvie" and the "King of Caveats." But he should have listened. In March 2004 Latham complained to his diary:

> He sounds incomprehensible in the media whenever he talks about Iraq ... Rudd wanted our policy on the troops to be a review when we got into government. Imagine the pounding we would have taken on such a wishy-washy stance, so I

overruled him and said yesterday that we wanted them home by Christmas. I've had a firm position on every other issue and it's worked for me; why not this one?

With that, Latham began his long slide in the polls. For months he had been dominating politics, but once he declared Labor's intention to withdraw the troops, he was pounded. Howard was triumphant once more. Labor slouched towards another defeat.

Rudd got on with his ceaseless work. Neither his demands nor his methods appeared to have changed from his Brisbane days, but now, instead of a staff of eighty-plus to call on, he had only two or three. He drove them hard. They came and went. One told me:

His office is chaotic. He would schedule staff meetings at bizarre times – like 10 p.m. on a Sunday night when parliament is sitting next day. And because he is busy doing other things, the 10 p.m. meeting doesn't start until 1 a.m.

Because everything is on the go at once and he's interrogating the detail of everything, nothing comes out until the last minute. Bringing work to a conclusion was focused around the next media hit. He loves an announcement.

He has an enormous appetite for raw information. He believes if you shake the raw material the answer will fall out all of its own accord. He wants the data. He likes the material organised in matrixes – big spreadsheets showing who knows what when.

He doesn't trust his advisers to give advice, so they become glorified research assistants. The Parliamentary Library was also researching – rather than analysing – for him. He had them tied in knots with every request. They pushed back a few times when the load got too heavy. But he does read everything he asks for.

He is a strange beast behind closed doors. He is so focused on the day-to-day tasks that he loses the social niceties. They are neither here nor there. Staff are interrogated beyond what's reasonable to expect them to know. And if you don't know, the atmosphere changes. Not a blow-up. It becomes very quiet. But he doesn't deliberately push his staff to this point.

For all the effort, he doesn't come up with particularly interesting solutions to problems. His policy positions aren't breakthroughs, not particularly new or exciting. After all that work they are dull.

It was always hard grind. Even when you had big wins, the mood was: well, what's next?

By this time Rudd had acquired Alister Jordan, a slight, sharp-eyed man dubbed Mr April by the rest of the staff. "There was no reason to expect the 22-year-old who'd answered a newspaper job ad would survive any longer than the others, Mr January and Mr February," explained Phillip Hudson in the *Sydney Morning Herald*. A recent political science graduate from Queensland, Jordan was first office manager, then adviser and finally Rudd's chief of staff. He is still there after working 100 hours a week for the man for nearly ten years. Jordan became part of the Rudd family. He is said to be the only person in politics Rudd trusts.

Marge Rudd died at the age of eighty-three on the day before the country went to the polls in October 2004. The knowledge that he had spent the last days of his mother's life campaigning for a man he could not respect filled Rudd with rage. He judged that Latham was on the skids and that it was time to broaden his own appeal with the party and the public. But Latham refused Rudd the promotion he wanted and bitterly accused him of leaking to the press. In one of the most notorious passages in his diary, Latham wrote:

> He appeared surprised, protested his innocence and then broke down badly, sobbing over the

recent death of his mother, just before polling day. Rudd was in a very fragile condition. I told him to leave work and go back to Brisbane to rest with his family. But he wouldn't give up. Even though he was crying, he kept lobbying to be Shadow Treasurer. It was becoming quite sad.

But Latham was the one who had the breakdown. First he retreated with his family and then, goaded to fury by press complaints that he'd failed to respond decently to the Asian tsunami, he called the press to a bleak park in Western Sydney and resigned from public life. Rudd, up in Aceh to inspect the damage and offer bipartisan support for Howard's billion-dollar gift to Indonesia, flew home to canvass support and found Beazley once again blocking his road.

Australians loved Beazley. They might not vote for the Bomber, but they loved to see him leading the Labor Party. The polls of late January 2005 spoke with a single voice: Beazley was the man. Rudd was stuck where he was at the last challenge: in the low 20 per cents. Behind him with a swathe of Latham's votes was a new contender, the left-wing Victorian Julia Gillard. Her public support was in the high teens. Rudd and Jordan spent the weekend of 22 to 23 January canvassing caucus for support. Against Beazley they could muster only seventeen or eighteen votes. His colleagues disdained his bid. Again he threw in the towel. A deal was done at this point: in return for allowing the old leader to be re-elected unopposed, Rudd would be next in line should Beazley fail. Such deals are, of course, notoriously unenforceable.

The party showered Rudd with praise for standing aside. "I've got a field marshal's baton in the backpack," he told the press. "It's just that during the current term of the Australian parliament it's not possible to take that baton out." Beazley wanted to shift him to education. He absolutely refused, for education would take him out of the public eye. Another long haul lay ahead and foreign affairs would keep him in the news all the time. Beazley had no choice. Rudd also insisted that trade be added to his responsibilities. Rudd now had authority to talk across the economy.

Nine months later, Paul Volcker, the former chairman of the US Federal Reserve, revealed that AWB Limited – formerly the Australian Wheat Board – had paid $300 million in kickbacks to the regime of Saddam Hussein. Volcker's investigation of the UN Oil-for-Food Programme had identified AWB as the biggest single source of corrupt payments to Iraq before the invasion. The Howard government, after working hand in glove with AWB for some time to keep a lid on the scandal, was forced to hold a public inquiry into the wheat sales. But the terms of reference given to Terence Cole QC were carefully crafted: he had no authority to delve into the government's role in the affair.

Rudd was made for the attack he sustained on the government for the next year. The rich and complex detail of the story Rudd mastered effortlessly. Few but the lawyers knew the case so well. Once more he had Downer in his sights, for the minister for foreign affairs had signed permits for 292 ships to carry wheat worth over $2 billion to Iraq – and almost every contract was laden with kickbacks that breached UN sanctions. Night after night on television, day after day in parliament Rudd lashed the government for turning a blind eye, failing to heed warnings, lying, covering up, pretending to know nothing and now refusing to allow Cole to investigate Downer and his department: "The terms of reference make it possible for a firing squad to be put together for the Australian Wheat Board while taking the Howard government out of the firing line altogether."

Rudd was painting the prime minister as a habitual liar. Grandees of the Canberra press gallery sneer at the issue – aren't all politicians liars? – but Rudd's attack was highly effective, wounding Howard and simultaneously fashioning his own image as professional and truthful. The big essay on faith he wrote later in 2006 would argue for Christianity as the religion of truth-tellers, indeed of martyrs for the truth. A panegyric for Dietrich Bonhoeffer, "whose political theology is one of a dissenting church that speaks truth to the state," it would end in a magisterial attack on Howard the liar: "The prime minister's now routine manipulation of the truth poses significant problems for the long-term integrity of our national institutions ..."

This relentless pursuit of Howard won Rudd the friends he needed in the party. Hawker argues: "The real breakthrough was the wheat scandal. It made him in the eyes of caucus and the powerbrokers." The Christian Rudd with a passion for diplomacy was not the man they wanted. They were after a fighter, a smart and determined fighter, to defeat John Howard's union-busting WorkChoices. The NSW unions under John "Robbo" Robertson, who had masterminded a brilliant television campaign against the legislation, were becoming impatient with Beazley's failure to gain traction on the issue in Canberra.

Every Friday, Rudd flew to Sydney for *Sunrise*. The show was working better than ever. The "Big Guns of Politics" segment had been moved to the highest-rating slot on the highest-rating day of the week. He and Hockey pulled off a television triumph in 2006 by climbing the Kokoda Track together to celebrate Anzac Day live on *Sunrise*. Rudd would have breakfast with Hockey after the show every Friday and then do his rounds of the town, usually calling at Sussex Street, where early 2006 found him in conversation with Robertson over the party leadership. After backing Beazley through thick and thin – he was on a crash diet at this time to impress the voters – the forces of the NSW Right, the king-makers of Labor, were splintering. Most were ready to switch to Rudd.

Rudd's position was suddenly complicated by Gillard, who in April began overtaking him in the polls. The two had very similar problems. Both had worked hard at building high public profiles, but both were thwarted in caucus: he by distrust and distaste, she by coming from the Left. At no time in living memory had Labor chosen anyone from the Left as its federal leader. That winter, Rudd and Gillard recognised their mutual interest and began to talk. A battle between them would see both wiped out. Yet if they could unite, Beazley was gone for all money. Gillard was ahead of Rudd in both the polls – 31 to 27 per cent – and in the caucus – about twenty-eight votes to his sixteen – but he would not run on her ticket.

On the last Monday of November, Cole's five-volume report on the AWB scandal was tabled in parliament. It may have been as late as that week that

Rudd and Gillard finally settled their pact. They deny a Kirribilli clause governing the succession. She was taking her chances: if they failed to win the next election, it would be her turn after that. Bob Hawke rang to say Beazley should be left alone. Rudd says he replied: "Get fucked." He asked the NSW Left MP Anthony Albanese to stand in for him that Friday on *Sunrise*. Rein said "Go for it," and he walked down the corridor and told Beazley the fight was on.

The execution had been exquisitely choreographed. The press was in the dark. As Rudd returned from Beazley's rooms, the first Labor member rang a designated journalist at AAP to say she was supporting Kevin Rudd's challenge called that morning. His supporters continued ringing AAP through the day. Jordan and Rudd were confident they could win but not sure of having the convincing victory they needed. Caucus loved Beazley, not the challenger. Though the three-year charm offensive had warmed a few hearts, Rudd still had not many friends and no solid faction. But over the weekend the party professionals moved in behind him. Old enemies were canvassing on the contender's behalf. Labor had to come out of this bloodletting looking as if it had finally made up its mind. And no one in caucus doubted Rudd's determination. "I've seen some driven politicians in my time, but I have seen no one more driven than Kevin," Senator John Faulkner told me. "But this is a good thing, not a bad thing. It's what the Labor Party needed after that long period of Liberal government. You have to be driven to succeed. You have to be driven to overcome the advantages of incumbency."

On Monday, 4 December 2006, Beazley lost to Rudd thirty-nine votes to forty-nine. Howard's strategist and pollster Mark Textor was not happy: "As a professional of fifteen or twenty years' standing, I was deeply worried almost immediately after the leadership change." Rudd would prove the party's most potent electoral machine since Bob Hawke, but this was not clear at first. Beazley already had Labor well ahead in the polls, but similar leads had disappeared as he campaigned in 1998 and 2001. Latham had been way ahead of the government in 2004, but that lead had evaporated too. The challenge for Rudd was to hold Labor's lead all the way to the ballot box. One advantage over Beazley lay deep down in the figures: Rudd would magically restore the party's primary vote. He straddled a vast political divide: Greens on the Left and Christians on the Right would give their first vote to Labor under him. Also clear in a Newspoll published on the morning of his caucus victory was the public's enthusiasm for the Rudd/Gillard team (52 per cent support) and weariness with the old Beazley/Macklin leadership (27 per cent support).

But the voters continued to admire the prime minister as a *person*. On none of the usual measures – e.g. "decisive and strong," "in touch with the voters," "has a vision for Australia" – did the change of leaders trump Howard.

Then Australia saw Rudd in action. In the media blitz of those first days, he returned to the themes he had brought with him into politics: compassion, fairness and decency. There was clunky talk of forks in the road and bridges too far, but what caught the national imagination at this low point in our politics was a fresh, young, smiling leader backing simple, old virtues. The man the party chose for his fighting qualities was embraced by the public for promising to bring sweetness and light to politics. Addressing parliament as leader of the Opposition for the first time, Rudd gave one of the most eloquent performances of his career, delivering, essentially, his maiden speech all over again:

> Compassion is not a dirty word. Compassion is not a sign of weakness. In my view, compassion in politics and in public policy is in fact a hallmark of great strength. It is a hallmark of a society which has about it a decency which speaks for itself. For us in the Labor movement from which we proudly come and have come this last century, these values

of security, liberty and opportunity are not incompatible with equity, with sustainability and with compassion …

So the battlelines are drawn in this great battle of ideas between us. In the ten days or so ahead, when we leave this place, I will be travelling the country, taking this message out. This is not just a battle for ideas; it is a battle on the ground as well. I say to those opposite: we intend to prevail in this battle of ideas, on the ground, right through to the next election. We intend to prevail.

He did. The more Australians saw him, the more they liked him. Petty scandals were brushed aside. Drinks at a strip club, covert contact with a Labor bagman, the row with the Lows over the Eumundi eviction, calling dawn early on Anzac Day for the convenience of *Sunrise* – that saw the end of the "Big Guns" – rumours of a filthy temper and news that his heart had been patched up left his popularity untouched. Indeed, he emerged from these tabloid smears a little stronger each time. From early 2007 he was the most popular Opposition leader since polling began in Australia.

That summer he took a camera crew to Eumundi and shot a commercial that went to air on Australia Day. It was masterful: back home had come the boy once desperate to escape, now a politician claiming his due as a son of the land. The text was superior boilerplate: stuff about Mum and Dad, education, a strong economy and a fair go. But tucked in there was something Rudd really believed in, something his return to Eumundi proved true: "Some call us the lucky country, but I believe you make your own luck."

The polls showed Australians wanted Rudd to be prime minister and Labor's two-party-preferred vote threatened the government with something like anni-hilation. The man caucus had regarded for so long as a try-hard chameleon was thought far more trust-worthy (67 to 49 per cent), far more in touch with voters (76 to 50 per cent) and much more likeable (82 to 55 per cent) than the prime minister. Howard was not despised. A Nielsen poll in June showed voters still thought him the better man to handle the economy and even foreign policy. But young Rudd was thought way ahead of old Howard in his grasp of social policy (68 to 43 per cent), understanding of climate change (71 to 37 per cent) and overall public approval (63 to 50 per cent). This was a man who could do superbly what all who crave high office must do: harvest a nation's hopes.

Yet all the way to victory night at the Suncorp Stadium there was a question in the air: can Australia have a leader who's an ash-blond, unfit, smiling nerd? The answer that night was yes. Nerd leaders are fine by Australians. We like experts. We like ideas. We value competence in our leaders. We choose them much as we choose an electrician: because they can be trusted to get on with their complicated work. We have a long tradition of electing such leaders. The campaign of 2007 was a face-off between two nerds: eleven years of power hadn't altogether disguised the gawky, opportunistic policy wonk that was John Howard. As the polling analyst Andrew Catsaras told me: "The Paul Hogan era is over. Australians want their leaders to be competent, intelligent and able to do the job."

Rudd was sworn in at Yarralumla on 3 December 2007. The Queen's name did not pass his lips. Instead of allegiance he swore to "well and truly serve the Commonwealth of Australia, her land and her people, so help me God." On his first day in office, he signed the Kyoto Protocol. On the first day of parliament he delivered an apology to the stolen generations into which he threw what was most authentic about his politics: his instinctive sympathy for children and for the survivors of wretched childhoods. His coarse – but popular – intervention in the controversy over Bill Henson's photographs the following May flowed from the same source. "Absolutely revolting," he declared after a few seconds' scrutiny of redacted images on a television monitor. "Kids deserve to have the innocence of their childhood protected. I have a very deep view of this. For God's sake, let's just allow kids to be kids." Hovering over his attack on Henson as much as the extraordinarily fine Apology are the ghosts of Eumundi and Ashgrove.

The Apology had not come easily. Having trouble drafting his speech, Rudd went to see Lorna Fejo, who had come down from the Territory for the occasion. Fejo had been ripped out of her mother's arms by white police and a black stockman in a bush camp in Tennant Creek in the 1930s:

> I asked Nanna Fejo what she would have me say today about her story. She thought for a few moments then said that what I should say today was that all mothers are important. And she added: "Families – keeping them together is very important. It's a good thing that you are surrounded by love and that love is passed down the generations. That's what gives you happiness." As I left, later on, Nanna Fejo took one of my staff aside, wanting to make sure that I was not too hard on the Aboriginal stockman who had hunted those kids down all those years ago. The stockman had found her again decades later, this

time himself to say, "Sorry." And remarkably, extraordinarily, she had forgiven him.

It was a great day for tears. Inside the house, on the lawns of parliament, in squares and streets across Australia, crowds were weeping, more with relief than anything that the country's sorry business had finally been done. On his first day in parliament the new prime minister walked into the history books. It seemed we had elected a man of principle and courage.

Man for All Seasons

S hriven, blameless, fresh from communion, the prime minister stands at the lych-gate of St John's Canberra and takes questions from the media. Although he rarely does the rounds of the Sunday morning current-affairs shows, Rudd stands at the gate of the old church on Constitution Avenue, available for the cameras, whenever Sunday finds him in Canberra. The message is clear: this prime minister mixes faith and politics. It makes Rudd an odd man out among Labor prime ministers. The last keen believer to lead a Labor government was Scullin. Not since the Second World War has Australia had a self-confessed God-botherer of any political persuasion running the country. The sight of a prime minister using a church as backdrop for a press conference sets many Australians on edge. But it's authentic Rudd and he knows it plays surprisingly well to the electorate.

Who is Rudd? A political Christian. After Labor's defeat in October 2004, Rudd took command of an operation to win believers back to the party. A strong religious undertow had worked against Labor in the campaign. Atheist Mark Latham with plans to cut the cash flowing to rich church schools was pitted against John Howard the prince of Family Values. Howard was employing some of the tricks and rhetoric sweeping George W. Bush to a second victory in those same weeks in the US. A shrewd deal to swap preferences with Family First, a party set up by the Assemblies of God, put Steve Fielding into the Senate and on Rudd's analysis cost Labor at least four marginal seats. A month after the poll Rudd declared on Channel Ten:

> We will not for one moment stand idly by while either the Liberals, Nationals or Family First assert that God has somehow become some wholly owned subsidiary of political conservatism in this country.

The fight to reclaim Christ for Labor began with a PowerPoint presentation in Rudd's parliamentary office in late November. Spilling from his room into the hallway was nearly a third of the caucus: believers and non-believers from all factions. What they planned was unfamiliar work, but if winning meant grappling with God, then it had to be done. Rudd found an ally in Jim Wallis, a visiting American preacher who was out here to promote his book *God's Politics*. Wallis was to become a key figure in the claw-back of Christian votes by US Democrats. The operations in America and Australia moved roughly in parallel. The two men kept in touch.

Rudd was appealing to a bigger audience than the 8 per cent of Australians who join him in prayer on any given Sunday. Australia remains – to the despair of rationalists – a largely Christian country. Rudd puts the figure at about 70 per cent, but that's oddly sloppy for a professional politician. The true figure is a still very strong 50 per cent. But the potency of Rudd's appeal to faith is felt even beyond that constituency because, as Marion Maddox explains, even non-believers in Australia admire Christianity:

> Look at atheist parents who send their children to church schools and agnostic voters who support contracting out welfare to the Salvation Army, Anglicare or Mission Australia. They don't go to church, but they want "values." And they want to be reassured their leaders have some.

Early in his time in parliament, Rudd joined the Monday Night Group, a collection of Christians drawn mainly from Coalition ranks. These were deeply conservative and rather strange figures to sit with each week and swap ideas about life, death and eternity: Ross Cameron, Bronwyn Bishop, the ultra-Catholic Brian Harradine and the man he would one day face across the despatch boxes, Tony Abbott. Membership of the group was another item in the caucus indictment of the Member for Griffith back in those days. "One of my Labor Party colleagues said to me, 'Kevin, never pray with the bastards, because if you do it makes it harder to hate 'em. And half of the business of this place is hating them, because we want their jobs.'"

Rudd had been as shy of discussing his faith as his childhood until politics demanded it. But once the campaign to recruit Christians was underway, Rudd spoke and wrote about his faith in revealing detail. It came to define him as a new kind of politician: soft-hearted, hard-headed, courageous, visionary, even pure. Two women in two remarkable interviews dug down to his fundamental beliefs. To Geraldine Doogue he confessed his debt to his mother's CWA Catholicism:

> When you see people in strife, I cannot be indifferent to that because that's the way I've been brought up. And I've given that as an adult a form of political expression called the Australian

Labor Party, which is, by the way, as flawed and
as failed as I am. But we try.

Would he be in politics but for his faith, she asked.
"That's a fantastic hypothetical," he replied. "Probably, I think. None of us are devoid of ego." Faith, he
said, helps him battle pride and keep things in pro-
portion even as it offers glimpses of the sublime. He
told Julia Baird on the ABC's *Sunday Profile*: "For
me it is pretty grounding and also at a deeper, I suppose philosophical, level it's a deep personal wonder-
ment at eternity."

Early 2005 saw Rudd researching religion and
voting patterns and conducting a media blitz starring
himself as the Opposition's shadow spokesman for
Christ. His immediate target was Howard's moralis-
ing version of family values:

> Surely a family's ability to put food on the table is
> a family value; surely a family's ability to afford
> proper health care for its children is a family value;
> and surely making sure our children have access
> to a decent education is equally a family value.

WorkChoices gave Rudd magnificent opportunities
to mock the government when Howard and his treasurer, Peter Costello, demanded, on this issue, the

churches keep out of the debate: "The message from Howard to the churches is speak out when it suits the government, but shut up when it doesn't."

Rudd's strategy caused disquiet in Labor ranks, particularly on the Left. For decades the party had had to fight clerics in order to pursue social reform. Battles over abortion, birth control, divorce, drug reform, IVF, censorship, homosexuality etc. had been made hard by the churches. The supposedly secular soul of Labor was always under threat. And here was Kevin Rudd inviting the Christians back in. Rudd argued he only wanted them to be given a fair hearing:

> A Christian perspective on contemporary policy debates may not prevail. It must nonetheless be argued. And once heard, it must be weighed, together with other arguments from different philosophical traditions, in a fully contestable secular polity.

And as always he offered a personal assurance: "I am a Jeffersonian separatist."

Australians warmed to his homemade, rather secular faith. An umbilical cord still stretches to Rome, but he worships with his family in the Anglican Church. "Denominationalism means virtually nothing to me." All claims of infallibility – from popes, bishops and preachers – are absurd. No ecclesiastical authority can tell him what to do or what to believe. Christianity has no monopoly on morality. Man's ultimate guide is an informed conscience. As he prepared to vote on stem-cell research in 2002, Rudd turned to his mother for advice. This was not an abstract issue: Marge Rudd had Parkinson's disease.

> My mother was a Catholic from central casting. Her response when I put to her the question of what I should do in this vote was: "In the great traditions of the Church, Kev, that is a question for your conscience, not mine."

Rudd's record on conscience issues is deeply conservative by community standards but falls short of the rigour demanded by Rome and the Pentecostals. He voted in the end for stem-cell research – "as one of that bill's most reluctant supporters" – but couldn't take a further step four years later and vote for the cloning of human embryos. He voted against euthanasia but supported the use of the abortion drug RU486. His position on homosexuality remains messy. He is not troubled personally – many of his best friends etc. – and does not believe Christ backs the harsh sexual teachings of conservative faiths:

I see very little evidence that this preoccupation with sexual morality is consistent with the spirit and content of the Gospels. For example, there is no evidence of Jesus of Nazareth expressly preaching against homosexuality.

He sends his best wishes each year to Sydney's Gay and Lesbian Mardi Gras – a practice John Howard abjured – and backed legislation to wipe from all Commonwealth laws the last traces of discrimination against gays and lesbians. But there are limits – personal and political – to his sympathies. He has made no move to bring homosexual men and women under the protective umbrella of the *Anti-Discrimination Act* and he opposes anything resembling gay marriage. On *Q&A* in May 2008, he dodged the question as long as he could, then, to jeers from the audience, admitted the definition recently introduced into the *Marriage Act* – the union of a man and a woman – "is the position of my party and that is the position I hold personally." That would change.

Rudd does what he can to keep off such ground, minimising doctrine and maximising values. Christ's teaching on poverty is where his politics and religion merge most comfortably. It's the gospel of Eumundi, Ashgrove and Nambour; a message of hope for those who have, like the Rudds, "run into one of life's brick walls." In one way or another he has been making the same argument for over thirty years:

> What do you do about people who can't look after themselves? People who are poor? People who are oppressed? Do you walk by on the other side of the road, or do you do something about it? Jesus taught us that love requires action.

But nothing radical. Rudd's drift from Rome had not transformed him into one of those campaigning evangelicals who drove the anti-slavery movement and fought for women's suffrage. Rudd sees himself on a transformative mission, but there will be no upheavals along the way. As one of his aides explained: Rudd is not out to abolish poverty so much as see the poor are treated decently.

Sally Warhaft, eccentric and brilliant editor of the *Monthly*, was looking for someone to profile Rudd, the man nibbling at Beazley's heels. No writer was right for the job. So she turned to Rudd himself: would he write her a substantial piece on faith? Just as *Sunrise* had given Rudd his speaking voice, constant practice on the nation's opinion pages had taught him how to write. The 6000 words he gave Warhaft a fortnight later were very fine. The appearance of "Faith in

Politics" in the first week of October 2006 caused a sensation:

> Above the Great West Door of Westminster Abbey are arrayed ten great statues of the martyrs of the Church. Not Peter, Stephen, James or the familiar names of the saints sacrificed during the great Roman persecution before Constantine's conversion. No: these are martyrs of the twentieth century, when the age of faith was, in the minds of many in the West, already tottering towards its collapse.
>
> One of those honoured above the Great West Door is Dietrich Bonhoeffer, the German theologian, pastor and peace activist. Bonhoeffer is, without doubt, the man I admire most in the history of the twentieth century ...

Rudd presented himself here as a conviction politician of rare courage. His claim to be following in the footsteps of the great was taken seriously. The essay didn't have to be read: the fact of it lifted him out of the ruck. But on reflection, this fascination with Bonhoeffer was odd for a man with Rudd's ambitions. He wryly acknowledges a martyr's example is not much help for a politician. Bonhoeffer was a brave man on the other side. He wasn't dealing with the moral conflicts that inevitably come with government. He told the truth to a vicious regime and paid with his life. What is it about Rudd and martyrs? It's a fascination that goes all the way back to his schooldays. In the essay he called Bonhoeffer "the Thomas More of European Protestantism." Could there be somewhere in him the death wish of a pious schoolboy: some trace of an old hankering to go out in a blaze of moral glory?

Two months after "Faith in Politics" appeared – provoking news reports, opinion pieces, television interviews, panel discussions and outrage from the Opposition – Rudd defeated Beazley for the leadership. The pollsters had already discovered switching to Rudd would dramatically improve Labor's primary vote – mainly by bringing Christians back into the fold. The claw-back had worked, but more for Rudd than the party: the faithful weren't planning to return to Labor but to Rudd Labor. Twelve months later the election confirmed that "Kevin 07" was catnip for believers. "While the blue-collar workers provided the grunt with the national swing, the religious activists provided the leverage and the key seats," John Black of Australian Development Strategies told the *Australian Financial Review*.

> Black says the profile of the Rudd majority "looks a little like a 1970s Gough Whitlam rally held in a

Queensland rural church hall – Blacktown meets
Nambour – with high-school educated, skilled
and unskilled blue-collar workers sitting side by
side with the evangelical and activist religions –
and making up the numbers are kids, lots of them,
from babies up to ten-year-olds."

The morning after his strange victory speech at
the Suncorp Stadium, the Rudds worshipped at their
parish church of St John the Baptist, Bulimba. Standing afterwards at the gates the prime-minister elect
gave his first press conference. Rather woodenly he
listed phone calls received from the great – Bush,
Brown, Yudhoyono – and ran through the adminis-
trative details of the coming days. He promised to
govern for all Australians and departed. It was, in its
way, as odd as his performance the night before. The
Age's Tony Wright wrote:

Here he was, the winner, and he was offhand,
almost disengaged, not a smile to be had. There
was a cold purpose about him ... As to any detail,
any hint of a spark of humour ... nothing doing.

"Politics is about power," Rudd had said nine years
earlier when he stood for the first time to address
parliament. Now he had power. He appeared not

exultant but profoundly satisfied. If the pursuit of power had anything to do with repairing the wreckage of his childhood, then at this moment all the bits and pieces of Kevin Rudd were coming together at last. He was just fifty and had power in his hands.

Prime ministers learn on the job. There is no school to prepare them for the task. That he had taught himself so diligently to be a candidate, a contender and leader of the Opposition did not guarantee he could now teach himself to run the country. But Rudd has form: he had at each step of the way exceeded all expectations. And no prime minister had arrived at the Lodge with a CV quite like his, a point he turned into a *Yes, Minister* joke: "I'm probably the first bloke for quite a while who has been at one stage in his life both Humphrey, Bernard and now the minister, and in this case the prime minister, so there is very little I haven't seen before."

But how would he now reconcile his faith and politics? "Anyone who says that it's easy is not telling the truth," he told Geraldine Doogue. On one hand were "questions of conscience" and on the other "the inherent compromise of the political process." Rather grandly for a party politician he concluded: "I think any person in the public political process must first and foremost answer to their conscience."

Doogue pushed him: did he ever feel his faith being sidelined by politics? "The techniques of politics are mind-boggling," Rudd replied. "And there's a danger that you see at the end of that the suffocation of the soul." Doogue was taken aback. "I mean it," he assured her, "because I've seen it." In others? "Judge not lest you be judged. But it can happen. And I think when you sense the extinguishment of the light or the message inside of you in terms of what you want to do for the community – and the country and beyond the country for the world – it's time to pack up and go." But Rudd has a problem: the backers he finally found for himself in the party don't think like that. The NSW Right pursues hard-line, nuts-and-bolts politics. Key figures from the Sussex Street machine are Rudd's advisers. His decent ambitions are at odds with – and appear to have given way to – their "whatever it takes" approach. They don't spend political capital on great moral challenges. What they do best is staying in power. Suffocation of the soul comes with the territory.

Rudd has delivered for Christians. He inhabits that prudish world where respectability, upbringing and faith merge in a kind of resolute caution. This informed his instinctive response to the Henson photographs and to radio foul-mouth Kyle Sandilands quizzing a young girl about rape: "Really off."

Decent prudishness is the common spirit of his government and Howard's. So is a meagre commitment to liberty. Christians are not by nature on the side of freedom: they have dedicated their lives, after all, to serving the greatest power known, Almighty God. Rudd's government is bravely facing down all opposition to its plans to filter criminal material from the internet – not just child porn but, say, discussion of euthanasia techniques – while abandoning plans for a timid charter of rights.

On 22 November 2009, Rudd addressed the national conference of the Australian Christian Lobby. His mission: to announce Labor would provide another $42 million to bankroll the National School Chaplaincy Program until the end of 2011. Howard's original scheme was greeted with public protests. This is not the state funding church schools to teach, and church hospitals to treat the sick. The High Court has blessed such arrangements. This program bankrolls chaplains to be chaplains.

Rudd is unperturbed by such naked funding of religion by government. He clings stubbornly to his claim of Jeffersonian purity while acknowledging tacitly that no such scheme would be allowed under the US Constitution. Here in Australia, Rudd argues, the scheme is rescued by choice: schools can choose the denomination and faith of the chaplains.

"The Australian attitude to these things is, I think, quite practical," he told me. "The dividing line in this country is not providing anyone a platform to mandatorily impose a religious view using the agency of the state. That principle is alive and well. That is the dividing line." He is equally unperturbed by the constitutional challenge to the scheme now underway. "That's why we have the High Court."

In Opposition no policy was more firmly at the centre of his Christian agenda than the humane treatment of boatpeople. It is the unhealed wound of Australian politics. He wrote in the Bonhoeffer essay:

> The biblical injunction to care for the stranger in our midst is clear. The parable of the Good Samaritan is but one of many which deal with the matter of how we should respond to a vulnerable stranger in our midst.

Even so, Rudd was responsible for the expensive vaudeville of processing on Christmas Island and had talked tough on the eve of the 2007 poll about perhaps towing boats back to Indonesia. He declared people smugglers "scum of the earth" who might "rot in hell" and his government is now considering legislation that would throw Oskar Schindler in the clink. But even now he talks of following the example of the Good Samaritan.

Why not Christ, I asked the prime minister. Wasn't he a refugee? Didn't he only survive to do his work because of the generous refugee policies of Egypt? Rudd wouldn't play: "I'll leave the theological analogy to yourself."

He is hardly more comfortable with the politics. Ask about the passions generated by boatpeople and he replies curtly: "The Australian people will react as they choose fit. All I can do is respond to the objective facts concerning the numbers." He rattles off figures. But there is no fight in the man here, no sign he's willing to mount a bigger political or moral argument to rein in these passions. He presents himself as a spectator at the wreck. "How [the numbers] are reported and how they are responded to by the wider public, that's a separate matter over which I have no control."

But couldn't he use his authority as prime minister to urge Australians to calm down? He dismisses the idea as pointless, indeed counter-productive. He suggests I read Hansard. "I would draw your attention to what I have been saying consistently for a long time, a long degree of time."

Perhaps admitting this country has racial anxieties is the one thing a leader can never do? "If you have a view of the Australian heart and soul, which

I think I do – as someone who's grown up in rural Queensland, worked abroad, works nationally – this is a very good-hearted country. There are always going to be people who have real fears and anxieties in any country. You see that throughout Europe; you see it throughout North America; you see it elsewhere in the world as well. But this is a very good-hearted country with a deep instinct for a fair go at home and abroad."

But that, of course, is not what the polls say. Rudd knows it, for a couple of days after our conversation the processing of all Sri Lankan and Hazara boatpeople was suspended indefinitely. The overflow from Christmas Island was flown to John Howard's mothballed detention centres in the desert. In the face of tough polls after a brutal campaign over the boats led by another professed Christian, Tony Abbott, Rudd had caved in. The more humane policies of the new government had lasted barely twenty months. Faith had not sustained him. The old days were back.

Only recently I stumbled on some video of Rudd promising the same Australian Christian Lobby that Labor would, if elected, abolish John Howard's harsh refugee regime. They were pleased. Rudd is thought to be hardly touched by time, but this is footage of a younger man. A few years in government have changed much and aged him. But in August 2007 he answered the lobby's questions with steady confidence:

> I want to make sure this country maintains an open heart ... If we are seen to walk away from all of that, it says something very bad about us internationally. But even worse than that, if we as one of the initiators of the post-war Refugee Convention consensus are seen to be fragmenting it at the edges, we are also part and parcel of frag-menting the global consensus and machinery for dealing with refugee challenges into the future. I never want to be part of any such government that does that.

Parts per Million

Canberra was Brisbane all over again. The same demands, the same chaos, the same kids' brigade, the same high hopes, the same obsession with the news cycle, the same delays, the same business of keeping people waiting – for several hours in May 2008 the chief of the defence force, Air Chief Marshal Angus Houston – the same certainty of being on a great transformative mission, the same ceaseless work – but much, much more power.

Labor had never given such muscle to a prime minister. With victory approaching, Rudd insisted the old tradition of caucus electing the ministry would end. He said: "Part of modernising the Labor Party is putting all that stuff behind us." The power the factions lost, Rudd gained. All but a few heavyweights sitting at the Cabinet table owed their place to him. It has never been harder for Labor ministers to stare down a prime minister.

Nor have Labor Cabinets ever been so circumscribed. From the time Rudd's government faced its first crises, more and more big decisions were made by four key ministers alone – Rudd, Gillard, the treasurer, Wayne Swan, and the finance minister, Lindsay Tanner – sitting as the Strategic Priorities and Budget Committee. In early 2010 Laura Tingle reported:

> When ministers arrive for federal cabinet meetings, they find a folder waiting in their spots which they can look at but not take out of the room. Inside are decisions already taken by cabinet's expenditure review committee and the ultimate power within the Rudd government – the Strategic Priorities and Budget Committee (SPBC). Ministers are expected to endorse the decisions without discussion, and usually do.

Two other Cabinet systems have broken down. Submissions once circulated ten days before Cabinet meetings began to turn up in ministers' offices only the night before. And scrutiny of submissions by inter-departmental committees has largely given way to scrutiny by the prime minister's office and department alone. Rudd is the choke point again.

"This is a Cabinet-led government," he told me. "There are Cabinet meetings each week. There are Cabinet committees who determine the core decisions of the government and that is the way which we have operated this government from the beginning ... I'll be engaged as the chairperson of a number of those committees ... whether it's macro-economic management, whether it's the investment in and reform of the education system, investment in and reform of the health-care system, whether it's the future of climate change and water – these core decisions of the government, including the national security agenda – surely people would expect that the prime minister was intimately involved in those core agendas as I am through the Cabinet committee structure for which I make absolutely no apology."

Rudd had clearly learnt one lesson from Brisbane, where he earned the nickname "Dr Death" for the ruthless sacking of department heads when Goss came to power. Way down the line, public service bosses were made to re-apply for their jobs. However necessary, this was deeply resented. The slide and fall of Goss can be put down in part to the alienation of Queensland public servants – natural Labor voters and indispensable allies in government. Rudd guaranteed continuity when he came to power in Canberra. While he dressed up the "no spill" principle in the rhetoric of Westminster conventions, the decision to keep Howard's department heads and ambassadors in place was good, cautious politics, however much it distressed the Labor faithful. Bureaucrats under Rudd might find themselves exhausted and baffled by his demands, but their jobs would be secure.

With so much power concentrated in Rudd's hands, access to the prime minister becomes a crucial issue of government. Since before Machiavelli, courtiers have whinged about access. "It's easier to get in to see the Pope than Kevin," one disgruntled backbencher told me. "He's always rushing," a junior minister told me. "You have fleeting meetings." At the top of the ministry is a small group of men and women with easy access to the boss, though it's said there are times and moods when even these heavyweights have trouble getting through the door. They are regarded as conduits to power. John Faulkner told me: "People have come to me and said: will you tell Kevin this? It's presumed I have better access to him. But I say to them: you're the one who should talk to Kevin."

Senior ministers with urgent matters to settle with the prime minister can find themselves waiting and waiting – even flying with their staff to another city only to wait fruitlessly for the door to open. The minister for communications, Stephen Conroy, had to put himself on a couple of VIP flights with Rudd in April 2009 to break the bad news that the tendering process for the national broadband network had failed. "Like most of Rudd's Cabinet ministers,

Conroy had trouble finding an opening in the prime minister's program," Peter Hartcher reported in the *Sydney Morning Herald*. Time can also be in short supply for distinguished citizens co-opted by Rudd to pursue his visionary plans for the future. "There comes a point when these big ideas need prime ministerial time, and it isn't there," I am told by Richard Woolcott, Rudd's special envoy to the Asia-Pacific community. "It's a disjunction."

David Epstein, Rudd's chief of staff, bailed out in November 2008. He had lasted a little over eighteen months at Rudd's side, trying to bring order to his office as leader of the Opposition and prime minister. At forty-four, Beazley's former chief of staff was the oldest man close to Rudd. Epstein left before the government celebrated its first birthday. Reports at the time spoke of Rudd still diving into every issue in depth, still not separating wheat from chaff, still operating in logistical confusion. Epstein's place was taken by Alister Jordan. Other staff came and went, but Mr April had lasted eight years to reach the post he had always wanted: chief of staff to the prime minister. He is available fourteen hours a day, seven days a week. He's believed to keep a sleeping bag in the office.

History doesn't worry much about the work practices of the great. Churchill slaved for ridiculous hours and drove his staff to distraction. No one in retrospect gives a damn. Rudd isn't Churchill and this isn't the Second World War, but what looks like dysfunction in Canberra will seem mere eccentricity if the results are worthwhile. Rudd's big brain and prodigious energy save him from many of the perils of his own hyperactivity. When his attention is engaged, he is a formidable distiller of complex information. The process is not efficient and might not end in the best policy, but his understanding of the issues is superb. It all takes time, as an unnamed bureaucrat explained to Laura Tingle:

> You can't go to Kevin and say, "Well, Prime Minister, here is the issue, here are your potential options for dealing with it, here is what we recommend you do, you just sign here," and get it done in a two-hour meeting. He wants to synthesise the information himself, so instead of a two-hour meeting, you'll have a 35-minute meeting where you have to tell him everything known about a subject so that he can go through the intellectual process of considering it himself. Then there will be a few more meetings.

Part of the problem is Rudd's ambition to find "decent" solutions to the nation's problems. Decency is personal, intuitive, hard to delegate. It calls for the sort of scrutiny only he can give. Marry that to a sense of indispensability that is right off the Richter scale, and you have what looks like a recipe for ruin. He takes command of top-shelf policies – the emissions trading scheme or the new health arrangements with the states – but when other policies come under attack, Rudd requires ministers to brief him down to the smallest detail. He responds to pressure by burying himself in detail. This passion to know everything does what it did in Brisbane: makes life around him, and the business of government, hard.

Rudd is proudly the prime minister of fine detail. Mastery of detail ensures good policy outcomes, he told me. It ensures accountability: "The prime minister is required to answer in detail across the entire breadth of government decision-making." So he is satisfied with the flow of business through his office? "Absolutely. There is a structural criticism here which will be levelled at any private office of any head of government, state or federal, Labor or Liberal, which has been around since time immemorial. People should read the literature."

He has never lost his love of showing he knows more than anyone else in the room. Facts pour out of him as they have ever since he was that Jaycees kid speaking for Australia. His Press Club debate on health policy with Tony Abbott in March 2010 was a demonstration of how powerfully Rudd can marshal facts. At other times they emerge in a dazzling and somewhat pointless display of mastery. He puzzled James Packer by sitting down with the young gambling mogul one day and telling him everything he knew about gambling in China. His knowledge was encyclopaedic.

Information is a great prerogative of power. Rudd has at his disposal a vast, highly skilled machine for gathering facts. The demands he makes on the public service quickly became legend. So did his chipper response to complaints of bureaucratic exhaustion:

> I understand that there has been some criticism around the edges that some public servants are finding the hours a bit much. Well, I suppose I've simply got news for the public service – there'll be more. This government was elected with a clear-cut mandate. We intend to proceed with that. The work ethic of this government will not decrease, it will increase.

Hours aren't the issue. Bureaucrats don't mind working hard, long days. They object to feeding material in when nothing much comes out; demands made at midnight that might be made at midday; wild flurries of activity driven by petty media squalls;

calls for detailed briefing on fourth-rank issues that need never go near a prime minister; and urgent requests for material they know to be sitting in Rudd's office already. They mind *wasting* their time. And they worry that not much good policy can come from a strange mix of rush and delay. The new government was always pressing forward while leaving unfinished business in its wake. Labor had been in office less than a year when Phillip Coorey of the *Sydney Morning Herald* came up with this perfect image:

> Rudd is starting to resemble the home handyman in a house full of half-finished jobs, while still eager to begin more. He's out in the backyard building a shed while the wife is yelling at him to finish the kitchen renovation and rehang the screen door out the front.

None of this affected Rudd's popularity for two years. All through this time he was living in a paradise of immense approval. Newspoll had registered something like a national orgasm in his first months in office:

> 84 per cent of us thought him decisive and strong,
> 89 per cent thought him a man of vision,
> 86 per cent though him likeable, and
> 79 per cent thought him trustworthy.

These enthusiasms would cool a little. More of us came to think him arrogant and fewer saw him as a man of vision. But the nation's trust in his intelligence, capability, capacity for hard work and honesty was hardly touched before Copenhagen. Yet Rebecca Huntley of Ipsos Mackay research noticed hesitation in the focus groups. "People warmed to Rudd quickly," she told me. "But the affection hasn't deepened. He's seen as bright, not beholden to the party warlords, competent, his own man, really keen to have the job, a breath of fresh air. But who is he? The feeling is: we've been on lots of dates, but we haven't got to the next level."

First and foremost, he is the engine that drives him. Every witness to his life since Nambour talks about the phenomenal machine inside this man. He turns many faces to the world, but the engine under the hood is the same 5.4-litre V8. What you see of Rudd at any particular moment depends on the destination and the terrain. He is a *sui generis* off-road vehicle whose driver is only glimpsed in passing, a shadow through the windscreen.

He can be so good: turning up without fuss at a bedside or a funeral; sitting on the floor at 2020; delivering the Apology; staying on to yak with the party faithful; charming a table of distinguished Americans at lunch or a bunch of weary doctors in a hospital courtyard; posing time and again for photographs with families and kids when he's out walking; or dazzling a delegation from the China National Peking Opera Company with half an hour's patter in Mandarin.

And he can be so bad. He has a way of ignoring people once their usefulness is past. Before his challenge to Beazley he was ringing John Robertson of Unions NSW half-a-dozen times a day. With victory the calls stopped. He passed in the corridor the man who made him leader of the party without a nod. Text messages to journalists whom this self-confessed media tart had courted for years dried up when he became prime minister. Something of this was inevitable: prime ministers have new and onerous preoccupations. But his neglect of obvious courtesies is a strange flaw in a politician so determined to do his chores perfectly. He switches on and switches off. He shows marked disdain for the feelings of those who are already on-side. It's not clear if their hurt registers. Perhaps other people's feelings are a closed book to him.

He stands on his dignity. He makes a display of little grudges. He is untroubled by the impact of behaviour that is, by any measure, startlingly rude. The party has not forgiven him for failing to turn up to the funeral of John Button, one of Labor's favourite sons, in April 2008. He took a teddy bear instead to the bedside of Cate Blanchett. His request to the BBC not to be seated next to Madam Fu Ying, the Chinese ambassador to Britain – the request was refused – raised diplomatic hackles on a couple of continents in March 2009. The sight of Rudd shuffling his papers as the New South Wales premier, Kristina Keneally, warmly welcomed him in early 2010 became a defining bad look of his prime ministership. He and his ministers spent weeks fixing the mess with flowers, smiles and long walks through the grass for television cameras.

He can be beguiling company. His mind is full and rich. He has read a lot and remembered it all. A love of playful argument survives the grinding routine of political confrontation. That he finds being one of the boys so difficult is hardly a hanging offence. Leaders are often awkward in just this way. Those sitting with him as he guzzles peanuts and swears wonder why he tries so hard. It makes people uneasy rather than relaxed. The cussing comes and goes and so does the Australian demotic. Exclaiming "Fair shake of the sauce bottle, mate" on Sky News provoked a torrent of mockery. Defending himself, Rudd let slip a clue to his bifurcated way with words: "I grew up on a farm in country Queensland and my father always used to say, 'Fair shake of a sauce bottle.' I'm the son of a farmer, for God's sake." He never heard such talk from his well-spoken mother, Marge: it's the ghost of Bert Rudd talking to an eleven-year-old.

Everyone wishes he had more sleep. "Kevin starts at around six in the morning," Thérèse Rein told Annabel Crabb. "He might get to bed around one or two, or maybe three. He doesn't need a lot of sleep." That's debatable. From his caucus, his office and his ministry come reports that Rudd is a better man when he has slept. The moods are better, the tantrums fewer, the work easier when he has had something like a normal night's sleep. Moody people are judged – not always fairly – by their worst moods. When Rudd is fresh and things are going well, he turns an open face to the world. Exhausted and under pressure, he shuts down. He is a man who combines resilience and a brittle temper in quite unpredictable ways. On any day he can be both the boyish Tintin of Bill Leak's cartoons and Alan Ramsey's famous "Prissy, precious prick. One with a glass jaw, a quick temper and, when he loses it, a foul tongue."

On a grey afternoon in late January 2010, a well-dressed crowd stood on the hard floors of Sydney's Museum of Contemporary Art while Rudd delivered an Australia Day address. He is still as he was at Nambour High: most at home behind a microphone. Delivering speeches seems less a chore for Rudd than one of the perks of office. The Apology will have its place in any anthology of great Australian oratory. Yet Rudd can leave audiences numb with tedium. It is often and rightly pointed out that his syntax owes a lot to *The Book of Common Prayer*, but the strategy of his speeches owes more to the evangelical sermon, which must always, whatever the occasion, spruik for the redeeming virtues of Christ. Evangelists are always on the stump. So is Rudd.

Veterans of the talk circuit swear he spoke for forty-five minutes at the MCA. It may have felt as long but was half that time. This is the authentic Rudd few see and few forget once they have experienced it. He opened with the criminal record of his forebear, Thomas Rudd: five minutes. He mused on the mixture of "can do" and "fair go" that unites Australians: three minutes. A toast at this point would have launched the celebrations nicely, but Rudd was only warming up. An account of the government's triumph over the global financial crisis – four minutes – had guests gazing across the harbour. Surely, *surely* he would end soon? No. Carefully numbering each step along the way, he addressed the two challenges we face for the future, the three strategic options available and the three measures that must be taken: another twelve minutes.

In New South Wales, a 123 per cent increase in transport infrastructure; $1.5 billion for the Hunter Expressway; $600 million for the Kempsey Bypass; $1.8 billion upgrading the rail networks in the freight system of this state. Now on top of that when we roll out the National Broadband Network, an investment of up to $43 billion, this state representing a third of the federation will receive the bulk of that investment – altogether with one objective, to increase the state-of-the-art of our infrastructure here and across the country to enable our workers to work more efficiently in the future.

Glasses were long empty. Minds had wandered far away. What on earth did this have to do with Australia Day? The strangeness of such events is disturbing. Surely Rudd knows how boring and out of place this is? How insulting? Has he so little in his mind about Australia that the best he can do to celebrate our national day is give an interim report on infrastructure spending? Is he so vain he thinks he transforms this brass into gold just by delivering it? Or does he not really care what people think? He's there, these are the issues on his mind, and they can listen? He never rescues the situation by being blokey:

I don't know about you but I'm pining for a drink. I have one further, formal, solemn task to perform and that is to ask you to raise your glasses in a simple toast to our great land, Australia.

Political leaders are born to disappoint. They can never fulfil the hopes they raise. Letting the punters down lightly is a great political art. There are figures in caucus who say: this man has turned out far better than we feared. And there are those who reply: he is as rackety as we feared Latham would be. He is defended by the party, but more out of necessity, it seems, than conviction. He is the leader. Come what may, he must lead the party to the next election.

If disappointment with Rudd has a particular edge, it is because people have come to doubt his courage. Howard's courage was never in question. His values were. The opposite is true for Rudd and doubt is eating away at his goodwill. "What is courage?" Rudd asked at Yarralumla the day Trooper Mark Donaldson was given his Victoria Cross. "The answer perhaps lies best with those who have known the profession of arms." Rudd speaks with ease about the courage of nurses, fire-fighters, police and soldiers, but not often of politicians. He speaks of Australia being shaped by three great values: courage, resilience and compassion. He recognises what courage is: "Knowing the dangers that lie ahead on the road, but defying those dangers and taking the decision to proceed."

He is courageous pursuing those gut issues that connect somehow to the mess of his early years: child protection, education, health, homelessness and China. Signing up to Kyoto and making the Apology were symbolic acts of great distinction, though by the time they happened most opposition had melted away. The polls gave Rudd permission to sign up and say sorry. He shows little ticker for brawls over big abstract issues that go to the soul of the nation. The rights agenda has been casually junked. The republic is postponed to a date to be fixed.

A shrewd old bureaucrat who has worked with a few prime ministers wonders if Rudd really understands the way power works at the top. He isn't afraid to pick a fight but doesn't then behave like a prime minister: he involves himself so much; puts himself on the line so quickly; doesn't exercise authority by keeping his distance. These problems of technique are odd in a man who has had a long fascination with power. Tracking down the powerful, picking the people he has to know, began as a diplomatic duty and became a lifelong passion. He is a determined networker. But perhaps it's his deep respect for power that makes him so careful not to put powerful forces offside. His drive to acquire power is extraordinarily strong – the work of a lifetime – but he shows less enthusiasm to exercise it. His instinct is to hoard rather than spend.

Certainly, at first he overrated the power of business. He prides himself on understanding business – and talks of "deep kissing" big corporations – but those who deal closely with him doubt he grasps its inherent strengths and weaknesses. In his first couple of years in office he took business protests too seriously. He jumped when they barked. His emissions trading scheme was almost whittled away to nothing as a result. Now he has picked a brave fight with the mining companies to tax their mega-profits. A leader with a reputation for cutting and running has set himself a defining test of courage.

"My name is Kevin," he quipped as he greeted the party's national conference in 2007. "I'm from Queensland and I'm here to help." He's not good at jokes. But the limits of Rudd's courage can't be grasped without remembering he comes from up there: he's a son of the DLP, nephew of the Country Party, raised in a state where Labor had been on the outer forever. A Labor grandee told me: "Rudd seems to measure what's worth fighting for by Queensland standards. Never forget the extraordinary caution of Queenslanders." And hovering over Rudd are the failures of the Goss enterprise: all that effort to craft evidence-based policy and the people turned against them. On the tenth anniversary of Labor coming to power in Queensland, Rudd admitted failings – not his but Wayne Goss's: "His belief in what was good policy would often obscure what many regarded as that which was politically sustainable." So what lessons did he learn about himself from those years? He admits to none. He defends his methods and his policies. The way he sees it, Queensland had a brief interregnum of National Party rule – the result of a protest vote gone wrong – and has been Labor ever since. The people saw the light.

A few days after being sworn in, Rudd found himself on Sydney's Radio 2UE, where Peter FitzSimons asked: "Will you use the power of your office now to continue investigations into AWB and finally get to the bottom of it?" Rudd waffled:

> I said prior to the election and just after that once we form government – that was only on Monday of this week – we'd take advice on that and that's being prepared. But that will take some time to prepare and to deliberate on. I've regarded that as a, and I regard it still, as a matter of gross failure of public administration …

Rudd has never done a thing about AWB since becoming prime minister. In the United States, oil executives have served time and companies have paid penalties of more than $100 million for giving kickbacks that were a tiny fraction of the massive sums AWB paid to Saddam. In Australia, civil charges have been laid against a few of the company's executives, but the searching investigation of diplomats and ministers Rudd demanded in Opposition has never happened. As this essay goes to press, not a soul has been held to account for their role in the biggest corruption scandal in the nation's history. Rudd is not going to hold an inquiry that stares deep into that pit.

Many failures of courage have followed, but confronted with the global financial crisis of late 2008 he displayed true resolve. His response to that calamity was, in many ways, the making of him as prime minister. He had been puddling round until then. Rudd has been condemning the pretensions of neo-liberal economic theory ever since he entered parliament. They were the subject of a second huge essay he wrote for the *Monthly*: "Howard's Brutopia." The collapse of the machinery of capitalism proved his worst fears true. He was propelled by the urgent advice of the treasury secretary, Ken Henry, to pour money into the economy. Rudd has never been afraid to spend money. The strategy was decided independently of Cabinet by the Strategic Priorities and Budget Committee, which served to cement in place its key role in the government. Speed was of the essence. But the failures of the home insulation scheme and the schools building program are part of a wider critique of Rudd's passion for speed and the dramatic announcement of programs to start, if possible, as soon as yesterday.

When Rudd talks of political courage, he talks of Gough Whitlam. He is unabashed in his praise. The prose is purple. Hawke and Keating were never so effusive. Whitlam's is one of the few Australian political lives Rudd appears to have studied deeply. They come in order of interest: Whitlam, Andrew Fisher – Queenslander and acolyte of Keir Hardie – and Bob Menzies. Even after all this time, Gough's "audacious and historic" dash to Beijing still fires Rudd's imagination: "That trip took real political courage." Perhaps Whitlam is another of the martyrs he so admires, offering everything for the cause, crashing through or crashing. At the launch of Jenny Hocking's biography of Whitlam in 2008, Rudd spoke in the grandest terms of him having:

> … a political style and a policy program characterised by unbounded optimism, unbounded passion for the progressive political project and an absolute fearlessness in assaulting the citadels of conservative political power.

This wasn't mere sentimental praise for the alert bundle of old bones who had come to the launch in his wheelchair. Rudd sees himself as a progressive nation-builder in the Whitlam mould. "Today," he declared to the solemn crowd, "we continue that tradition, through a new era of national reform." He is way out of his league here, a thought that should surely have crossed his mind as he stood at the microphone reciting Whitlam's radical record. Only in one sense is he truly Whitlam's heir: in his dealings with China.

At Peking University in March 2008, Rudd directly admonished the Chinese government for its human-rights record in Tibet. He did so, he said, as a true friend, or *zhengyou*:

> A partner who sees beyond immediate benefit to the broader and firm basis for continuing, profound and sincere friendship … It is the kind of friendship that I know is treasured in China's political tradition.

His courage that day was recognised around the world. In April 2010 he repeated those words, birched China once again for its human-rights record and deplored the country's friendships with "Regimes around the world that others seek to isolate because of their assault on the integrity of the international system – from the Sudan to Burma." To those who say he has no great plans as a leader, Rudd replies that he is keeping an eye on China. What will our world be like, he asks, when China is once again the great power it was three centuries ago?

The defining failure of Rudd's time in office was the slow collapse and abandonment of his plans to address global warming. Another of the eloquent passages in the Bonhoeffer essay – a document which seems now to have been written in another age – urged Christians to "speak robustly to the state" on climate change:

> The planet cannot speak for itself. Nor can the working peoples of the developing world effectively speak for themselves, although they are likely to be the first victims of the environmental degradation brought about by climate change. Nor can those who come after us, although they are likely to be the greatest victims of this inter-generational injustice. It is the fundamental ethical challenge of our age to protect the planet – in the language of the Bible, to be proper stewards of creation.

Outside Australia he would face formidable obstacles – the intransigence of US industry and of China's leaders – and by the time he left for Copenhagen the political obstacles within Australia were hardly less daunting: the Opposition had risen against his emissions trading scheme, deposed its leader and installed a cadre of climate change deniers intent on blocking the legislation. But even before these political obstacles became perhaps insurmountable, Rudd had shown a particular lack of courage in formulating Australia's response: two years of lobbying by the country's most powerful corporations had left the ETS in tatters. Instead of deterring dirty industries from burning carbon, Rudd's scheme would subsidise coal burning for decades. Trade-exposed industries were to be given free permits galore. So massive were the subsidies proposed for power generators that they drew a public rebuke from the extraordinarily discreet adviser to the government, Ross Garnaut:

> There is no public-policy justification for $3.9 billion in unconditional payments to generators in relation to hypothetical future "loss of asset value." Never in the history of Australian public finance has so much been given without public-policy purpose, by so many, to so few.

The result was a messy, expensive policy the public could neither grasp nor enthusiastically rally behind. This was diplomacy more than politics. Everyone signed. Face was saved. Whether the scheme would work was a second-order issue. It promised to achieve so little at such cost that the failure of Rudd's efforts at the Bella Center in December 2009 was greeted with relief by many who think, as Rudd perhaps still does, that global warming is the greatest economic and moral issue of our time.

When he abandoned the ETS in late April 2010, relegating it to the Siberia of his late second term, scorn poured down on Rudd's head. He was clearing the decks for the elections; he had a brawl on his hands with the mining industry; he had a new national health agreement to bed down and a budget to introduce – but the decision to abandon the ETS was greeted with contempt. He collapsed in the polls. The conviction politician was seen as a man of empty words. His love affair with the Australian people – always more respectful than romantic – hit a rough patch. For the first time since he became Labor leader, the people were thinking of voting for the other side.

Face Time

The manager of this waterfront pub in Mackay has put on a few jewels and stationed herself in the foyer to miss none of the fun. Prime ministers and their staff are not her usual line of work. "We serve the miners," she explains. The place is frantic. Aides come and go, sometimes in running gear but always on their phones. Out on the terrace where things will turn ugly later, Rudd holds court with the usual suspects: the mayor, the editor of the local paper and the Labor candidate. Mackay needs a big new road to get coal trucks to the wharf. The price is high. Alister Jordan takes notes. Waiting patiently to shuttle Rudd's people around the town is a taxi driver who has, at his own expense, packed an esky of ice-cold mineral water for his passengers. He says: "I've been Labor all my life."

At sundown Rudd suggests a walk and we set out in bare feet along the weed-strewn beach. Security guards walk at a distance fore and aft. A passing straggler calls out: "You are the best prime minister

ever." The clichés of the day drop away. He talks
about himself as a child with great affection but oddly,
as if that kid in Eumundi was someone else entirely.
The memory of Ashgrove is still blazing away. He
was a sick kid then, he says, but he is someone who
has grown stronger as he grows older. By this time he
is puffing a little as we slog along the sand. That Rudd
is still a puritan is beyond doubt, but he's not the prig
who preached in Burgmann College. Prime Minister
Rudd isn't touting the virtues of Calvin's Geneva.
He laughs to hear some think he is a creationist. Not
true. Once or twice he shies away from questions,
declaring he's just not a reflective person. I don't
believe him: I sense no one is more curious about the
mysteries of Rudd than Rudd himself.

People come out of the dark to shake his hand. He
grabs young kids with obvious delight. Perhaps the
happiest version of himself is Rudd the father. Rudd
the leader is a loner: it's been a lonely business all
along and gets lonelier the higher he climbs. "I think
it's just inevitable. Ultimately you have to make calls.
And that is an individual and solitary business." So
many of the people I met writing this essay spoke of
Rudd as a loner, but not a loner by choice. They see
him wanting, if only he knew how, to be part of the
in-crowd – in the Nambour playground, in Goss's
office and in caucus. A man who has taught himself

so much appears not to have been able to master this: the business of belonging among his fellows. It is one point on which even colleagues who despise him feel human sympathy. He seems so stubbornly alone.

There is no force-field around him. As we eat dinner, people drop by the table to chat. "I'm Kevin," he says. They know. Years ago when he was first presenting himself to the public as a human being, he was asked to name his favourite book, film and composer. The list has changed since 2003. *The Brothers Karamazov* now trumps *Crime and Punishment*, *Babette's Feast* beats *Dr Strangelove* – though his eyes light up at the memory and his right hand half-rises in a Nazi salute – and Mozart is now the master, not Beethoven: "Over Easter I listened to the Requiem again and it's just sublime." The painters he most admires are the pre-Raphaelites. "They saw poverty for what it was and had, you know, certain Christian overtones." I struggle to remember something from my childhood: the knock at the door? "Yes, *The Light of the World*." And out pours the history of Holman Hunt's image of Christ standing with a lantern in his hand knocking at an overgrown doorway: one of the great recruiting posters of Christendom.

Almost as he is leaving the table he asks me the argument of this essay. It's a man-to-man question, so I tell him. I'm pursuing the contradictions of his life: the farmer's kid who runs away to China, the politician unloved by his own caucus who turns out to be such a potent electoral asset; a decent man with decent political ambitions who leaves so much wreckage in his wake; an orator of skill who can be a bore; a man with modest policy ambitions but a strong drive for power. And I'm wondering if his government will go the way of Goss's.

I don't notice his face changing at first, but by the time I finish giving this bare-bones account I realise Rudd is furious. I have hurt him and he is angry. What follows is a dressing down which registers about a 3.8 on his Richter scale. He doesn't scream and bang the table as he does behind closed doors. We're in the open. The voice is low. He is perfectly composed. From the distance of the next table it would be hard to tell how furious the prime minister is. Indeed, some boys come over in the middle of it all to ask to have their picture taken with him. Later, he says politely and returns to his work. What he says in these angry twenty minutes informs every corner of this essay. But more revealing than the information is the transformation of the man. In his anger Rudd becomes astonishingly eloquent. This is the most vivid version of himself I've encountered. At last he is speaking from the heart, an angry heart.

Face to face, it's so clear. Rudd is driven by anger. It's the juice in the machine. He is a hard man to read because the anger is hidden by a public face, a diplomat's face. Who is the real Kevin Rudd? He is the man you see when the anger vents. He's a politician with rage at his core, impatient rage.

He finishes, leans over the table, shakes my hand and strides inside, walking straight past the boys waiting so patiently for their photograph. An aide rushes after him. He will not come back out onto the terrace. The boys go in to him. A flash bursts inside and the prime minister disappears.

11 May 2010

Afterword

The plotters who pulled Kevin Rudd down a month after this essay appeared didn't know their man. They knew he was making a mess of government and had lost support in the caucus. They could see his immense popularity fading. But they didn't realise that Rudd would never give up, the wounds would never heal and he would never go away.

His self-belief is bottomless. There were dark nights for Rudd after his defenestration but it remained a constant comfort that he had never been rejected by the Australian people. His quarrel was with his party, a quarrel he was ready to resume whenever the opportunity allowed.

Rudd had never had an army of supporters in caucus. Nor did those who worked closely with him in his early years have much to say in his favour. As a diplomat, public servant and shadow minister, Rudd had an unhappy knack of making colleagues loathe him.

But the public saw another figure altogether, a new kind of Australian politician, a man of intellect and values. He sounded right. He looked fresh. He was not mired in old Labor conflicts. He seemed a conviction politician of rare courage, a thinker who could take the country into the future.

Whatever the party's suspicions, their pollsters told them Rudd bridged the old divide in Labor's following. The fearful were comfortable with him. So were the intellectuals. He pulled votes from the radical left and the Christian right, from the Greens and the Tories. They made him leader in December 2006, but not out of admiration for the man. They did it for the party.

He won a mighty victory over John Howard in 2007. He was loved. What followed was the longest honeymoon in Australian political history. A fresh spirit swept over the country after the rancour of the Howard years. His government handled the global financial crisis superbly. The Opposition collapsed.

But at the height of his popularity the flaws began to show. All this might not have mattered if the results were good. They weren't. And it turned out that Rudd couldn't bear to be disliked. He was oddly unwilling to draw on the bank of goodwill at his disposal. He saw himself as an agent of transformative change but in practice he was a trimmer. Reverses knocked him about badly. He wasn't resilient.

Australia's love affair with Rudd began to sour after Copenhagen. A bipartisan pact to deal with global warming had collapsed when the Opposition dumped the urbane Malcolm Turnbull for one of the great head-kickers of Australian politics, Tony Abbott.

Abbott got under Rudd's skin. The great mistake of Rudd's career was to fail, in early 2010, to take the country to an election fought on climate change, an election he seemed certain to win. Instead he floundered about for six months making dramatic but poorly thought-through policy decisions: to take charge of the hospitals of the nation and to tax the super-profits of the mining boom.

He failed to pull off either policy coup. His government was logjammed. His popularity was slumping and an election was looming. At this point, his party made a catastrophic tactical error: instead of confronting him, pulling him into line, imposing discipline on his office, making all that was positive about the man work for the Labor government, they sacked him.

He was only fifty-two. His ambitions were untouched. And he has, since childhood, taken defeats very, very badly. The belief that he leaked against the new leader, Julia Gillard, in the election campaign that year earned him fresh enmity in caucus. The poll he would have won comfortably left Gillard running a minority government.

And Rudd never went away. Though Gillard twice demonstrated he didn't have the numbers to topple her, Rudd didn't give up. His belief in himself was untouched. As her fortunes collapsed, the polls kept giving caucus the same old message: that whatever they thought of Rudd, the people had not given up on him. He might yet save the party from ruin – perhaps not win an election but save Labor from a historic wipeout.

So, three years almost to the day since he was toppled, despite everything that went wrong the last time, Rudd was restored – for the sake of the party. The election was only weeks away. That would play to his strength. This time he didn't have to govern. He only had to campaign.

1 July 2013

POLITICAL ANIMAL

The Making of Tony Abbott

I am not asking the Australian people to take me on trust but on the record of a lifetime and an instinct to serve ingrained long before I became opposition leader: as a student president, trainee priest, Rhodes Scholar, surf life-saver and volunteer fire-fighter, as well as a member of parliament and as a minister in a government.

—TONY ABBOTT, to the Federal Council of the Liberal Party, 30 June 2012

For what shall it profit a man, if he shall gain the whole world, and lose his own soul?

—MARK 8:36.

Prince Hal

Australia has never shown much enthusiasm for the man. In the old days when pollsters asked us who should take over from John Howard or Brendan Nelson or Malcolm Turnbull, we put Tony Abbott way down the list, usually at the bottom. As the years passed and the number of Liberal contenders dwindled, we always picked someone else: Peter Costello even after he gave up the leadership without a fight; Malcolm Turnbull even after the climate sceptics brought him undone; or Joe Hockey the untried hulk from morning television. We never wanted the man the Liberals gave us in December 2009. Abbott was their choice, not ours. And the party was almost as stunned as the nation. "God almighty," one of the Liberals cried in the party room that day. "What have we done?"

The Canberra press pack was held behind ropes waiting for the result. Bob Ellis was treated as comic relief as he buttonholed us with predictions of an Abbott victory. All alone in a nearby anteroom the

Reverend Peter Rose sat reading the Bible in front of a blank television screen. "There was no rancour in there," the priest told me. "That's what I was praying for." Hadn't the poor man noticed that parliament was a palace of rancour? It had been for weeks as Turnbull was torn to pieces by his party. Labor was gloating. Kevin Rudd was once more sailing along at the top of the polls. And the press had it wrong. The Liberal whip walked down the corridor, stood at the precise spot indicated on the carpet and announced Abbott's victory without a trace of pleasure.

Journalists swore, hit the phones and scattered. Out in the parliament gardens, pundits began talking to cameras. There was little evidence of jubilation in the corridors. Doors were closed. Abbott and the press faced each other in the party room about forty minutes later. It wasn't crowded. A little pack of supporters had come along to cry "hear, hear" from time to time. They had the shattered look of people given what they'd wished for. By her new leader's side stood the deputy perpetual, Julie Bishop, smiling and smiling. As the voltage of her smile dimmed, you could see her will it back to life. Once or twice she turned on Abbott a look of coquettish amusement but her eyes were dazed.

"I accept at times I have stuffed up," he said. "I suppose I should apologise now for all my errors of the past and make a clean breast of them." But he didn't go into detail. Long practice makes him good at confession. It's in his blood. The most Catholic thing about this profoundly Catholic man is his faith in absolution. The slate can always be wiped clean. Over the years he has said and done appalling things that might have sunk another politician. But charm and candour and promises to do better have seen him forgiven so much. The loudmouth bigot of his university days, the homophobe, the blinkered Vatican warrior, the rugger-bugger, the white Australian and the junkyard dog of parliament are all, he would have us believe, consigned to the past. Another self has walked out of the wings. "The Australian public are very fair and are always prepared to give a leader of a major political party a fair go," he told his little audience. "I believe that when you become leader, you make a fresh start."

We have not seen a contender like this before. Though he admires them and studies what they teach, Tony Abbott is not another Bob Menzies or John Howard. He is more conservative than both, more quixotic, a man of another faith that leaves him deeply troubled by the drift of the world. Heroes play a large part in his imagination. He dates the first stirrings of his interest in public life to the Ladybird books his mother read him as a child. "These usually turned out to be about great figures in history: Julius Caesar, Francis Drake and Henry V," he wrote in his book *Battlelines*. "The lesson, invariably, was that duty and honour carried the day." Spoonfeeding heroism to children of the Empire since World War I, Ladybird books were still going strong on Sydney's North Shore in the 1960s. In their world, power has magic. The handling of power is the greatest moral test a hero faces. Power transforms and challenges them. Abbott's favourite Ladybird book seems to be the one about wastrel Prince Hal who turns into heroic Henry V. Heroes excite Abbott. A few days after becoming leader of the Opposition, he was given a quick quiz by Josh Gordon of the *Sunday Age*. Favourite film? "*Gallipoli*. Seen it many times." Film star? "John Wayne." Book? "I'd have to say it's probably *Lord of the Rings*. It's the book I've read most." The best personal advice? "Avoid the occasion of sin."

For a long time he saw himself as a man on a quest. So did old friends and political colleagues. Peter Costello called him "a Don Quixote ready to take on lost causes and fight for great principles." Knights on horseback make odd figures in politics. They can be comic. They can be malevolent. They can be inspiring. They have a way of seeing the everyday world not quite as the rest of us do. It's unsettling. Sometimes they are right and we are in their debt. Often they find themselves, lance in hand, searching for windmills. A few of these types are always about in politics, attractive bit players on the left and right. But they rarely come so close to power as Abbott has. One of the many puzzles about this man is how much of the Don Quixote survives under the armour of caution he has begun to wear in the last few years.

We haven't warmed to him. As he set about his job of wrecking Labor he saw off one of the most popular prime ministers in the history of the federation and weeks later nearly beat the man's successor at the ballot box. That 2010 campaign dashed Labor's early hopes. Abbott didn't stuff up. He held his nerve and he very nearly got there. In those weeks, Australians extended a measure of respect, even admiration, to Abbott. But once that near-miss was passed, the polls have recorded deep dissatisfaction with the man. For most of the time he has been leading the Opposition, about 60 per cent of us have disapproved of his performance.

That figure is only a little less worse as 2013 begins. We think Abbott more arrogant and narrow-minded than ever. Few of us credit him with vision. Most have never thought him good in a crisis. Despite his unrelenting assault on the prime minister's integrity since the last election, Australia trusts neither leader much – and him no more than her. An Essential poll in mid-January found 61 per cent of us think him arrogant, 56 per cent narrow-minded, 55 per cent aggressive and 54 per cent out of touch with ordinary people. It's a devastating verdict. The two qualities we have always acknowledged in Abbott are his intelligence and capacity for hard work – but even our faith in his intelligence has faded since the Coalition handed him the job of ousting Labor.

By all the old rules, to be so unloved should make Abbott political road-kill. He is not. He survives as a rare figure in Australian politics: a disliked leader of a popular Opposition. The polls for him and the polls for the Coalition he leads have been, at times, worlds apart. They seem to be falling into step now. Even so, his strategists are banking on us doing something we have never been keen to do before: vote out an unpopular prime minister on behalf of an unpopular leader of the Opposition. It may be only a flicker in the polls but Australians seem now to be saying: "Maybe we can." A vast political terrain lies between now and then, but it seems this unliked and unlikely man is heading for victory.

Tricky to read at the best of times, Abbott grows more opaque as he sees himself approaching office. The big political unknown of 2013 is not the Coalition platform – that will be clear enough before polling day – but what power might do to Tony Abbott.

It is a question that has intrigued him all his life. He has himself on a tight rein. He is campaigning hard but giving little away. The junkyard dog is in the kennel. His minders want him to be even more cautious, more hidden, less visibly himself. He is talking about the needs of the nation. His ferocious attacks on the prime minister these days come tinged with regret. He hopes to go on rattling the government while no longer rattling the public. He has not cared much about that before. Destruction has been everything. But what Australia has never really given him now matters: love and respect.

Fighting the Revolution

H is mates called him Abbo. "He was wild," says a student from those years. "Wild even for a wild college boy." From the moment he arrived at Sydney University in early 1976 he showed himself to be a muscular reactionary of extraordinary, boisterous energy. Turmoil followed him everywhere: drinking, writing, arguing, fucking and playing rugby. The study of economics and law never engaged his imagination. Politics did from the start. His home base was St John's, the Catholic men's college under its gothic tower. His political base was the tiny Democratic Club, one of a network on campuses across the country set up and guided by Bob Santamaria's National Civic Council. For the next five years he would speak, write and campaign for NCC causes. The background noise of his university years was the clatter of roneo machines. Within days of his arrival on campus he was putting out the club's newsletter, the *Democrat*. The targets he chose for his debut as a fighting journalist were lesbians, homosexuals and the Students' Representative Council (SRC):

> Most students will be interested to know that Orientation Week's Gay dance was a financial failure. Not only did the SRC make good this loss but it collectively howled down a speaker against the motion ... it is a foregone conclusion that only motions supporting subversion, perversion and revolution will be passed.

The high hopes the Abbotts had for their son had not quite been realised at Riverview, the Jesuit school in an Italian palace on the upper reaches of Sydney Harbour. Dick Abbott was a popular dentist who had taken to Catholicism in his teens. The circumstances of his conversion were peculiar. Dick's father had made a bargain with God that were his family to survive a voyage to Australia in the early months of World War II they would go over to Rome. Untouched by torpedoes, the Abbotts converted with some fervour. Dick was keen to be a priest but opted in the end for dentistry. He returned to England after the war where he met Fay "Pete" Peters, an intelligent, energetic Australian dietician. She converted. They married. Tony was born in London in 1957. A couple of years later his mother drove the return to Australia. As Dick Abbott's practice prospered, the family moved higher up the North Shore until they were living in a beautiful house on the edge of the bush in Killara.

Three daughters were born but the family's ambitions centred on little Tony: "His mother and I knew pretty early on that, with Tony, we had produced something out of the box." The girls adored their brother. The boy worshipped his father. The mother worshipped the boy. He was in his mid-teens when his mother told a table of dentists in Sydney that Tony would one day be Pope or prime minister. There was some tension in the family between these ambitions. The girls favoured politics. Justin Rickard, a law student who dated one of the daughters at university, remembers: "Even in those days Tony was spoken very highly of in his family, with great awe and respect, and the phrase 'future PM' was often whispered or should I say yelled around the family table."

At any other school his record would have been regarded as outstanding. But at Riverview it was merely solid. He was neither head boy nor dux. Despite his father's protests, he never made the first XV or the first eight. He didn't debate. His name was not on the honour boards nor was it everywhere in the school magazine. In his final year he won the Paul

Meagher Prize for Modern History and His Eminence the Cardinal's Prize for Religious Knowledge. It was not a shower of glory. He made his name at Riverview with a wonderful larrikin moment at speech day in October 1975. The governor-general, John Kerr, was giving the prizes in the midst of the supply crisis. "Sir John, this must be frightfully boring for you," said young Abbott as he shook the vice-regal hand. "Why don't I take you to the Liberal Party rally in town?" Kerr laughed but the quip caused quite a stir. The boy was with his mother at Reuben F. Scarf's a couple of weeks later buying a new suit for the end-of-year formal when a shop assistant broke the news that Whitlam had been sacked. "Pete" Abbott said: "Fantastic!" Tony Abbott backs Kerr to this day.

A priest at Riverview had cast his spell on the boy when he was only sixteen, a spell that has never been broken. Emmet Costello offered him an example of a priest in society, a man of faith in the world of power. Getting about Sydney in a Bentley or BMW, this heir to a gold-mining fortune from Fiji ministered to the rich, pursuing death-bed conversions in harbour mansions and bringing distinguished lapsed Catholics back into the fold. Costello's much-touted triumph was the return to mass of Tom Hughes QC, attorney-general in John Gorton's government.

Costello encouraged robust faith rather than pious introspection. Habits of worship were vital. Costello's rule was: mass early and often. Life was to be lived and forgiveness was always available to the penitent. Social justice was not Costello's bag. His life's mission was to find and shape leaders in the interests of his order and his faith. He drilled into his boys the Jesuits' imperative that they hang onto their souls while tilting for the world.

Costello has never been shy of touting his role in Tony Abbott's life. "I first met him in 1974 and he was then in Year 11 at Riverview and from the moment I met him he was different. He walked into my room – I was a chaplain for the boys – and he projected an image immediately of high intelligence, ambition, drive and leadership and I thought this guy is worth following." The boy was dazzled, too: here was a worldly priest confirming his own high faith in himself. One day Costello casually suggested Abbott might become a priest. The idea nagged at him for the next dozen years. Abbott would come to rate Father Costello second only to his own father as "the most important male influence on my life."

In their last weeks at school, Catholic boys of particular promise were taken aside and invited to rather mysterious "Peace with Freedom" weekends to prepare them for life at university. Though not invited, young Abbott tagged along: "Some instinct whispered that this was not an opportunity to be missed." In the heady atmosphere of that secret forum in the summer of early 1976, the course of his political life was set: young Tony was recruited for Bob Santamaria's Movement. The men who did the work were Peter Samuel, the *Bulletin*'s cranky political correspondent; Warren Hogan, the embattled professor of economics at Sydney University; and Joe de Bruyn, a hard-line Catholic union official about to assume lifetime leadership of the shop assistants' union. Looking back on this moment over thirty years later, Abbott wrote:

> It was a thrill to meet people of influence and authority in public life. It was exciting to think that I might be able to make a difference to the wider world. Most of all, it was good to learn that there was a way to get involved immediately through joining the Sydney University Democratic Club.

He pledged his troth to Santamaria. It would be a year before he met the man face to face but he fell in love that weekend. "I have been under the Santamaria spell ever since." Until the old man's death in 1998 Abbott regarded him as "the greatest living Australian."

Few shared his awe. Inside and outside politics, inside and outside the Catholic Church, Santamaria was also widely hated. His venom was phenomenal; his energy inextinguishable; and his fears legion. In the Whitlam crisis just passed he had privately discussed the need to raise a secret army to defend democracy against the scourge of Labor. Now, in his sixties, he was seized by a profound sense of failure. Despite all he had done – purging the unions of communists, splitting Labor, founding the breakaway Democratic Labor Party and guaranteeing the conservatives a long haul in power – he felt he had failed in his larger purpose. The DLP was busted. Australia was not the good country of his Catholic dreams. Revolution still threatened the world. His sense of mission was sustained by an absolute conviction that he stood for fundamental truth in a world of superficial values. Others might think him a fanatic, an alarmist and a bully, but his latest recruit would find him: "A philosophical star by which you could always steer."

Abbott is a man with mentors. Most were old men with embattled beliefs: true believers; relics of lost causes; men with a high view of their life and mission; men who believed in the magic of the crown, the church and old institutions. And they loved him: so unlikely, so promising. The chance to ride out with them to confront the zeitgeist touched something deep in young Tony. He was a kid with a powerful wish to serve. To stand for old ideas and old authority in the late 1970s took courage of a kind, and deep faith in faith. He believed the path Santamaria was inviting him to take was essentially religious. In the old man's obituary a couple of decades later he wrote:

> His real role was to create a type of secular religious order, something like a band of political Jesuits, a group of men and women whose religious values translated into strong commitment, not necessarily to any political party, but to a set of social principles.

The tactics were not so lofty. The Democratic Clubs were small and their membership carefully controlled. The correct line was strictly enforced. They used tactics Santamaria developed to fight Reds in the unions: provocative campaigning, ceaseless leafleting and infiltrating rival organisations. They called themselves moderates but their position was extreme: as far to the right as the Maoists and Trotskyists on campus were to the left. They were accused of rough-house tactics and wrecking what they couldn't control. The student newspaper *Honi*

Soit reported: "This organisation has a long history of politically motivated violence – whether as vigilantes for vice-regals, smoke-bombers for Saigon, poster pullers for political reaction, or bullies for by-elections."

Among the young cocks on the campus, Abbott quickly made his name. Thousands of words of campaigning journalism poured out of him, an extraordinary number of them attacking homosexuals, male and female. He proudly announced the Democratic Club had established a Heterosexual Solidarity Society. When he decided, with astonishing cheek, to seek election in his first year as a student fellow of the university senate, Abbott ended his lofty manifesto by claiming: "As an infrequently practising heterosexual and drunkard I feel I have significant community of interest with many students ..." He lost the vote narrowly and his temper publicly. "He came down to the SRC and kicked a glass panel on the front door in," reported *Honi Soit.* "Not that he meant to mind you, things just seem to happen to Tony."

His fellow warriors loved him in a slightly protective way. "Tony was a warm, sociable individual, a ton of fun," recalls Joe Bullock, who is now state secretary in Western Australia of de Bruyn's shoppies' union. "People warmed to Tony. He was very personable, very quick with the common touch he still has. But he was enthusiastically hated by those who hated him. He was seen as a very worthy opponent with a capacity to win. We all thought Tony would be a force to be reckoned with when he grew up and we're still waiting." Great things seemed to be at stake. Bullock says: "Everyone thought they were engaged in a bigger battle. I thought I was engaged in a battle between good and evil." Though the young man failed to enter the senate in that first turbulent year on the campus, he did win a place on the SRC and in the university's delegation to the Australian Union of Students (AUS). Over the next three years Abbott would throw all his political energy into gutting both.

This mighty wrecking operation was being conducted by Democratic Clubs across Australia to prevent revolution spilling out of campuses and tearing society to pieces. "It was as necessary to break the revolutionary base in the universities," Santamaria declared, "as it was to contain it in the unions." Communism still flourished in the universities and communism in all its forms – soft, hard, Russian, Maoist and Trotskyist – was enemy number one for Santamaria. But his fears went far deeper than that. He had with spectacular scorn denounced in his memoirs the yet unfinished revolution of the 1960s. Santamaria deplored the Pill, homosexuality, rampant materialism, married women in the workforce, environmentalists, drugs, abortion, anarchy on campuses, economic rationalism, dissident theologians, divorce without proof of guilt and the cult of the moral autonomy of the individual. What he saw at stake here was the authority of family, church and state, indeed legitimate authority in every field of life. The fear was a new Dark Age coming out of the universities. The precedent was Paris in 1968. To blame were:

> The present crop of professors, lecturers, teachers, journalists, politicians, bureaucrats, media experts, bankers, and – I regret to say it – not a few of the clergy, in other words, the people who actually run society.

Young Abbott took all that on board. The question is: how much has he jettisoned since? Communism is utterly beaten and only nutters fear revolution these days. Abbott is not one of them. He never shared his master's monkish asceticism or his profound pessimism. But Abbott's years in the service of this strange Catholic warrior mark him to this day. Like Santa, he is not driven by money. He's not a social climber or a snob. He's never lost the protégé's sense of being on a mission, an essentially religious mission in a secular world. Humanity is fallen. Society is fragile. Western civilisation is in flux. The world according to Abbott may not be in the immediate danger Santamaria feared, but it is heading the wrong way. That is the nature of things. From Santamaria he took values rather than policies, values and attitudes beyond the ordinary reach of politics in this country. His conservatism is coloured clerical purple.

After a summer in Western Australia spent surfing, carousing in pubs and selling pots door to door, the young delegate turned up at Monash University in January 1977 for his first AUS conference. He was determined to fight the good fight and make a name for himself. In both he exceeded his own high expectations. A wilderness of factions were in play, factions often controlled, as the Democratic Clubs were, from beyond the university gates. The right's determination to seize or crush AUS had been revitalised by the AUS decision a few years earlier to support the Palestine Liberation Organisation. The anti-PLO campaign brought together the Liberals, the right of the Labor Party, the National Union of Jewish Students and Santamaria's people. It proved to be the training ground of a new cohort of leaders on both sides of politics: Abbott, Peter Costello, Eric Abetz, Michael Yabsley, Michael Danby, Michael Kroger, Nick Sherry and, a little later, Julia Gillard.

The *Weekend Australian* asked Abbott to report the conference. It was a remarkable break and his attack on this "tragic farce" filled a leading page under a banner headline:

I ACCUSE
Phoney student thugs
Use spit and abuse
To create terror ...
By TONY ABBOTT

He wrote of scuffles in corridors, angry confrontation, factional bastardry – always of the left – fear, provocation, systemic danger and facile causes in which nothing of any consequence was achieved.

Generally the air was heavy with the not-unpleasant odour of marijuana. The conference hall was gaily decked with gaudy Maoist flags and communist slogans.

Some delegates wore badges cheerfully urging the "smashing" of Fraser and the shooting of Kerr. Books on sale covered everything one wanted to know about abortion, street fighting, subverting universities, indoctrinating the young, and homosexuality.

These thousands of words – ending with a pure Santamaria flourish about the great risks these influences posed to "those who will eventually lead society" – were Abbott's debut in mainstream journalism. Whether his account was fair or wildly exaggerated is by now impossible to judge. What matters – and what infuriated his opponents – was that at the age of nineteen Abbott was writing with such authority. He had found a public voice. His name was everywhere as the battle raged for control of AUS. He was making his mark. But these wild times and all they promised for his future seemed suddenly about to end.

His girlfriend, Kathy McDonald, was three months pregnant. It was the old Catholic catastrophe: no chastity, no contraception, no abortion and, it would turn out, no marriage. They were lovers at school, having met at a high tea for Riverview boys and Monte Sant' Angelo girls in Year 11. The *Bulletin* would report:

> She was infatuated immediately, dazzled by this intellectually precocious, outrageously funny, albeit conservative seventeen-year-old boy who could quote Shakespeare and recite the great poets – and not always just for effect ... "We were both confident, out there people and we adored each other."

The affair between the Catholic rugger-bugger and the sweet lefty art student was a complex business. "I loved uni," Abbott would later say. "Having the romance with Kathy was all part of the magnificent, exuberant boisterous time." But he had not abandoned the notion of one day serving his church. "I was sorta wrestling with this idea of the bloody priesthood, and I kept saying, 'No, no! No sex! Against the rules!' Then I'd say, 'Oh, all right.'" A priest took McDonald aside at some point and urged her not to get in the way of Tony's vocation. As it happens she had also practised Vatican roulette once or twice with her flatmate Bill Kensell. But neither McDonald nor Abbott doubted, when she discovered she was pregnant, that the child was Tony's.

He would excoriate himself decades later for being callow, insensitive and psychologically unprepared for marriage. But many an unwilling Catholic boy had found himself at the altar at his age. At first Abbott was going to marry her but then he pulled back. Marriage would not only rule out the priesthood but also his more immediate ambition to win the Rhodes Scholarship. There was a tradition of rugby players from Sydney going on to Oxford and his footy mates were saying to him: "Abbo, you ought to think of going for the Rhodes." But the scholarship was open only to single men and women.

Abbott called the shots. "I decided that Kathy and I were not going to get married and that adoption was the right thing to happen." They split up in the seventh month of her pregnancy. She said: "I wanted him ... to be a white knight on a charger and fix it up for me, but he couldn't so I ended the relationship." Abbott came to the hospital in July 1977 and held the child for a few minutes before the boy was given away. "I just wasn't ready for it."

Abbo had a great season on the football field that winter, even playing a few games as tighthead prop for the university firsts. He was no longer living at St John's. That place is a paradise for men like him but he was gone after only a year and the college has never much celebrated his successes. A decision had been made that Tony was spending too much time in the pub. Now he was back home with his parents in Killara but putting in long hours on the campus playing football and politics.

Santamaria was determined to keep student funds out of dangerous hands. Every student at Sydney University had to pay $10 a year to the SRC. That was risky enough, but each SRC across Australia then handed $2.50 of that fee over to AUS, which meant about $700,000 a year was available for leftist causes. The plan pursued by Democratic Clubs and their allies on the campuses was first to make SRC fees voluntary, and then to cut all links with AUS. In that way there would be little or nothing to spend in ways Abbott attacked week after week in the *Democrat*:

> When AUS champions the women's movement; homosexual liberation; the anti-Uranium campaign and anti-Kerr campaign, it is moving beyond the scope of unionism. Whatever their merits, these causes are quite divorced from the real needs of students.

According to the roneoed flyers he and his friends were handing around the campus, there was trouble brewing everywhere in universities: gays, strikes, sit-ins, the debauching of academic standards by Marxist lecturers, Palestine, abortion, the financial woes of AUS Travel and continued disrespect shown to the man who sacked Gough Whitlam. It had to stop. The first great political campaign of Abbott's life – which he would pursue by one means or another for nearly thirty years – was to drain the money from student politics.

His aim was to become president of the SRC and collapse it from above. For that he needed a bigger base than the Santamaria faction. It was Joe Bullock's idea to take over the Liberal Club. "I said we need a banner to fight under. We've got to have something that can draw people to us. The Labor Club was extreme left. There was no chance of knocking it off. But the Liberal Club was a dreadful bunch of dilettantes and social climbers. And there were not many of them. So I said: 'Let's knock off the Liberal Club.' But Tony was really reluctant. 'Oh, no, I don't want to join the Liberal Club.' He made it clear his loyalties were to Labor. Eventually I persuaded him against his better judgment to join."

The 1977 race for the presidency of the SRC was the first political contest that really mattered to Abbott. He was the great hope of the right. The campaign that winter term was bitter and he lost, heavily, to Barbara Ramjan. Though she was of the left, her work as the SRC's welfare officer had made her a popular figure across the factions. Her victory was declared on the evening of 28 July in the SRC's rooms in the basement of the Wentworth building. It was an especially dismal time for Abbott: his defeat came two days after the birth of the child he thought was his son.

A science student was using the cheap photocopier in the SRC foyer when trouble erupted around him. He had many friends in the SRC but was not politically active. Now a professor of biomedical science, he told me: "Suddenly a flying squad of yahoos led by Abbott came down the stairs. Abbott is unmistakable. Everybody knew Tony Abbott. He was all over campus all the time. He walked past me quickly but his gang screamed 'commie' and 'poofter' and the guy behind him grabbed me by the shoulders and threw me against the wall. I was furious. I picked myself up and immediately followed these thugs down the corridor."

Ramjan was in the corridor. As Abbott approached, she thought he was coming to offer his congratulations. "But no, that's not what he wanted. He came up to within an inch of my nose and punched the wall on either side of my head." She recalls with cold disdain: "It was done to intimidate."

Two "great logs of guys" were obscuring the science student's view. "I saw Abbott raise his elbow above his head and his fist was clenched and then he drove his fist down. I did not see a punch land. As I pushed along the corridor, I saw Barbara being helped up very ashen-faced." He has no doubt who it was. "These two polarising figures on campus were unmistakable and here was Abbott acting as he did all the time. He was a bit of a thug and quite proud of it I think." He never forgot the incident: "I have been talking about it for a long time."

As Abbott and his mates disappeared down the corridor, Ramjan looked about for her campaign manager, David Patch. Years later he would write in the *Sydney Morning Herald*:

Ramjan found me. She is a small woman, and Tony Abbott was (and is) a strong man. She was very shaken, scared and angry. She told me that Abbott had come up to her, put his face in her face, and punched the wall on either side of her head. So, I am a witness. Her immediate complaint to me about what Abbott had just done had the absolute ring of truth about it. I believed Ramjan at the time, and still do. Barbara Ramjan has been telling that story about Abbott ever since.

Patch, now a senior barrister in Sydney, was provoked to write in 2012 because thirty-five years after the event Abbott decided to deny the punch ever happened.

I know what happened. I write not to land a blow on (or near) Mr Abbott, but to ensure that the debate about the character and suitability of a potential Prime Minister is fully and accurately informed.

All the authorities agree this was a terrible year. September saw another night of bad-boy behaviour at the SRC, with allegations of flashing, intimidation and sexist abuse. Four students wrote to *Honi Soit* condemning Abbott on another charge: heckling the SRC's new ethnic relations officer, Takis Constantopedos: "Comments like this directed in a mocking and denigratory manner are a reflection of the racist attitudes of reactionaries." Abbott denied almost everything. True, his mate had pissed on a tree: "I really don't think urinating against a tree is such a terrible crime. It was quite late at night ..." But otherwise he accused his "extreme left" opponents of acting like Goebbels by spreading "brazen and outright" lies.

October saw him heckling speakers at the Ku-ring-gai College of Advanced Education. Helen Wilson, a trainee teacher, was at the microphone defending AUS when she heard a voice shouting, "Why don't you smile, honey?" and says she felt a hand groping between her legs. "I jumped back, turned around, and saw Tony Abbott laughing about two feet away. The people in the audience began laughing and jeering." Abbott was charged with indecent and common assault. He would be acquitted after giving the court a rather different account and producing a number of witnesses to support him: "She was speaking about me in a highly critical way, calling me an AUS basher and noted right-wing supporter. To let her know I was standing behind her I leaned forward and tapped her on the back, about the level of her jeans belt."

Abbo and his mates reckoned humourless people took them the wrong way. They were just having a bit of sport, pranks and larks. And if there was ever any argy-bargy it was only to counter the bad behaviour of the left. The left started everything. The left was always to blame. Veterans of those days still talk of the mayhem Abbott generated around him, of the packs of hecklers and the flying squad of mates, of him storming platforms and grabbing microphones to denounce lesbians and abortions. "At times it was all rather childish," Abbott confessed years later. "At times it was a little bit scary. But it was always bloody good fun."

Ramjan doesn't let him off so lightly. "He was the most in your face. That's what set him apart. There were, of course, other Liberal Party and DLP types on campus but they weren't offensive and they weren't rude. They were people you could talk to. You could sit down and have a cup of tea with them. I would never do that with Tony Abbott. He's not that sort of person. I don't care what your politics are, you can still engage with another person. You don't have to be threatening. You don't have to be just that awful person." She called the year that followed – with her as president and Abbott on the SRC executive – the worst of her life. "I have no doubt Tony was a most charming man when he wanted to be. It was a very conscious choice he made. I doubt there would have been any moment in that year that he would have been charming towards me."

But Abbott's noisy behaviour and hard-line views were winning him a following. And he was learning some political lessons. He didn't have to be a nice guy. He didn't have to go with the flow. It was possible to stand against the political tide. Tyro journalist Malcolm Turnbull watched Abbott at the AUS conference of early 1978. He wrote in the *Bulletin*:

> The leading light of the right-wingers in NSW is twenty-year-old Tony Abbott. He has written a number of articles on AUS in the *Australian* and his press coverage has accordingly given him a stature his rather boisterous and immature rhetoric doesn't really deserve.

AUS was on its last legs. Its income had nearly halved. Eleven campuses had seceded. AUS Travel had collapsed among allegations of corruption. Turnbull acknowledged the growing support on campuses for the Democratic Clubs and for Abbott, and asked a question he must look back on now with rather grim irony: how could a student of Abbott's views hope to be a national leader?

While he can win support from students because of the shocking state of affairs in AUS, he cannot take the next step because of his conservative moral views. Abbott is opposed to any legalisation of homosexuality and generally presents an old-fashioned DLP image. The students may be more conservative than they were a few years ago, but they have not swung back to the right as much as that.

One night that winter of 1978, the Sydney police ambushed a demonstration in Kings Cross, bashing and arresting lesbians and gay men. The paddy wagons were followed back to Darlinghurst police station by angry demonstrators. Arrests continued. One policeman dragged an unconscious woman by her hair through the station door. Four or five beat a young man's head against the station's iron gates. A woman was hit hard in the face as she sat in the dock. A man in the cells was beaten so badly he was taken, after some hours, to St Vincent's Hospital. By dawn, fifty-three men and women had been charged. As a wave of outrage swept the city, the SRC executive carried a motion unanimously condemning the "unprovoked and unnecessary police violence" and declaring: "this SRC actively supports and promotes equal rights for all lesbians and male homosexuals."

The minutes explain how unanimity was achieved: "Abbott was out of room." He returned to cast a lone vote against the SRC's decision to deliver its protest to the NSW premier.

Abbott's name was scrawled on lavatory walls. He was attacked in *Honi Soit* as an extremist, fascist, careerist, parasite and stooge of the NCC. But in September 1978 he tasted the first real victory of his career when at his second attempt he won the presidency of the SRC. He had power bases all over the campus: he was also president of the Democratic Club, still in control of the Liberal Club and a newly elected student fellow on the university senate. But the SRC presidency was the office that mattered and he won it without being less than himself: bully and charmer, speaker and writer, hard-line advocate and tireless recruiter. He could usually count on the St John's crowd, though things sometimes went awry. Peter Costello recalled in his memoirs addressing an anti-AUS meeting at Sydney University:

> Tony settled on a plan to get his college mates to vote with me. He would assemble them at a nearby hotel for beer and then lead them en masse to the rally. But as the afternoon wore on, the beer proved far more compelling than the rally. They never made it. The vote was lost.

To win the presidency, Abbott campaigned hard around the conservative faculties of engineering and medicine. He called on the footy crowd to back him. "We used to go along to watch him for sport," one recalls. "He was extremely right-wing at a time when everyone was extremely left-wing. He used to bait them, particularly lesbians. There were a lot of lesbians about then." He addressed the men's colleges. He boasts of earning an ovation at St John's by promising to tear down the posters of Che Guevara at the SRC and replace them with portraits of the Queen and the Pope. He convened rowdy meetings on the university lawn. He heckled and he dealt with hecklers. He was not afraid of losing skin in the game. For the rest of his career there would be skin everywhere.

He was a lonely president. On a council of thirty members, he had no more than three or four supporters. He didn't build alliances; he fell out with the moderates; he created and dramatised division. He didn't like the SRC and made no secret of being happy to see it bankrupt. "I can't recall a constructive policy for the benefit of the student body that he ever put forward," says a distinguished Sydney lawyer who was active in university politics then. "My lasting impression is of negativity and destruction. For those he did get on with, he was well liked. He also generated an enormous amount of hostility verging on vitriolic hatred from those who were his political opponents."

They tried to prevent him taking office. The farce that followed involved police, rival teams of locksmiths, mobs of angry students, lawyers and university officials. Abbott's car aerial was snapped. He slept in his office under siege. He tried to fire SRC staff. Even those on the executive supporting his right to take office thought his behaviour "senseless, futile and provocative." This battle didn't take up all his time. The *Sydney Morning Herald* revealed in the middle of this madness that the "newly elected president of the Sydney University Students' Representative Council, Mr Tony Abbott" had joined the British morals campaigner Mrs Mary Whitehouse on the platform of a rowdy Festival of Light rally in Sydney Square to protest abortion, child porn and the permissive society. Pies and cream cakes were thrown. The *Herald* reported the Reverend Fred Nile "escaped with cream in his hair." No pies hit Abbott.

The NSW Equity Court confirmed his election a few days later and he took command of his office, waging war on graffiti, tearing down political posters, banning homosexual activists from reception, cheerfully calling the welfare officers "sluts" and berating SRC staff by name in the pages of *Honi Soit*. Abbott was running a one-man campaign to wreck his own organisation. Week after week he attacked the SRC in the student paper. The writing is sharp, fearless and provocative. One week he took readers on a tour of the SRC offices:

> Luckily, it is lunchtime, so we are able to watch a meeting of the SRC women's collective (men from a distance, as only women are allowed into the "women's" room). Grim faced, overall-clad, hard, strident, often lustfully embracing in a counterfeit of love ...

He invaded the Women's Room with a Channel Ten news crew and cub reporter Mike Munro. The issue was voluntary fees. The point was ridicule. When asked to leave the room, Abbott declared for the cameras: "This is a man's room for the moment." On ABC *Nationwide* he was calling for the slashing of both university funding and student numbers. This was to be done in the name of restoring academic rigour to Australian universities by denying Marxist lecturers the wherewithal to teach, for instance, the politics of lesbianism. He was spouting pure Santamaria: "Marxists realised that the universities now play a crucial role in the education of the elite of modern society, and they understand if they destroy the academic standards, and perhaps even the moral standards of that elite, well then they have perhaps fundamentally and fatally undermined liberal democratic society."

His footy mates loved him. "Shut up, Abbo," they'd say when he started talking politics. "Shut up, Abbo," was a familiar, affectionate taunt on the field and in the pub. They forgave him his outrages. They loved the daredevil in him. One night he was drinking at the Bald Rock Hotel in Rozelle when a fire broke out in the house next door. Law student and school friend Greg San Miguel told the *Sydney Morning Herald*'s Deborah Snow:

> Flames were shooting from the roof and we could hear kids inside ... within a minute or two it was so hot it was hard to get near the house. Meanwhile Tony had jumped the fence and by force of will had pulled the bars off the windows and got the kids out. He disappeared off the scene straight afterwards.

At about fifteen stone he was much bigger than he is now, a good front rower, playing in the university seconds and thirds with occasional games for the firsts when their star props were touring with the Wallabies. The rugby crowd had no idea Abbo was still thinking of the priesthood. They should have kept a closer eye on *Honi Soit,* which ran the SRC president's address to new students in Orientation Week, 1979:

> All physical objects, all human works are quite insubstantial in the parade of eternity – only God endures. In all ages progressive thinkers have announced the death of God. My friends, He has made more comebacks than Mohammed Ali. For most of us, he refuses to die. This is the FUNDA-MENTAL TRUTH that has been forgotten by the university in its rush to be fashionable ...

He had a rough-house brand of Catholic evange-lism. One day in late 1979, Greg Sheridan brought him into town to have a beer with some journalists on the *Bulletin.* Sheridan was also a Democratic Club warrior, another Santamaria acolyte out to save the world. He later wrote: "Tony and I became boon companions, deep friends and allies in the great strug-gle of the late 1970s, to break decisively the grip the far Left then had on university politics." Sheridan now had a job on the *Bulletin.* The magazine's designer Lindsay Foyle remembers Abbott in the pub that afternoon immediately threatening fisticuffs for the faith. "The main point of contention was a woman's right to control pregnancy, either via contraception or

abortion," he recalled in a wry account of that afternoon published twenty years later in the *Australian*.
Abbott "decided the quickest way to settle our differences was for him to take me downstairs and demon-
strate how I was wrong by punching my head in."
Sheridan told his heavy-set university mate to back
off. No fists were raised. The bizarre outburst was
over in a minute. Foyle wrote: "Within a few years all
those who were in the bar that evening worked on the
same magazine and, as is the nature of things, became
friends." None queried the story when it appeared in
2001. All denied it when it was republished in 2012.
Foyle stands by his account.

Abbott organised two plebiscites on the campus.
One to cut all ties with AUS was passed handsomely.
But a second to end compulsory fees for the SRC
lost heavily. Abbott did not give up. He put all his
efforts into persuading the university senate to defy
the student vote and use its own authority to decide
the issue of SRC fees. This was the young man's idea
of liberal democracy. He told his fellow senators:
"The SRC is unnecessary and superfluous." The senators turned him down. Next he haggled over old
provisions for conscientious objection to paying the
fees. Who would be exempt? He demanded guaran-
tees in writing that anyone who opposed the SRC
funding "the Active Defence of Homosexuals on

campus" should not have to pay fees. The senators gave no guarantee.

While he was battling this out, he stood for re-election to the senate, striking a heroic pose on the campus as a man of high principle who had "trodden an individual and even provocative course" that had to be understood in the light of his urgent purpose:

> Otherwise high-handed and precipitate actions have, I think, been justified by the potentially grave danger posed to university values and ordinary standards by certain trends on campus.

He lost – to his ally Tanya Coleman, later Costello – but like a dog with a bone didn't let the funding matter alone. He tried to persuade the senate to cut the SRC fee by $2.50, the sum no longer being sent to AUS. The motion was lost on the voices. He demanded a show of hands. It was lost again and he announced he had no option but to resign from the senate. It was not a particularly impressive gesture: this was his last meeting anyway. As he walked from the room, the chancellor, Herman Black, remarked dryly that if he wished to resign, he should do so in writing. Abbott's letter arrived three weeks later.

At last, in his final year, he put aside politics and studied. In November he was awarded one of the great scholarships of the world: two years at Oxford courtesy of the diamond-mining fortune of Empire loyalist Cecil Rhodes. For Anglophiles and rugby players, the Rhodes was died-and-gone-to-heaven time. Winners must be scholars fond of sport who display "moral force of character and instincts to lead." The award to Abbott came as a surprise to some who had seen him up close on the SRC. One jibe at the time was: "Second-grade footballer, third-rate academic and fourth-class politician." But Abbott impressed a panel of worthies chaired by the governor of New South Wales, Sir Roden Cutler. That's what mattered. Abbott used the announcement in the *Sydney Morning Herald* to have a last whack at student funds being spent fighting Kerr, Fraser, uranium mining and other "extreme causes."

He arrived in Oxford a free man, free of the expectations that had driven him at Sydney. He didn't have a pack to lead. Bob Santamaria was a long way away. Oxford was saving civilisation from the abyss without any help from him. And they did things so differently: goon squads heckling lesbians won no applause in that university town. The Rhodes had taken him over the threshold of the Establishment. Power was everywhere around him: in the history of the place, its traditions and its connections. His tutors were men with world reputations. The Catholic community of the university was in every way ambitious. As the old expectations lifted from his shoulders and he felt himself free to start again, Abbott did what he always does as he enters a new world determined to impress: he found himself a mentor.

Paul Mankowski is now a divisive figure in the Jesuit order: blunt, uncompromising, hard-line, a man of great masculine charm, foe to all things modish and friend to every traditional practice of the church. "Mankowski is a piece of work," a leading Australian Jesuit told me. But the priest has his admirers and Abbott is among them. When they met at Oxford in late 1981, this American was studying Aramaic, living with extreme frugality – dressed, according to Abbott, in the clothes of dead priests – and boxing. He gave Abbott a skipping rope and put him in the ring. It's said of Mankowski that he wasn't much of a boxer, he just liked to be hit. Abbott was smitten and still is today. "I doubt that I have ever met a finer man than Paul Mankowski."

Boxing was many things to Abbott: contest, glory and discipline. When he talks about his life, this is the point in the story where he begins to rhapsodise about discipline. Abbott's accounts of his Oxford years suggest his tutors and Mankowski were telling him the same thing: that to make something of his contradictory talents would take discipline. Boxing was a place to start. "The thing about boxing," he told ABC *Grandstand* in 2012, "is that it requires an enormous amount of discipline because you've got to discipline yourself to overcome fear and inevitably you are frightened before you get into the ring." In *Battlelines* he wrote of meeting Mankowski and falling in love: "Within a couple of weeks, the challenge of a new and ferocious discipline naturally had me hooked."

On a bus taking some Australians down to London to see the latest Edna Everage extravaganza in the West End, Abbott met a law student at Magdalen. He and George Brandis were very different men moving in different circles. But from a distance Brandis watched Abbott over the next couple of years becoming "not just one of the most recognisable but one of the most popular people in the university." There was his (rather small) April 1982 pro-Margaret Thatcher march to counter the big anti-Falklands War rally at the Martyrs' Memorial at Oxford. And there were the boxing matches reported in the local Oxford paper: four games and four wins including two victories over Cambridge. No one ever praised Abbott's style in the ring. One of his sparring partners told Mark Dapin years later: "Tony used to club them into submission." The last fight in early 1983, and Abbott's most famous victory, was like all the rest:

He waded in and he just kept punching until the point of exhaustion. He was getting so tired, and he was breathing heavily, and his hands were coming down, and I thought, "If his opponent survives into the second round, I don't think Tony will recoup enough to win the fight," but the ref stopped it.

Abbott had a wonderful time at Oxford. He left an even more committed Anglophile than he was when he arrived. "I loved the rugby. I loved my studies. I loved the opportunity to mix with a remarkable group of people from all over the world and, yes, I loved the boxing." He didn't win a first- but a solid second-class honours degree in history and politics. Lord Blake, his history tutor, sent him back into the world echoing Emmet Costello's reservations: "Mr Abbott needs to temper his robust common sense with a certain philosophic doubt." And the departing student had a surprise for Brandis:

a few of us were engaged in that perennial late-night discussion among university students: what are you going to do when you graduate? Glittering careers in public life, academia or the professions were envisioned. When it was Tony's turn, he said simply, "I'm going to be a priest."

Puppy Love: Canberra,
26 June 2012

"Where are the animals?" David Speers asks as he climbs out of the Sky News car. It's cold at the dog pound on the outskirts of Canberra where the press is gathering for today's attack on the carbon tax. I give Speers the lie of the land. In the office is a woman with a white rat called Bijou on her shoulder. Out the back, a pit bull bitch called Yserah is waiting for the leader of the Opposition. They see a lot of pit bull pups at the RSPCA, her handler had told me. Why? "Because young guys have pit bulls and they are idiots and they don't desex their dogs." A sign on Yserah's empty cage says the bitch is "Zealous."

The press pack has been to so many of these carbon tax outings over the last two and a half years. Abbott's office digs into its database day after day, issues another "media alert" and out the press heads to another outfit about to be ruined by the Great Big Tax on Everything that has lately morphed into the

Toxic Tax Based on a Lie. Six months ago there were rumblings in the party that the strategy was exhausted. But to the delight of the leader's office – and the exasperation of Labor – these jaunts are still putting Abbott's face on the news. Mind you, something of the fun has gone out of them now that he no longer turns up occasionally in strange body-hugging gear. His minders – and perhaps his wife – have said no to Speedos and Lycra. Even so it can be said that never in the political annals of this country have so many seen so much of so little.

The press is perky. The dog pound promises better pictures than another visit to Bill Lilley Mitsubishi of Crawford Street, Queanbeyan. We're still hoping Abbott might tackle something a little more complicated one day than greasing a wheel nut or ironing a shirt. Maybe a hip replacement. Gathered in the car park are journalists from AAP, the *Australian*, the *Canberra Times* and the *Sydney Morning Herald* plus Paul Bongiorno and his crew from Ten and Speers of Sky News. Over by the gate, a woman with purple hair is climbing into a chicken suit. Her placard is lying on the ground:

The sky isn't falling!
Carbon Price = Good for Jobs
& our future!

Abbott and Greg Hunt unpack themselves from a Commonwealth car. Abbott is spotless. He walks as though he has to will each leg forward. It's curious in a man who is so obviously fit. His face is skin and bone. He smiles but his eyes are hooded. The overall effect is faintly menacing, as if he's about to climb into the ring. No pollsters will ever be able to tell us how much of the vote he loses just for looking so uncomfortable in his own body. Bijou is presented as he crosses the foyer. His response is faultless. Patting the little rodent, he says: "I suppose I should show my professional respects."

The press has given up saying so but Abbott and Hunt are denouncing what they once supported: a price on carbon and an emissions trading scheme. The Opposition spokesman on climate change wrote his thesis at Melbourne University on the benefits of countering global warming by taxing polluters. And Abbott's support for emissions trading helped persuade John Howard to adopt that policy. Only the politics have changed. From the moment he became leader of the Opposition Abbott has driven a scare campaign to convince us Gillard's tax will destroy the economy. He's done so with flair and immense determination. But Abbott's wild hyperbole is about to be tested. The tax is only days away.

Yserah has vanished. "I was told I wasn't allowed to use a pit bull," says her disgruntled handler. At the end of her lead now is Mars Bar, a beautiful young Rottweiler. What's the difference? As it happens, the press pack is not going to crack jokes today about attack-dog politicians. The cameras barely record the self-confessed junkyard dog's encounter with the Rottweiler and get to work only as the politicians begin to cuddle a couple of part Staffy puppies, Gloves and Mittens. The names had been chosen only that morning. They run through a lot of names at a dog pound. As the flashlights blaze Hunt mugs for the cameras: "Gorgeous, and the puppy's pretty too."

We huddle among the kennels, hiding from the chicken lady. It smells like a nursing home back here. "The RSPCA is one of Australia's great charities," says Abbott once all the microphones are set. "It is a household name and justly so. It is one of the many organisations which is going to be damaged by the carbon tax." He speaks with grave regret. "I will be travelling the length and breadth of Australia in the first fortnight of the carbon tax's introduction just pointing out to people that every family's cost of living is going to be harmed. Every Australian job is going to be less secure and it is not actually going to reduce emissions."

Michael Linke, the society's local CEO, tells us the carbon tax will cost the RSPCA $180,000 across Australia. Jobs will go. "There is absolutely no way that I'm going to compromise animal welfare." As he walks away from the microphone I stop him to ask the obvious question: what's the RSPCA's national budget? "$90 million." What are we doing here?

That night Abbott and Hunt are on television cuddling those puppies while denouncing the brutal impact of the carbon tax on the RSPCA. There are also a few clips of Julia Gillard's mockery in the House: "I can tell the leader of the Opposition, on the first of July, cats will still purr, dogs will still bark and the Australian economy will continue to get strong." Next morning the *Sydney Morning Herald* shows Abbott petting the rat. (Typical.) Over the next days, the RSPCA deals with a storm of criticism for taking part in this political exercise. Animal lovers are assured the RSPCA supports action on climate change. Gloves and Mittens find a home.

Fathers and Son

In the subdivisions of Emu Plains, Tony Abbott came to doubt his vocation. He was nearly thirty. He had spent two unhappy years in a seminary and ordination was still years away. In summer at the foot of the Blue Mountains he found himself teaching scripture to kids, running a youth group and occasionally preaching at Our Lady of the Way. A spiritual apprenticeship in the suburbs was not, he wrote, without its rewards. "But I found it difficult to believe that this was meant to be my life."

This wasn't what he had in mind at Oxford. But Oxford had played on his love of history, old institutions and heroic sacrifice. Mankowski had fanned the flames of a fire he saw had never quite gone out.

Meeting Mankowski, a contemporary who was both the embodiment of muscular Christianity and fully acquainted with the cross tides of modern life, made me think that it might be possible to become a priest and stay "normal." Perhaps it was "meant to be."

He was not driven by piety. He always imagined himself a leader of the church. He might have studied for the priesthood in England or Rome. He did not cast his lot with the Jesuits but took himself to St Patrick's Seminary at Manly. Father Michael Kelly, a confidant at the time, explained: "He wanted to be Archbishop of Sydney." It was not an ignoble ambition but ahead of the young man lay a long and celibate road.

His sisters were put out. "We were all just horri-fied, because we felt the priesthood was not the career for him," said his sister Jane Vincent. They believed him destined for politics. "It's what he's cut out for. It suits his character, and the way he's been brought up ... he's exactly the right sort of person to be prime minister." Undeterred, Abbott turned up at Manly in February 1984 full of fervour and determi-nation to excel. He was an amazing "get" for the church: footballer, student leader and Rhodes Scholar. The historian Father Edmund Campion was one of his teachers: "He wasn't so much a big fish in a small pond as a whale in a swimming pool. People felt swamped by his intellectual achievements and by the force of his personality."

Abbott didn't disappear from view. He kept up with old school and university friends like Greg San Miguel. "He didn't strike me as starkly changed on his return." Oxford had not turned a lout into a saint. San Miguel knew his friend had always had serious ambitions. "At Oxford Tony let his serious side advance." But old campus adversaries were surprised to find a gentler Abbott explaining himself in the pages of the *Australian* soon after entering the seminary:

> As time went by it seemed to me the real issues were not so much political but spiritual; the important arena was not Parliament, the economy or the strategic balance but the human heart; the great qualities were not ambition, ability or eloquence but love. It's been said I have a martyr complex, that I like to rush off and engage in heroic struggles for lost causes. I hope that's not true. We humans have something very deep in us which is repelled by the idea of God. I think that's our pride and the Christian is in a sense constantly at war with the world and often at war with himself.

To his dismay, Abbott found himself in an institution as confused, often vapid and unsure of itself as left-wing student politics had been. Once again, authority was under attack. This time the trouble-makers were theologians at war with the Vatican. St Patrick's was too camp for his taste, too gay. There was too much navel-gazing. He was much older than his class, much brighter and more a man of the world. He quickly loathed the place. He found no mentor there. Things grew worse in his second year when a new man arrived to run the place, a priest with superficially democratic ideals and deep faith in what Abbott took to be psychobabble.

"Tony wasn't one to walk on the headland with beads in his hands," says Noel Debien, an ABC broadcaster and fellow St Patrick's seminarian. "He was not a meditator. He loved good music and was moved by ceremony. But he was impatient with frip-pery. He was not one of the squeaky-black-shoes and soutane brigade. He was orthodox and straight-forward. His attitude was: 'Tell me what's required and I'll do it. I do not need to go on a fucking *jour-ney*.' He took it all so seriously. Tony didn't warm to the very black, camp sense of humour in the place, a way of dealing with the difficulties of it all. It was difficult. Celibacy is hard. It is not an easy thing to be in the prime of your life and you can't even wank."

Abbott couldn't help himself: he took the problems of St Patrick's to the press. An article for the *Catholic Weekly* was never published but a letter appeared in the *Northern Herald* explaining why so many seminarians dropped out:

> St Patrick's is a microcosm of the Church where the tensions only too evident in contemporary Catholicism are brought into sharp and often painful focus. This is the central reality of St Patrick's ... the real reason for the drop-out rate ... include ennui, psychosomatic illness and unwillingness to conform to whatever model of priesthood happens to be momentarily fashionable.

The letter was a bold move, says Debien. "Talking to the press was a sign you had given up on the church. I thought he was a hero. He was pressing the self-destruct button but thank God someone was saying this stuff."

The cardinal was furious. Abbott was swiftly in Emu Plains. After a few months out by the mountains he was shifted to North Rocks, closer to the city. All this time he was negotiating the terms of a return to the seminary. A way was eventually found but he'd had enough. At football training on Sydney University oval – he had been coaching since his return from England – he announced he was quitting. The response was enthusiastic and ribald. Abbott would later write in the *Bulletin*:

Three years' grinding struggle to meet the Church's standard was over. But a dream had died, as well – the dream that I could join that splendoured company founded by Christ which has angered, amazed and enthralled the world ever since.

His many accounts of the death of this dream make it clear the fundamental issue wasn't celibacy – though surely that would have become impossible in time – but the bleak conviction that "serving a local church at a time of disillusion and decline" wasn't worth the sacrifice. The power of Rome was in question; the authority of the priesthood was in doubt; and the modern church was deliberately downplaying its own mystique. What was the point of giving up so much for so long to become a bishop in a church that had abandoned its heroic mission? It was a prospect of little power and no glory. Besides, what might have dawned on him in his school days but for mentor priests whispering about his vocation was now inescapably clear: his deepest interest was politics.

Once out of the seminary, Abbott was offered two jobs. One was to write for the *Bulletin*. The other was to be an organiser for the latest front Santamaria had set up to peddle his vision of doom, the Council for the National Interest. Abbott's letter turning Santamaria's offer down was one of two key letters he wrote to the old man in these years as he struggled to map his future. They should never have seen the light of day but were accidentally released to editor Geoffrey Browne and reported in the *Australian* in late 2012 by Ross Fitzgerald and Stephen Holt. The embargo by the Santamaria estate is once again firmly in place. Fitzgerald and Holt summarised Abbott's reasons for saying no:

> Things would be different if he were still 21 and fresh out of university, or 35 with an established professional reputation. But this was not the case. He had just dropped out of the priesthood and could no longer risk "another great gamble." His life to date, Abbott wrote, combined "much promise but little actual performance." He believed that the time had come for him to build a career so that he could show a future wife and employer that he was solid and dependable ... He felt he could do more to advance the values of the NCC by writing for the *Bulletin* as opposed to working directly with Santamaria in Melbourne.

He met John Howard. Under siege from both his deputy and the corrupt premier of Queensland, Joh

Bjelke-Petersen, the leader of the Opposition gave the young man forty minutes of his time. Howard had done his homework. He knew this was the former student politician, the footballer, the Rhodes Scholar, the ex-seminarian. He found him "Very intelligent, easy to talk to, had a lot of views the same as me; was traditional about a lot of things, but he was also somebody with a great enquiring mind ... he saw Australia as something of an outpost of Western civilisation and values in the Asian Pacific region, and having to combine the history and the geography of our country, which he thought we could do ... I thought he had real political talent." No commitments were made on either side. Abbott still saw himself as fundamentally Labor. Howard made a vague offer of work somewhere down the track. A few weeks later he lost the 1987 election to Bob Hawke.

Abbott began at the *Bulletin*. The old magazine was a revolving door for the politically ambitious. Bob Carr had only recently left for the NSW parliament but still called in from time to time. Malcolm Turnbull had gone to the bar on his own path to parliament. Lindsay Foyle was still there. He and Abbott easily patched up their differences. Abbott joined the Australian Journalists' Association and led a little strike. Later he would oppose a big strike at the *Australian*. "He would make aggressive speeches at meetings," recalls long-time unionist Alan Kennedy. "I think he saw himself carrying the Santamaria banner into battle against us commos." Among themselves, journalists began calling him the Mad Monk.

Drinking next door at the King's Head that winter, Abbott met Margaret Aitken, a New Zealander working in Sydney for the Rothschild bank. Abbott's biographer Michael Duffy writes of her being instantly attracted to this large, loud, friendly figure who "chatted about the intricacies of the Labor Party split of the 1950s, a subject with which she, not surprisingly, was unfamiliar. Indeed, she was not at all interested in politics." It became swiftly clear to both of them that they would marry.

Abbott was straining at the leash, desperate to enter the political fray. On 8 December that year he wrote to Santamaria again. With astonishing chutzpah he told the man he revered so deeply that the NCC was finished, doing little more than carping from the sidelines. Santamaria did not dissent. Abbott's letter is again under lock and key but Fitzgerald and Holt summarised his argument:

He wanted to change society by working from within. This meant sharing the fears and concerns of the "common herd." It was crucial to "make the compromises that life requires, be wrong, get blood on one's hands – but at least be in it." For "vigorous, self-starting people" such as himself, the real issue was to secure a direct parliamentary presence.

But on which side?

"To join either existing party involves holding one's nose," he wrote. "Either way would upset some. But to do nothing dooms us to extinction."

Abbott dismissed the Liberal Party:

It was "without soul, direction or inspiring leadership," while its members were divided between "surviving trendies and the more or less simpleminded advocates of the free market." The Liberal Party's mixture of "hand-wringing indecision or inappropriate economic Ramboism and perhaps their lack of political professionalism" struck Abbott as a fatal combination.

Abbott urged Santamaria to lead his followers back into the Labor fold:

Labor's previous 30 years of hostility to Santamaria weighed against it but Abbott wrote, "our roots and the origins of our political culture are there" … if the ALP was not "dominated" by Santamaria-style ideas, it would succumb to "the grip of the Left or of soulless pragmatists." This was intolerable.

Labor had been sounding out Abbott even while he was in the seminary. Carr was from time to time asking if he might be interested in a career with the party. Abbott told Santamaria:

The NSW Labor government led by right-wing stalwart Barrie Unsworth was due to fight an election in March 1988 and this was surely "a window of opportunity" to be exploited.

Santamaria said no. He mocked "the reptilian Liberals" and acknowledged there was an opportunity for Abbott to pursue "a real apostolate in Labor ranks," but in a forceful, forensic reply to the young man, the weight of Santamaria's scorn fell on the Labor Party:

Santamaria rejected the suggestion of the NCC "going back to our Labor origins in an organised way, as our central strategy." Santamaria noted that Catholics had largely run the NSW ALP since the 1950s but that the only result of Catholic influence in Labor governments, both in NSW and federally, had been "jobs for the boys."

Santamaria's instinct was always to block Labor. Starving it of the talent of young Tony was a tiny detail in a lifetime of hostility. Abbott was not immediately persuaded to ditch his fundamental allegiance – he voted Labor in that state election – but the man he called his "philosophical star" had given him his bearings.

Abbott left the *Bulletin* in the autumn of 1988 and found a job running a batching plant for Pioneer Concrete, the company of a "prominent member of the wider Jesuit network" Sir Tristan Antico. In spring, the Abbotts were married by Emmet Costello in the Riverview chapel. A few weeks later, Abbott bumped into John Howard at the funeral of the DLP dinosaur Jack Kane. Duffy wrote that at around this time Abbott "found the Liberals more attractive" and sometime in this year of shifting alliances he joined the party. He wasn't active. Then he abandoned concrete for the *Australian* where he wrote editorials for the next twelve months. His first daughter was born. But his political prospects were not growing any brighter. Howard was no longer leader of the Opposition and the Coalition lost once more to Hawke in March 1990.

At this nadir in the fortunes of his party, Howard invited Abbott to lunch. There was a job going as one of the press secretaries of the new leader of the Opposition, John Hewson. Twenty-four hours later, Abbott was in Canberra. He had found the mentor who would mean almost everything to him in his political career. It wasn't Hewson. Abbott and his boss were very different men – a Catholic idealist, Abbott would later say, serving a Baptist technocrat workaholic – but things began well. Hewson found him bright and hard-working. "Diversity of opinion is an enormous asset," he says. "Tony was the furthest to the right of my advisers. He was, with that DLP background of his, always about hard-line social policy. He was very good at defending a case in argument." And Abbott was excited by the commitment to principle he saw in Hewson:

> He had called his advisers together, and we were talking about the coming couple of years leading up to the 1993 election, and John said something like this: losing an election would not be the end of the world, but going to an election without a policy, or a set of policies, that I really believed in – *that* would be the real failure.
>
> Now I was thrilled to hear this, and I thought to myself, in the tradition of B.A. Santamaria, this

is a *man*, not a political weathervane. Whether you like him or dislike him, whether you support his policies or not, this is a *man* in politics.

But Hewson didn't use Abbott's speeches. "I spoke off the cuff most of the time. But I remember getting him to draft a speech for some housing awards and there were two words on housing and the rest of it was a defence of the monarchy. I had to say that wouldn't do. It happened quite often." Abbott was included in meetings but not part of the inner circle. And he was learning to deal with the press almost from scratch. He was an opinion writer, not a reporter. He had no contacts in and no experience dealing with the Canberra gallery. It didn't help that he and Hewson were instinctively wary of the press. Alan Ramsey wrote:

> In twenty-five years in Canberra, I remember no Opposition leader who blitzed the press gallery boxes with as many pieces of paper as does Hewson. His office churns them out at a furious pace, often pages in length. Yet the gallery hardly ever gets to talk to the man behind the words.

This is when I first met Abbott. *Four Corners* was doing a profile of Hewson. Standard stuff. But

Abbott was demanding the impossible: all questions in writing in advance. We refused. The result was a mess that didn't play well for us or Hewson. The press gallery was whingeing about a press secretary "who keeps very close counsel indeed." The nickname Mad Monk became public currency.

Abbott's most important task at this time was to turn the opening chapters of *Fightback!* into prose. Hewson's Australia was to have a goods and services tax and Hewson's impeccable approach was to stage a year's debate before putting the tax to the people at the coming election. *Fightback!* was the end of Hawke. Within weeks Paul Keating was prime minister and hard at work attacking this great big tax on everything, a tax which in his heart he deeply admired. Abbott gave the Labor leader useful ammunition, drafting a speech for Hewson with a few lines of Killara snobbery that would haunt the Opposition leader all the way to the ballot box and beyond:

> In any street, of course, it's always easy to tell the rented houses. They're the ones where the lawn isn't mowed, the plants aren't watered and the fences aren't fixed.

Hewson was a bad-tempered boss. Abbott handled the outbursts well but relations between them deteriorated. He wasn't getting on with people in the office: his teasing got under people's skin. Hewson said: "He was one of the most interesting and challenging people on the one hand, and one of the most frustrating people I've ever met in my life." In February 1992 he shunted Abbott aside, leaving him with the vague task of looking after "political and communications strategy in the lead-up to the election" which was over a year away. Abbott's great consolation at this difficult time was growing closer to Howard. This increased the tension in Hewson's office. "While I always knew that he was running his own and Howard's race," said Hewson, "I was never really sure when he was running mine."

Abbott couldn't just leave. His second and third daughters were born while he worked for Hewson. The Liberal Party in New South Wales was looking for a new director but Barry O'Farrell got the job. By the time the election of 1993 rolled around, Abbott had left to work for the party secretariat. Hewson's loss shocked Hewson, the country, the party and Abbott. Determined to remain leader of the Opposition, Hewson announced *Fightback!* was dead. Abbott wrote to him: "How can you sacrifice your principles to save your job, when you would not sacrifice your principles to save the election?"

Abbott cites sending this note – which Hewson

has no recollection of seeing – as a clarifying moment in his career. He had seen deep conviction frankly expressed make his boss unelectable. More finesse was required, more discretion. Fifteen years later he urged Santamaria loyalists at a dinner for their newspaper, *News Weekly*, not to abandon principles. "If you don't have them, what is the point of life in politics?" But principles must be pursued "intelligently and sensitively" so as not to frighten the public:

> The art of effective democratic statesmanship is of presenting your principles, presenting your convictions, in ways which sufficiently impress the public such that you are seen as a man or woman of principle, but which don't so worry the public that they think you would be a risk if you found yourself in a position of power.

After witnessing the Hewson catastrophe at first hand, Abbott began to wear a mask. Since then he has grown and changed. Life and politics have taught him a great deal. But how this has shaped the fundamental Abbott is carefully obscured. What has been abandoned? What is merely hidden on the road to power? It is hard to tell, especially as he continues to insist he is a politician of enduring values. What makes people so uneasy about Abbott is the sense that he is biding his time, that there is a very hard operator somewhere behind that mask, waiting for power. He came away from those years with Hewson convinced more than ever that a real *man* must win: "Unless you're in a position to make executive decisions, it is – dare I say it? – but sounding brass and tinkling cymbal."

Safety of Life: House of Representatives, 27 June 2012

Out in the Indian Ocean another rescue is underway. This time Australia swiftly sent help to the stricken vessel. The last boat in trouble was left unrescued for over thirty hours as Australia tried – and inevitably failed – to persuade the Indonesians to take its human cargo back again. Over ninety drowned. Death has brought the boats issue back to life. Question Time is suspended. Gillard is pushing Malaysia again. The Opposition is insisting the government capitulate utterly: abandon Malaysia, resume processing refugees on Nauru and defy Indonesia by returning refugee boats to the Java coast.

A little cohort of Liberals long troubled by the race politics of the boats is threatening to cross the floor. Greens and senior Liberals take the dissidents aside by turns. Julie Bishop kisses Mal Washer. It is a peck of gratitude. She has his vote. While negotiations continue in clumps around the chamber, Opposition politicians queue at the dispatch box to sing arias to human rights. Even Kevin Andrews, the jailer of Dr Mohamed Haneef, is caterwauling about the vulnerable needing rights. It is an arresting, complicated and contradictory scene. Conservative politicians who have ridiculed every effort to entrench human rights protections in Australian law for fifty years are weeping in the House of Representatives about the Hazaras and Tamils who would be left unprotected if dispatched to Malaysia.

"We have always believed in offshore processing with protections," intones Abbott. Not quite. As if rising from the grave, John Howard's old immigration minister Philip Ruddock gets to his feet to remind the House that it was Labor that insisted during the *Tampa* crisis that fundamental human rights be incorporated in the Pacific Solution. "This matter turns on the very question of whether or not you walk away from those obligations on offshore processing now. We are seeking ... no more than Kim Beazley demanded of us at that time."

Abbott is looking particularly earnest as he faces the cameras later in the gardens of parliament. Each sentence comes with a reflective little pause. "We did try hard today to reach what we thought was a principled compromise." This is risible. He had held his rebels in check by promising to increase the quota of refugees an Abbott government would take. Nothing more. Earlier in the day he had spoken of consulting his conscience. There is none of that now. He bats press questions away, hardly pretending to address them. He knows there is no guarantee Nauru will work. He knows boats can't be towed back. He knows that unless the big parties can come to some agreement, the Greens will block both their plans in the Senate. The stalemate he brought us out here to condemn is his work as much as anyone's. This is a happy politician with a grave face.

WikiLeaks told us how keen the Coalition is to exploit the boats. In late 2009, in the dying days of Malcolm Turnbull's leadership of the Opposition, a "key Liberal party strategist" popped in to the US embassy in Canberra to say how pleased the party was that refugee boats were, once again, making their way to Christmas Island. "The issue was 'fantastic,'" he said. "And 'the more boats that come the better.'" But he admitted they had yet to find a way to make the issue work in their favour: "his research indicated only a 'slight trend' towards the Coalition."

Abbott found the way. That Christ himself was a refugee doesn't trouble him one bit. He has a Jesuitical line he offers troubled constituents that is almost too embarrassing to put down in black and white: the flight into Egypt, he says, took the Holy Family to the *nearest* sanctuary. Hazaras, by contrast, are travelling all the way to Australia. For such journeys there is no Biblical backing. They should have stayed in Pakistan. Abbott's Christian conscience sees nothing standing in the way of taking political advantage of boat people. In the Abbott analysis, Howard saved his skin by stopping the boats. The argument goes something like this: Howard won the battlers in '96, almost lost them in '98 with the GST but enough stayed around to let him squeak home. Then he won them all back in '01 with strong border protection.

Abbott cast himself as a hero in the battle of the boats the moment he became leader of the Opposition. The old derogatory rhetoric was deployed with fresh aggression: Australia was under invasion; Australia had lost control of its borders; Labor lacked the will to protect the nation; Labor was "rolling out the red carpet" for these "illegals." Compassion is "moral vanity." Abbott even mused one morning on Perth radio that it was un-Christian for refugees to come by sea. He licensed his immigration spokesman, Scott Morrison, to link boat people with exotic diseases, the drug trade and gun-running. At one point Abbott faced open revolt in his party after backing Morrison's complaints about money spent flying survivors of a boat wreck to the funerals of their families. Briefly it seemed his leadership might be under threat after a member of shadow cabinet, disgusted by what was going on, leaked to the press that Morrison had suggested the party capitalise on growing concerns about Muslim immigration. In the *Sydney Morning Herald*, Peter Hartcher reported: "He put it on the table like a dead cat." There was talk in the party of easing up on boat people. It was not to be. One Liberal MP told the *Courier Mail*: "It works incredibly well for us in outer metropolitan electorates."

Labor folded. In August, Julia Gillard eagerly accepted the Houston Committee's recommendation that she adopt almost all the Coalition's brutal policies to stop the boats. Few Australians doubt the parties play politics with this issue but that does not mean the nation has much sympathy for refugees crossing by sea. What little there was has been exhausted by years of attacks from Abbott and Morrison as boats continued to arrive from the north in record numbers. An Essential poll in late August revealed Australia's great enthusiasm for Air Chief Marshal Angus Houston's proposals. Nothing was too tough: 66 per cent of us wanted the boats turned back where possible; 67 per cent wanted the old camps on Manus and Nauru reopened; 47 per cent were happy for asylum seekers to languish there for several years; and 72 per cent of us were keen to prevent families joining those boat people we eventually accept to live in Australia. This enthusiasm wasn't matched by much confidence in the outcome. The same Essential poll published as Labor capitulated to Abbott in August showed only 31 per cent of Australians thought the Houston regime would be "very effective" or even "quite effective" in stopping the boats. This isn't about success. What's been whipped up here by the Opposition is a thirst for punishment.

The Member for Yesterday

S omeone up the back was rudely demanding the chairman say what side he was on: the crown or the republic? The hall of St John's Anglican Church in Gordon was stuffy. The heckler wouldn't let up. The young man's question was fair but astonishingly abrupt by the standards of Sydney's upper North Shore. Malcolm Turnbull had given his spiel. Paul Keating had appointed him the day before to chair a committee of eminent Australians to advise on the shape of the republic. The rather courtly barrister Lloyd Waddy delivered his defence of the crown. As the meeting broke up, the heckler introduced himself to Waddy. "This very possessed, good-looking, solid man came out of the crowd and said: 'If you're looking for anyone to speak up for the monarchy, mate, I'm your man.'" It was Tony Abbott.

Waddy hired Abbott to run ACM, Australians for Constitutional Monarchy. "We never looked back from there. The monarchists were not being heard and he made us heard. He said to me: 'Mate, mate, we've got to set this up across Australia.' And he got the money to travel. And he got the most wonderfully representative groups of people together right across Australia: men, women, young, old, migrants." He rallied the troops, the bad cop to Waddy's good cop. He wrote a blizzard of press releases and opinion pieces for the press. "He was an absolute genius with the pen." The first killer phrase of Abbott's political career was: "the Keating republic." That he broke every preconception of what a monarchist was supposed to look like made him a particularly effective recruiting officer. He wasn't a forelock-tugging, elderly silvertail. He was this ocker.

Sentimentality and an instinctive hostility to change don't quite explain Abbott's attachment to the monarchy. He was still the "incorrigible Anglophile" of his childhood. No Fenian suspicions about the crown had rubbed off on him in his Catholic school days. The crown was history and heroism, romance and pageantry, one of the great institutions of Western civilisation. There is little sign in Abbott of a personal devotion to Elizabeth II, but he shared the old DLP reverence for John Kerr. Twenty-five years before he dismissed Gough Whitlam, Kerr was one of the brilliant lawyers stripping communists out of the unions for Santamaria. From the moment Abbott reached university in the months just after the sacking, defending Kerr from his detractors was a cherished cause. And now there was the raw political necessity of denying Keating a triumph. Abbott wrote: "Any republic that comes about under Keating will be Keating's republic and Keating's possession."

By the time ACM was up and running in the middle of 1993, Australia seemed to be drifting towards a republic. Half the country wanted to be rid of the crown. The political establishment was essentially republican and had been so for years. The press was republican. The rich suburbs were strongly republican. Labor, the Democrats and the Greens all officially backed the republic. More than half the Liberal caucus was personally committed to the cause. But there remained a stubborn third of the nation wedded to the crown and that would rise to a little over 40 per cent once ACM began making its mark. That is a powerful constituency. As he began putting ACM together, Abbott wrote a blistering article in the *Australian* to remind John Hewson that no issue was above politics and there were politics to be played here: he didn't have to be "relevant" and "swim with the community mood" and should he allow the Liberals even a free debate on the monarchy he risked months of "vicious infighting" that might destroy the party.

That was always the Santamaria way: when you haven't got the numbers, be vicious. It's called minority politics. Abbott would come to play them superbly, having learnt in the Democratic Club how small constituencies can cause big trouble. It's a matter of passion rather than numbers. The crucial weakness of the Australian republican movement was having not much more than reason on its side. By and large this is a country of milksop republicans. But Abbott, by engaging the anger of the minority, could turn the monarchists into a more formidable bloc than polling figures suggested possible. Walling in the crown was only the immediate aim. Across politics and across the country, the monarchists were doing something more, something big and vague. They were holding the line.

Abbott claims the campaign changed him. Until this time he had been all for an absolutely Australian Australia, not necessarily white but true to the Anglo ways Australians had always known. In 1990 he wrote: "There is no reason why a Vietnamese cannot become thoroughly Australian – provided he is encouraged to do so – rather than remain a Vietnamese who happens to be living here." In that remarkable piece in the *Australian*, Abbott backed Howard's right to call for a slowdown in Asian immigration; he endorsed Alfred Deakin's rationale for the White

Australia policy; he wrote of Asians making true Australians "feel like an endangered species through destruction of habitat"; and he demanded immediate assimilation as the price of entry for everyone arriving here from beyond the Anglosphere:

> The issue is the sort of Australia we want our children and grandchildren to inherit. Will it be a relatively cohesive society that studies Shakespeare, follows cricket and honours the Anzacs; or will it be a pastiche of cultures with only a geographic home in common?

But then he found himself at ACM working with Greek and Italian Australians who had not shed their old allegiances. Their passion for the monarchy grew out of their own home soil. They were fighting for the crown here because they believed Greece and Italy had gone to the dogs since becoming republics. They were Abbott's kind of people. No harm to Australia. It beggars belief, perhaps, but working with people like Sophie Mirabella née Panopoulos in his midthirties reconciled Abbott to multiculturalism. He told Paul Kelly about a decade later: "I had been altogether too ungenerous to migrants. I had it wrong and I made a mistake." But he cautioned that his idea of multiculturalism remained "very conservative."

After less than a year at the helm of ACM, Abbott had a call from John Howard. The seat of Warringah was about to fall vacant. Those waterfront suburbs – from Neutral Bay around to Middle Head and over to Manly – are among the best conservative real estate in Australia. They had not been on the market for twenty-four years. The man with the inside running would be Kevin McCann, a leading Sydney solicitor, company director and Liberal moderate. But Howard wanted one of his own in the seat. He urged Abbott to contest. The young man took a little time to consider. It was early February before his name began to appear in press lists of contenders. Though by far the most conservative man among these middle-aged professionals and failed state politicians, Tony Abbott would somehow come to represent the possibilities of a fresh start. It's a career pattern.

That he won Warringah with a single speech is a myth. Not in living memory had there been such an open, aggressive and competitive Liberal pre-selection contest as there was in Warringah in 1993. The rules had changed. Instead of fifty selectors under tight party control making the choice, the selection was now thrown open to a caucus of 200 with the rank and file having a decisive say. Abbott's referees included Laurie Oakes but most were monarchists. They included John Howard and Bronwyn Bishop, who had come down from the Senate to contest the nearby seat of Mackellar. She and her backers believed at this point that the leadership of the party was within her grasp. Santamaria saved Abbott's bacon by refusing to give him a reference. So besotted was Abbott still with the old man, he believed his backing would be a great help. In fact, it would have seemed ridiculous to the selectors of Warringah. Crucial support came from Radio 2UE's Alan Jones, who was commending the contender on air as a fine young fellow and the very best sort of Australian. Between them at this point began one of the great unconsummated love affairs of Australian politics.

The big day in Manly was Sunday 20 February. Good performances at candidates' nights had placed Abbott among the top three contenders. As always, he was writing for newspapers in his own cause; he was on radio calling for the Liberals to become "the party of ideas"; and he distributed a video showing the good work he had done for ACM on television. Jones had written a personal letter to each of the 200 selectors. Bishop, with all the allure of a possible leader, was working the phones. Howard praised Abbott as "a very good political scrapper." That Sunday, the candidate came quietly onto the stage of the Manly Leagues Club, moved the lectern to one side and, without notes, delivered a speech full of fight, short on detail and long on pride in the Liberal Party. He ended by pledging himself to a great cause: "reclaiming our political culture and helping Australia to achieve the greatness that we all know is within our grasp." He beat McCann by sixteen votes.

His maiden speech was also lyrical and far-ranging. He did all the right things: pledge his faith in politics, commend his predecessors in Warringah and thank all those who had inspired and supported him. A long list began with his family, mentioned the Jesuits, paused to remember Santamaria "who sparked my interest in politics" and ended at the feet of "the contemporary politician I admire most," John Howard. The new man pledged to be true to them all:

> May God and the ghosts of great men give me strength. May those who have laboured greatly to build this nation fortify my resolve to make a worthy contribution in this House.

What that contribution might be was up for grabs. The day after his by-election victory, and weeks before he gave parliament this elevated job description, he had told the press he was looking forward to being a "junkyard dog savaging the other side."

His own side was a mess. Hewson fell three weeks after Abbott entered parliament. Alexander Downer lasted only eight months. Howard returned like Lazarus from the grave and took the Coalition to a great victory in March 1996. But to the member for Warringah's immense frustration, the man he so revered kept failing to take him into the ministry. He believed someone of his "political horsepower" should be given a go. He had it out with the prime minister. Howard was unmoved.

A year later, Abbott discovered he had a traitor in the nest. David Oldfield was a suave conservative from Manly who had mustered votes for Abbott's pre-selection. His aggressive positions on migrants and Aborigines were no secret. Oldfield would say, "Abbott's concerns were the same as mine." That's been denied many times, but whatever the differences between them, the new member for Warringah had been comfortable giving a man with such a reputation a key role on his staff. Abbott went further, delivering a memorably savage attack in parliament on the reputation of Oldfield's opponent in the NSW elections of 1995. The fate of John Fahey's Liberal government depended on Oldfield winning Manly. He failed to do so after a bizarre and dirty campaign that saw the Liberals muzzling their candidate to disguise his unpleasant views. Bob Carr took office for a decade.

Abbott and Oldfield worked closely together in the federal campaign of 1996. But it wasn't long before Oldfield began plotting with the Queensland renegade Pauline Hanson to set up a new party. Abbott had no idea what was going on until April 1997 when Oldfield left with a glowing reference to work for One Nation. "Tony copped a lot of flak after I left," Oldfield told the *Sydney Morning Herald*'s Deborah Snow. "People asked him how I could be doing this without him suspecting anything. He, the assiduous networker, the insight man, the absolute operative, had had this happen in his own office – he'd had an operative he didn't know about." A humiliated Abbott blasted Oldfield: "He's a dangerous, snaky Rasputin who thrives on notoriety. Sure, I had him on my staff when I knew he held some unnaturally intense views on some things, but he seemed like a Liberal with a reasonable standing in the community. I'm not making any big claims for myself, but even Jesus had his Judas."

Howard was pussyfooting with Hanson. But Abbott began openly attacking her party as a fraud, especially after One Nation scooped up eleven seats in the June 1998 Queensland elections and delivered government to Labor's Peter Beattie. Behind the scenes Abbott was secretly assisting two court actions brought by disgruntled party members to prevent One Nation collecting public funding. "My view was that the situation was so dire that you had to take

David Marr

whatever allies you could find." In July he gave a
curious figure called Terry Sharples a handwritten
guarantee to cover out-of-pocket expenses from the
litigation. It was grossly unwise. It exposed Abbott
to the possibility of significant financial liabilities and
made it impossible for him, in the end, to cover his
tracks. In August, he lied to Tony Jones of the ABC's
Four Corners:

> Jones: So there was never any question of any
> party funds –
> Abbott: Absolutely not.
> Jones: Or other funds from any other source –
> Abbott: Absolutely not.
> Jones: Being offered to Terry Sharples?
> Abbott: Absolutely not.

A few weeks later Abbott set up a shadowy trust
called Australians for Honest Politics to meet the
costs of a second action to starve One Nation of funds,
this one brought by Hanson's aggrieved former secretary Barbara Hazelton. Abbott has never revealed
the names of the dozen donors who chipped in over
$100,000 to the trust. The Australian Electoral Com-
mission asked a couple of times over the years but
was always persuaded to back off. Hanson went
briefly to jail in Queensland. Abbott has since had to

live with the unanswered questions about this murky operation and that lie to Jones. He didn't help matters when he told Deborah Snow: "Misleading the ABC is not quite the same as misleading the parliament as a political crime."

Abbott's colleagues were in awe of his savagery but worried about his judgment. The One Nation mess left many wondering how capable he was of sizing up people and causes. His public stance against Hanson earned him a good deal of admiration inside and outside the Liberal Party but also the condemnation of many of his natural allies on the political right. The Sharples dealings intensified doubts that Abbott didn't know where to draw the line. He was seen to be a bit too keen to run crusades of his own. In unattributed briefings to the press, Liberal parliamentarians were calling him the unguided missile and the loaded dog of the government. And there was also, as if designed deliberately to exacerbate these worries, his defamation case against Bob Ellis.

The portly raconteur had defamed Abbott's old university ally Tanya Coleman, who was now Tanya Costello, wife of the nation's treasurer. In *Goodbye Jerusalem*, his latest volume of political reminiscences, Ellis wrote: "Abbott and Costello were both in the Right Wing of the Labor Party till the one woman fucked both of them and married one of them and inducted them into the Young Liberals." The story was a complete canard. And by not naming her, Ellis had also managed to defame Margie Abbott. The book was withdrawn and pulped within days of publication. The publishers were willing to apologise and pay damages. But the wounded parties decided to sue. On the far side of a deeply embarrassing trial was the prospect of more money. The comic element in all this was the decision of the men to join their wives in the action against Random House. What was the slur on them? The deputy leader of the Liberal Party and its most fearless attack dog told the court their reputations had been damaged terribly by the suggestion they were so "weak and unreliable" that they would abandon their political allegiances for sex.

When news of the case broke, the publisher's lawyers heard from many veterans of those years about Abbott's behaviour at Sydney University. They weren't called because his wild behaviour was not an issue in the case. But Abbott did a little back-burning to protect himself. A few weeks after *Goodbye Jerusalem* appeared he had his friend Christopher Pearson, the editor of the *Adelaide Review*, reveal for the first time the existence of the child born twenty years earlier. It was well done and big news. Abbott said: "Under modern adoption laws, it's quite likely that one day someone will knock on the door and

say: 'Hello, Dad.' I hope I can cope if it happens."
Confession and hoped-for absolution.

The trial opened in the ACT Supreme Court a few days after Howard's 1998 victory and proved a source of national amusement. I was as guilty as anyone. There were just too many jokes about Abbott and Costello to fit on a broadsheet page. The whole thing was clearly agony for their wives but in the end this purgatory of ridicule proved financially worthwhile: the Costellos were awarded $164,000 and the Abbotts $113,500. The best joke in all those weeks was a sight gag. One afternoon the seats reserved for Abbott and Costello stood empty. The court had given this pair with their battered reputations leave to go to Yarralumla, where Costello was sworn in once again by the governor-general as treasurer and Tony Abbott for the first time as Minister for Employment Services.

Waste Management:
Somersby, 5 July 2012

The Sulo factory is going flat out when the Commonwealth cars arrive at Somersby. We're all in Sulo's yellow fluoro vests, shouting over the noise of the mighty moulding machines pumping out their daily quota of wheelie bins. The machines will pause when the time comes for the leader of the Opposition to detail the impact of the toxic carbon tax on the biggest manufacturer of mobile garbage bins in the nation, SULO MGB Australia Pty Ltd. Turning out for the occasion on the NSW Central Coast are Joe Hockey and John Howard's former right-hand man, now senator, Arthur Sinodinos. They are enjoying themselves. The machines are heaving and pumping as Abbott begins attaching a pair of black wheels to a green bin.

He is just back from Darwin, where he had half an hour with Susilo Bambang Yudhoyono. "What will you say to him about your plan to turn back the boats to Indonesia?" David Speers had asked before Abbott flew north. He refused to answer then and is refusing to answer now. Good manners dictate discretion, he says. He will not indulge in megaphone diplomacy. Etc. It will emerge in a day or so after this jaunt to Somersby that he said nothing to Yudhoyono about the key Coalition strategy the Indonesians flatly oppose. They make that clear anyway, megaphone clear. No boats will be towed back to Indonesia. Gillard brands Abbott a coward.

Down south once more, the leader of the Opposition is facing the challenge of keeping alive the horrors of the carbon tax in the face of its undramatic debut four days ago. Not that all has been plain sailing. For days the tuneless Minister for Trade, Craig Emerson, has been singing his anti-Abbott ditty:

> *No Whyalla wipe-out, there on my TV.*
> *No Whyalla wipe-out, there on my TV.*
> *No Whyalla wipe-out there on my TV,*
> *shocking me right out of my brain!*

Abbott has always had a way of sidestepping blame for his own hyperbole. Even wild exaggerations are rarely held against him. He retracts a little and is forgiven a lot. "What you've got is constant colour and movement," says his old boss John Hewson. "He gets right in your face. He exaggerates; he grabs the headlines, even if he knows that the next day he's gonna have to back that off." Abbott has been grabbing headlines about Gillard's tax for eighteen months. Now it has begun and it seems hardly anyone has noticed. For a while Abbott seemed to be retooling for this moment by softening his rhetoric. "It's going to be a python squeeze rather than a cobra strike," he said in early June. It's a great line that went straight into the language. But as he crisscrosses the country now, attacking the tax on factory floors and in radio studios, the hyperbole is flowing as if he will never be called to account.

> It will make every job less secure ... play havoc with household budgets ... hit every Australian family's cost of living ... Every time you turn on a light, you pay. Every time you open the fridge, you pay. Every time you go to the airport or get on a bus or order a cup of coffee, you pay ... the carbon tax is going to make everything much, much worse ...

But week one of the tax reveals that Abbott and his front bench are out there alone. There is no uproar. Business is not manning the barricades. Those who hate the tax are leaving it all to Abbott and his team. Those who aren't fussed are hoping he will go away and let them get on with the inevitable. For the first time in a long time the leader of the Opposition is making himself available to heavy-hitting interviewers: Fran Kelly of ABC Radio National, Speers of Sky and Jon Faine of ABC Radio in Melbourne. He's testing himself against the best. They don't believe him when he talks crippling financial burden. Nor does the little knot of press gathered here at Somersby on the NSW Central Coast.

The machines are still, the cameras waiting and the leader of the Opposition is ready to give it another go. In politics we know repetition is everything. "This is an important local manufacturer. They are engaged in a never-ending struggle to survive and it is important that we don't make that more difficult." He tells us gravely that Gillard's tax will add $188,000 to the power bills of this factory: "A hit on their bottom line, a potential hit on jobs." I have a quiet word to one of the factory's owners, John Kernahan, who is standing over to one side watching the politicians and the journalists. He tells me Sulo's annual turnover is $85 million. So the carbon tax? "It's not a biggie."

The polls will soon suggest the same. Before July is over, half the nation will decide Gillard's "toxic tax based on a lie" isn't making much difference to their lives. No pain. Party polling will tell the leaders that voters on all sides don't really believe Abbott's blood pledge to repeal the tax on day one of his government. As the scare campaign dies that month, Labor's primary vote lifts a little.

Minister of the Crown

The new minister would stand in his office every day before Question Time rehearsing answers to questions that rarely came his way. "My department used to love it," a senior bureaucrat told me. "They made the hard questions harder and harder and tried to catch him out. It became a kind of game which they thoroughly enjoyed." Abbott gave these rehearsals his all, mastering the detail, practising his rhetoric, gestures and quips. He was determined to shine in parliament, determined to meet any challenges that might come his way. He wanted no balls-ups by himself or his department. He wanted to be on top of any major issues that might arise. But his first priority was his own political performance. "He wanted the assurance from the department that nothing was going wrong underneath. But as long as that was the case, he didn't really want to get into all the detail of how the Job Network was actually running. He was not hands-on. He was generally interested in employment but he was not one of those ministers who run their department."

Abbott's task was to sort out the problems of a signature Howard initiative: putting the work of the old Commonwealth Employment Service out to tender. First he had to clear his own patch by confronting his senior minister, Peter Reith. In *Battlelines* he wrote:

> On my first day as his junior minister, it was Peter Reith, not me, who chaired an officials' meeting addressing a funding crisis in the Job Network, even though it was my immediate responsibility. The next morning I fronted my ministerial boss to say that I had no intention of remaining a glorified errand boy.

Reith pulled back. Abbott was a problem-solver, a talker, a charmer. He mastered what needed to be mastered. He had the money to fix the problems. Though he went about the task with a will, he clearly did not share the ideological conviction that the jobless were better off without help from the public service. Abbott's default position is that governments are there to act, to solve problems, not to withdraw and leave things to the cut and thrust of market forces. His loyalty was to government and what government could achieve through intervention.

Abbott was a minister on the way up. Within a couple of years he would take over from Reith and enter cabinet; then in 2003 Howard would promote him to the behemoth portfolio of Health and Ageing, which he held until the government's fall. He began running a budget of a few hundred million and ended up with one of $30 billion a year. He began as a minor player and was quickly one of the best-known – at times notorious – ministers in the government. From beginning to end there were controversies. But there were no great catastrophes, no personal scandals. His ministerial career was packed into a decade: Abbott was still forty when it began and just fifty when it ended.

Bureaucrats like working for ministers on the rise: they have clout. The senior men and women who worked with Abbott over the next few years rate him among the better ministers, though with frustrating peculiarities. His handwriting is appalling. Even his numbers are illegible. Someone on his personal staff had to tell public servants what was actually scrawled on their submissions. He was reasonably efficient at turning paper around but not exceptional like Howard, who dealt with everything in forty-eight hours. They dreaded Easter when the minister disappeared on Pollie Pedal and would need to be tracked down in a crisis in some caravan park out in the boondocks.

Everyone got in his ear on these rides. He wasn't
bad at sifting out the rubbish but he did bring back
some odd ideas to his departments. "As with all
ministers," one bureaucrat remarked, "anecdote is
very powerful." He was admirably polite and kept
his temper, but staff dealings with him remained
formal. He was rather buttoned-up. You got to
know little about him. His public servants found it
strange that he did so much writing. To their intense
frustration Abbott would disappear for days behind
closed doors to write another 900-word opinion
piece for the *Australian*. He thought of himself as
thoughtful, even intellectual, and loved playing with
big ideas in this way. But they tended not to be
about the task at hand. There his contributions were
useful rather than original. For the most part he left
policy thinking to his departments. He and his office
were not a source of fresh ideas. Bureaucrats found
his staff intensely loyal and happy but relatively
weak. Abbott's experience with Oldfield had cast a
shadow, leaving him reluctant to hire figures of independent standing to work closely with him. A better
office might have made Abbott a better minister.
Clearly he was not excited by the business of public
administration. That had to be done well but it was
the responsibility of others. What engaged Abbott
most intensely in his decade in the ministry were the

political process and the possibilities of gung-ho government action.

By the time he had been in the job for a year, a third of the work once done by the CES had gone by tender to Christian agencies. Though the work was secular and the money – about $700 million a year – was public, some church agencies were demanding the right to hire only committed Christians to carry out their greatly expanded responsibilities. Buddhist community leaders protested. Jewish leaders went straight to the prime minister. As the controversy rolled on, there was no stauncher advocate for the prerogatives of Christianity than the minister. He argued that finding jobs was faith in action:

> It takes considerable resources of stamina and resilience to work with the long-term unemployed. The source of this commitment is of no concern to government. It could be an ideal of community service or professional pride as much as any religious belief in the brotherhood of man. What matters is that people working with job-seekers keep faith in themselves and in those they serve.

The Human Rights and Equal Opportunities Commission was equally certain that this was secular work being carried out with public money and should be performed according to secular rules blind to faith and sex. HREOC's draft guidelines were slammed by Abbott as "perilously close to discriminating against religion" and he railed against the depiction of himself in the press as a Catholic committed to protecting the privileges of his church. His rejoinder was lofty: "Any suggestion that practice of religion inherently devalues people's political judgments would be an ugly development in Australian public life."

But the criticism was fair. Abbott was protecting one of the most jealously guarded privileges of all churches, but particularly the Catholic Church: the right to employ in schools, hospitals and nursing homes only those who live according to the sex rules of the faith. Abbott put it this way:

> Organisations should not have to employ people who cannot support their fundamental principles. Expecting a church-based Job Network member to employ a gay activist, for instance, is as unreasonable as demanding that a Labor MP employ a leading member of the Liberal Party in his electorate office.

That's still the official church line: as enemies of the faith, homosexuals can properly be banned from teaching or finding jobs for the long-term unemployed. Few countries in the world extend this privilege to religion. Though Abbott had to accept the agencies could employ "sympathetic" non-Christians, he fought off all attempts to challenge the core privilege of the churches to refuse to hire homosexuals – or adulterers, single mothers, transsexuals or any sinners of the bedroom. In the year it took to resolve this controversy, Abbott made his name in politics. He entered the public imagination as a Catholic warrior.

Homosexuality still baffles him. He has long abandoned the mission against dykes and poofters he pursued at university. But he still finds it odd that a footballer from a good Catholic family could turn out to be gay. He has homosexual friends. Some of them adore him. Michael Kirby worked with him at Australians for Constitutional Monarchy and thought him attractive, intelligent, articulate and down-to-earth. When Abbott's old school invited the High Court judge to address the senior boys, he chose homophobia as his theme. The day before the talk, Cardinal Clancy attacked the Gay and Lesbian Mardi Gras. The Anglican archbishop backed him. Both demanded homosexuals live celibate lives. Kirby's theme was: "It's okay if you're gay." The impact was exactly as he wished: thoughtful questioning at the school and big press coverage afterwards. Kirby's biographer A.J. Brown reports:

Tony Abbott wrote to Kirby that he had trouble
with the idea that homosexuality should be
regarded as acceptable, rather than simply accepted:
"especially when the overwhelming weight of tradition holds that it is in some sense sinful."

He can't let it go. A couple of years ago he caused
a stir by telling Liz Hayes on *60 Minutes* that he felt "a
bit threatened" by homosexuality. He backtracked
swiftly, as he so often does, from his more arresting
statements, but on ABC *Lateline* a few nights later he
was still arguing that homosexuality "challenges
orthodox notions of the right order of things." These
days he is as likely to say that homosexuals are merely
different. But Abbott the true believer will not challenge his church. Not here and not, it seems, anywhere.
He does not like the language but does not dissent
from Vatican teaching on homosexuality. That his
sister Christine Forster is lesbian has not shaken his
faith. Politics Abbott talks mere difference but Values
Abbott believes, as he always has, that homosexuality
is, in the words of the church, an "intrinsic moral evil."

Abbott was under riding instructions from Howard not to talk outside his own portfolio. It wasn't
easy. It curtailed the range of the opinion pieces he
was churning out for the press, essentially vigorous
polemics on the virtues of the Howard government.

But on the great issue of these years, the monarchy versus the republic, everyone was free to speak and campaign. Support for getting rid of the Queen had risen to 57 per cent but the nation was divided on the kind of republic that should replace her, a division that proved the death of the proposal. This was minority politics – the power of the passionate minority to hold the line – played at a level of genius by Howard and with inexhaustible passion by his lieutenant Tony Abbott. The republicans have never recovered. Abbott can claim a good measure of credit not only for wrecking the republican hopes in the 1999 referendum, but also for keeping the republic off the agenda ever since.

The victory came at a price. Words are weapons, says Abbott, and ever since his university days he has shown how powerfully he can deploy scorn and insult. He denounced a proposal to remove non-citizen British from the electoral rolls as "ethnic cleansing" as bodies were still being dug up in the former Yugoslavia. He declared one or other of the Costello brothers – Peter the treasurer and Tim the Baptist minister – was "telling whoppers," an insult that ended the old friendship between Abbott and the deputy leader of his party. He accused republicans in his own party of conducting a "proxy war" against Howard. He threw into the mix Churchill, Pétain,

Charles de Gaulle, the failings of the Weimar republic and the rise of Hitler. In the *Sydney Morning Herald* at that time I set him some homework:

> Clearly explain how an Australian head of state with powers as proposed in the referendum could bring to office in Canberra a local equivalent of the most vicious dictator of the century?

He never justified the Hitler slur to anyone. His talent for personal abuse seemed depthless. Even friends in the press were reproaching him for going over the top. The prime minister began muzzling him. The monarchists won the day but the republicans romped home in most of the leafy suburbs of the nation, including those along the beaches and head-lands of Warringah.

After this victory Abbott was seen as a man to be reckoned with, a politician with a future. The press was interested. The first big newspaper and television profiles of him appeared. His story became known: university politician, boxer, would-be priest, monar-chist, hard man of the right, the first minister to be ejected from the House in nearly forty years. He was clearly a protected species, spoken of as the prime minister's protégé, a rival to Costello and perhaps a contender for the highest office one day. Even so, a single question was being asked more than ever after the referendum campaign: did Abbott know where to draw the line?

After Howard's third big win in 2001, Abbott hoped for promotion, though he had been in Reith's old job as Minister for Employment, Workplace Relations and Small Business for less than a year. Instead, Howard put the young minister's aggression to use by also appointing him Leader of the House, a position he would hold until the fall of the government. The hard calls of parliamentary strategy plus the tough line on the unemployed being pursued by the Howard government made it easier than ever to portray Abbott as utterly hard-hearted. He famously denounced "job snobs" and freely quoted Christ's remarks about the poor being with us always. He had a number of controversial but not untruthful things to say about the causes of poverty:

> We can't stop people drinking, we can't stop people gambling, we can't stop people having substance problems, we can't stop people from making mistakes ...

Under Abbott, the unemployed had never had to work so hard to keep the dole. While he was pilloried for enforcing a severe regime of punishment to force them into employment, he was trying behind the scenes to persuade the government to take another course entirely. He wanted tax breaks for those on welfare to encourage them to take work. This was his one big idea in the portfolio and he has cited it since as evidence that somewhere inside the Liberal Party the DLP was alive and well. But not very alive: the plan was killed by Howard.

Abbott knew he had to counter the caricature of the hard man of the right, the junkyard dog of government, if his leadership ambitions were ever to go anywhere. He began to give extraordinary, wide-ranging interviews which earned him something of a reputation as a thinker. No Australian politician in living memory had spoken quite like this. Politics Abbott was muffled by his place in cabinet, but Values Abbott had free rein. A 2003 interview with Paul Kelly of the *Australian* was the template for the pieces that followed. As they drove for hours through the bush one day, Abbott told Kelly he saw politics as a way of giving glory to God:

> This idea that politics is a managerial exercise, a simple question of resource allocation, I just think is dead wrong because politics is about inspiring people and persuading people there is value in what they do.

That day with Kelly he returned to his signature worry: the cohesion of the world. In his maiden speech Abbott had said governments must be an "instrument for giving cohesion and purpose to our national life." A decade later he told Kelly national survival was at stake:

> Every Australian needs to feel some kind of mystical bond and union with every other Australian. If that is ever lost, if it is just a sort of collective self-interest as tenants in the same building, that's not enough for a nation to survive.

Santamaria used to talk like that: another divisive man with a mission to hold society together. Abbott doesn't have the same sense that we stand forever on the lip of doom. But like Santamaria he sees the fragility of society as a bedrock argument against change, particularly change welcomed by most but passionately opposed by few. Cultivating the fears and harnessing the rage of minorities is a great conservative skill. Abbott has it in spades. His pitch to the fearful is the nameless dread of change in a fragile world. And the rest of us are urged to leave well alone or the fearful will tear politics apart. It is a profoundly conservative brand of politics that deals in panic and threat. Keating says: "You know what

Tony Abbott's policy is: 'If you don't give me the job, I'll wreck the place.'"

In his big-picture moods, Abbott's mind turns to the fate of Western civilisation. This is a vast grab-bag of everything he loves about the past and present: Christ, the Bible, Shakespeare, cricket, the welfare state – "an essential part of modern Western civilisation" – Winston Churchill and Edmund Burke. The list has grown over time to include "scientific and cultural curiosity, belief in the equality of man, freedom under the law, and a sense that diversity is a potential source of strength, not weakness." Western civilisation has Christian origins, a British bias and flourishes in the Anglosphere but its values are universal. "We don't support them because they're ours," Abbott says, "but because we think they are capable of being adopted by anyone, any place, anytime."

The Pope and the Queen represent "the oldest continuing institutions in Western civilisation." Other great defenders are Churchill, Santamaria and a number of obscure figures on the far right of Australian politics, including David Flint, the daffy gay lawyer who campaigned with Abbott against the republic. Abbott appears to count no one of the left among civilisation's defenders. Nor, despite his admiration for the United States, does Abbott count the Bill of Rights among the achievements of Western

civilisation. Freedom and rights are oddly discon-
nected in his analysis. All the American wars from
Vietnam to today were fought for civilisation's sake.
The Coalition of the Willing went to war in Iraq "to
uphold universal values ... if it's possible to engage in
an altruistic war, this was it."

Without hesitation Abbott declares "the whole
edifice of Western civilisation" to rest on the church.
Some might say the church had to be fought tooth
and nail to allow liberal democracy to emerge, but
Abbott claims we have the church to thank for "the
presumption of innocence, universal suffrage, limited
government, and religious, cultural and political plu-
ralism." But deeper than that is Catholic teaching on
birth, life and death, which he sees as "fundamental
to the ethical underpinnings of Western civilisation."
In a vast essay on the man and the papacy at the time
of Benedict XVI's visit to Australia for World Youth
Day, Abbott put his own worries about the fragility
of all of this into the pontiff's mind: "The question
haunting Benedict is whether our civilisation can
maintain these principles while rejecting the religious
insights on which they rest."

Such grand considerations hardly mattered for
Abbott in public life until Howard unexpectedly
promoted him to the portfolio of Health and Ageing in October 2003. Again there was a complex

problem to be solved. Doctors were threatening to abandon the public health system in the face of the looming failure of medical indemnity funds. Again Howard gave Abbott all the money he needed. He worked on the problems with the assistant treasurer, Helen Coonan: "He showed a great capacity to engage with people on various different levels: first of all the doctors, then insurance people at a fairly complex professional level – medical indemnity insurance and long tail insurance are pretty complex products – and he was quite able to empathise with patients. He managed to get everybody settled down on a temporary basis while we worked our way through it. We got a solution at last."

The medical profession liked dealing with Abbott. For the most part they found him sharp and refreshing. That he could muster so much money to address their worries naturally delighted them. After addressing the medical indemnity crisis, Abbott turned his attention very successfully to arresting the decline in bulk billing. But there were medicos who found their dealings with the minister puzzling. Adele Horin reported in the *Sydney Morning Herald:*

Ian Hickie, professor of psychiatry, and executive director of the Brain and Mind Institute at the University of Sydney, stood in Abbott's Canberra office arguing the case for more federal money for mental health. Abbott, then minister for health, was his customary engaging self. And Hickie soon found himself in a philosophical discussion about the nature of mental illness. "Abbott believed people should be able to control their thoughts and emotions; he believed they should exercise free will," Hickie says. "He admitted his own views made it hard for him to understand mental health issues."

Out of this exchange and an intervention by Howard came a $1.5 billion commitment to the first national mental health plan. A happy Hickie verdict on Abbott: "He's not a reformer; he's a great opportunist."

Abbott had moved from a portfolio where the Commonwealth ran the show to one where control of his vast responsibilities was shared with the states. He found this frustrating. He couldn't simply intervene. He had to work through others. He hated the muddle of federal structures. He liked to be able to make clean, final decisions. Officers in his department wondered if the minister was closing his door to write all those opinion pieces because they had the clarity his work now lacked. He could put his position without having to deal with the constitutional limits of Commonwealth authority or the difficulties of manoeuvring it through the COAG process.

Abbott's one big idea in Health was for the Commonwealth to take control of all the nation's hospitals. This required a shift in his thinking. In the Keating years he had declared that Australia had "a perfectly good system of government provided each tier minds its own business." He didn't think so any longer. "As a new backbencher, I had not anticipated how hard this was, given that voters don't care who solves their problems, they just want them solved." As Minister for Health he lit on a new guiding conservative principle: "Power divided is power controlled." He had in mind an enormous reform that would reshape Canberra's relations with the states. He was roundly mocked in cabinet. His senior bureaucrats put a lot of work into talking him down. Did he really want to be responsible for every asthma patient who had to wait too long in an emergency department? Eventually he was persuaded that Commonwealth public servants could not run hospitals any better than state public servants. This was the argument that got him, but he found it frustrating.

The health department was enormous. It had a budget as big as that of New South Wales. There were junior ministers, parliamentary secretaries and a team of deputy heads. Every parliamentary session Abbott brought them all together to discuss the issues that might emerge over the weeks to come. Such openness was unprecedented, kept everyone up to date and diffused the tensions that usually plague the parliamentary team serving a big portfolio. He was a good chair. He continued to hold a half-hour prep session before each Question Time. Now there was no lack of questions. Those working with the new minister were surprised by the contrast between his performances in the department and in parliament. Among the bureaucrats he was patient and polite. He would listen to – but not enjoy – criticism. There are ministers who relish slashing budgets, wielding the knife with macho pleasure. Abbott wasn't one of them. "He wasn't ruthless," said an observer of his time in the portfolio. "He didn't have an appetite for nasties. Cuts were never explored with relish. People find this amazing but he doesn't seek conflict."

Howard went to the 2004 elections having made cast-iron promises to keep Medicare's generous safety-net provisions. But after unexpectedly winning control of the Senate, Howard and Costello decided to renege. Abbott was distressed. He left Howard to announce the decision and withdrew to consider his future in the face of furious ridicule over this broken promise. "If we hadn't controlled the Senate, I would never have had to eat that particular shit sandwich,"

Abbott told Peter Hartcher many years later. "Getting control of the Senate was a curse. It allowed us to do things that we would not normally have been able to get away with and I think it tempted us to chance our arm in ways which ultimately did us significant political damage." In the end, he decided to stay in cabinet. He didn't bitch and moan to the press gallery. He went back to work.

One day he was asked how he, a Catholic, could preside over a system that funded 80,000 abortions a year. This was soon after he took over the Health portfolio and he brooded over the answer for five months. Then, at a rowdy meeting of the Adelaide University Democratic Club, he reignited a debate no federal politician had touched for twenty-five years:

> The problem with the Australian practice of abortion is that an objectively grave matter has been reduced to a question of the mother's convenience. Aborting a first trimester foetus is not morally identical to deliberately killing a living human being, but it's not just removing a wart or a cyst either. Even those who think that abortion is a woman's right should be troubled by the fact that 100,000 Australian women choose to destroy their unborn babies every year.

Abbott was being deliberately provocative and belittling. His was the language not of a politician, but a Vatican ideologue. He condemned women for taking the "easy way out" and declared abortion a national tragedy. He complained his constituents were more concerned with boat people than foetuses. It must have seemed to the minister like the old days of campus politics again as protesters were dragged from the meeting shouting, "Get your rosaries off our ovaries."

Abbott is still living with the repercussions of that speech. Women recoiled from him. Peter Costello went on air immediately to hose down fears that Medicare funding for abortions was about to end. In public Howard supported Abbott's right to raise the issue but was reported to be appalled in private. The Minister for Health seemed to have done his prospects in the Coalition great harm. "He's just too right-wing," Dennis Atkins reported a Costello backer saying. "You can't hold passionate anti-abortion views and lead a mainstream party, let alone lead the nation." The women of parliament organised to end his ministerial veto on the importation of the morning-after pill RU486. He was deeply hurt by this. He saw hypocrisy and scare-mongering all around him as the hullabaloo continued month after month. He stuck to his defence that he had spoken as a Christian but had *done* nothing about abortion as Minister for Health.

So why stir up this hornets' nest? The answer lies deep in his faith. Abbott feels obliged as a Christian to keep a lost political cause alive. Abbott the politician knows he can't roll back the law on abortion, but Abbott the rock-solid Catholic is not going to abandon the possibility. He cannot reassure the women of Australia that he will never try. In Abbott's book, Christian politicians are obliged to keep the faith and do as much as they can when they can. Unless it's a matter of the most extraordinary moment and a point of honour, there's no sense asking the public to do what it simply won't do. But the believer in office must always try to move the debate in the right direction. And they must be willing to wait. Those who wonder at the patience of figures like Abbott forget they have eternity in their heads.

Howard stepped in to shut the abortion debate down. A few weeks later, Daniel O'Connor, a 27-year-old television cameraman, contacted his birth mother for the first time. She was Abbott's university girlfriend, now Kathy Donnelly. What followed was excruciating for everyone and beautifully handled by Abbott. It is perhaps the only time in his career when the nation's heart went out to him. He was on his way to mass on Boxing Day, 2004, when a message came from Donnelly. After mass and a talk with Margie Abbott he rang. He met O'Connor. He thought the young man looked a little like his eldest daughter. The world was let in on the soap opera via a nine-page spread in the *Bulletin* with moody photographs and a contribution from Abbott that ended: "Margie and my daughters have accepted Daniel as a family member. For me, this is important, a new start, a second chance." The mother's university flatmate looked at the *Bulletin* pictures. The resemblance was so strong. DNA samples were provided. Three weeks after the news broke, the fairytale was over: O'Connor was not the long-lost son Abbott had imagined for so long was out there. "I'm sorry," he said, "that poor old Daniel has been dragged through the public spotlight as a result of a connection to me, which it now appears was never the case."

From the moment he entered cabinet, Abbott took more seriously than many of his colleagues the notion of discussing the nation's affairs around the table. "He was quite inclined to second-guess most things," says Helen Coonan. "Right at the end of a discussion he might say: 'A thought, can I offer a thought, Prime Minister?' And his thoughts were not bad ones. He's somebody who's capable of thinking outside the square. He used to be able to see other dimensions to problems. I think he irritated a lot of people who might not have taken too kindly to it. But I think he made a very useful contribution. And it's very Jesuitical, of course. I think he was true to his upbringing, his roots, his value system." He attended closely to deliberations that ranged far outside his own portfolios. At that point, ministers often discreetly work on their own papers. But Abbott liked to listen. He didn't come to cabinet with his mind made up about everything. He thought things through in the room. It was an unusual quality. That Howard allowed him such a long rein used to exasperate his colleagues, often the same ministers who despaired of his stream of suggestions for Canberra's intervention. Costello wrote:

> Never one to be held back by the financial consequences of decisions, he had grandiose plans for public expenditure. At one point when we were in government, he asked for funding to pay for telephone and electricity wires to be put underground throughout the whole of his northern Sydney electorate to improve the amenity of the neighbourhoods. He also wanted the Commonwealth to take over the building of local roads and bridges in his electorate. He wanted the Commonwealth to take over hospitals. He used to tell me proudly that he had learned all of his economics at the feet

of Bob Santamaria. I was horrified.

Costello and the hard right's Nick Minchin used to tease him as he proposed they intervene here or give money there. The tone was good-humoured. The verdict wasn't: "There he goes, channelling Bob again."

He certainly was when it came to the unfinished business of breaking student unions. As the boisterous president of the SRC young Tony had begged the Fraser government without success to intervene. Now three key figures in that old campaign – Abbott, Costello and the Special Minister of State Eric Abetz – were perfectly placed to pursue their old vendetta against left-wing student politics. A first bill for the abolition of compulsory student union fees failed in 2004 but it was back as soon as the government won control of the Senate. Old passions were rekindled on both sides. Such were police fears that in August 2005 Abbott was warned not to debate Julia Gillard in the Manning Bar at Sydney University. This was huge news. Abbott berated the police: "You have given a victory to the enemies of a free society." But the bill was also loathed by the National Party because it would drain university sporting clubs of cash. Out in the bush, those clubs and that money mattered. The bill passed by only one vote. Barnaby Joyce crossed the floor. Abbott had realised an old ambition but now the Nationals reckoned they were owed a favour.

Control of the Senate also let Howard pursue ambitions going back to the earliest days of his own politics: he would break the trade unions. This was not in Abbott's DNA. He thought WorkChoices harsh and bad politics: "A catastrophic political blunder because it undermined the Howard battlers' faith in the Prime Minister's goodwill." He and another Catholic warrior in the government, Kevin Andrews, contested the proposals in cabinet. They did not advance the underlying moral arguments but questioned how the politics would play out and whether WorkChoices would be seen to be going too far. Abbott was particularly concerned with the abolition of the no-disadvantage test, which had set a safety net under earlier workplace reform. He told cabinet: "It was always going to look as though we were exposing vulnerable people to danger." But Howard had his way.

Not for the first time, Abbott was left to defend a policy he deplored and his church opposed. Indeed, he faced an ecumenical wall of opposition. Abbott knew WorkChoices was damaging in Catholic circles because it was felt to be contrary to that strain of social justice the church had taken very much to heart. He had been through this before. Abbott was familiar

with the argument that Hewson lost in 1993 when the
Catholic vote deserted the Coalition over *Fightback!*
He knew how close Howard came to defeat in 1998
when the churches again came out against the GST.
He knew how lucky the government was when
George Pell, then the Archbishop of Melbourne,
broke ranks with his fellow bishops to declare:
"There is no one Catholic position on an issue as
complex as taxation." Howard had seized on that as
a lifeline. Abbott had also, in his time, suffered
Christian opposition to his government's approach
to native title, refugees and waterfront reform.

Being taken to task by clerics unsettles him. He
takes their attacks personally and his rhetoric in reply
is particularly insulting. It is easier for him when he
genuinely disagrees with his accusers. He simply
denounces them as partisan lefties, accuses them of
"moral snobbery" and claims they are just crawling to
their congregations:

> Finding fault with government is always more
> popular than telling parishioners to lift their
> game or confronting the church's own failings
> and has probably become the clerical equivalent
> of kicking the dog on the way home from a bad
> day at the office.

But it is tougher when, deep down, he agrees with them and Values Abbott finds himself at loggerheads with Politics Abbott. He and his critics in the church saw eye to eye on WorkChoices. He had signed up to the social teachings of the faith as a child. It was integral to the mission Santamaria sent him into the world to pursue. Abbott had never reneged on them. He believed they embodied values that helped hold society together. So when the crunch came over WorkChoices, where did his loyalties lie?

Politics won. As the government slid towards oblivion, Abbott's only loyalty was to Howard. It was an impeccably secular response. He put aside his own values. He respected cabinet solidarity. He did not, despite reports at the time, tell the clerics to butt out of political debate. He took them on. His language was memorably appalling as he demanded they get off the government's back:

> A political argument is not transformed into a moral argument simply because it's delivered with an enormous dollop of sanctimony. I do think that if churchmen spent more time encouraging virtue in people and less time demanding virtue from governments we would have ultimately a better society.

WorkChoices was killing Howard by early 2007. So was Kyoto. Howard had turned his back on the treaty as an act of solidarity with George W. Bush. But with the country locked in drought, Australians were demanding action. A few days after Labor installed its new leader, Kevin Rudd, the prime minister set up a committee of industrialists and bureaucrats who recommended an emissions trading system. But there seemed little or no hope that a deeply divided cabinet would sign up to the idea. The ultimate sceptic Nick Minchin led the hostile right and Malcolm Turnbull the enthusiastic left. Abbott was a swinging voter. He kept his mind open for a long time. He thought it through in cabinet. His support, when it came, was driven by politics not by science. Abbott's thinking, according to a close observer, was this: "There is a mood in the country: the bloody farmers think this drought is to do with climate change; we've got all these green initiatives but nobody thinks we're doing anything; we're going to meet our Kyoto targets yet we don't ratify. I think this is the time to go forward." Abbott helped Howard over the line. On 1 June 2007 the prime minister announced a cap and trade system, with targets to be set sometime after the election.

Abbott now faced a more agonising choice. Howard had been a father to him in politics for

twenty years. He owed every step on the ladder –
from his first job in John Hewson's office to the
mighty portfolio of Health – to this man's patronage.
He had, like an impatient son, opposed him at times,
but he had always been forgiven and favoured. Tony
was Howard's golden boy. Everyone in cabinet knew
this. He had absorbed most of the old man's politics
so long ago he might have been born with them.
Sitting with him in cabinet had been a masterclass in
leadership. *Battlelines* is a drab book on the whole
but there are passages like this that sing:

> Political leadership is not like running a company
> or being captain of a ship. Prime ministers can
> direct public servants, but, for all their promi-
> nence and influence, they can rarely give orders
> to their colleagues. Howard understood that
> respect had to be earned, affection had to be
> won, and authority had to be used sparingly if it
> was to be effective ... Howard's ability to be a
> successful prime minister for almost twelve years
> is the supreme personal achievement of modern
> Australian politics.

But by the winter of 2007, Howard's political
capital was exhausted. Peter Costello, the infinitely
gutless challenger, was standing by as Alexander

Downer began sounding out their cabinet colleagues on the margins of APEC. "We were in parallel universes," Costello wrote. "Face-to-face meetings with world leaders and meetings at night to canvass Howard's departure." Abbott faltered. On the afternoon of Wednesday 5 September, he had conversations with Costello and Downer that led both to believe he wanted Howard to step down. "Abbott thought a change might give us a chance to win," Costello wrote. But that evening, after more phone calls, Abbott rang Kirribilli House to pledge his undying support. Abbott would tell Liz Jackson of *Four Corners*: "From the very beginning of the government to its last day, I thought John Howard was the best man to lead the team."

He had a bad election campaign. He stumbled and told the truth one night: workers had, indeed, lost protections under WorkChoices. He lingered too long with Howard in Melbourne one day and was thirty-five minutes late for a debate with the shadow minister for Health, Nicola Roxon, at the National Press Club. They had a tight-lipped exchange as they shook hands for the cameras:

> Roxon: "You can't even get here on time, it must be a battle."
> Abbott: "It certainly wasn't intentional."

Roxon: "You can control these things, mate. I'm sure had you wanted to, you could."
Abbott: "That's bullshit. You're being deliberately unpleasant. I suppose you can't help yourself, can you?"

The microphones picked up the word "bullshit" loud and clear. It might not have done him so much damage were he not that day also under attack for abusing Bernie Banton. The dying anti-asbestos campaigner had turned up in a wheelchair outside Abbott's electoral office in Manly to mount a little protest over the government's reluctance to subsidise a new and expensive drug to treat mesothelioma, the condition killing him. Abbott took an ugly swipe at Banton. "Look, it was a stunt," he told Channel Nine. "Let's be upfront about this. I know Bernie is very sick but just because a person is sick doesn't mean that he is necessarily pure of heart in all things." In his trademark way Abbott was using the language of faith as an insult. He was left apologising all the way to election day.

At about 10 p.m. on 24 November Howard rang Rudd. He had lost government and his seat. A few minutes after conceding defeat he addressed the nation. He thanked the people of Australia and wished the new government "the very best of good fortune in the years ahead." Abbott's political world collapsed around him. He had kept his seat but lost his patron. Also gone were his ministerial salary and a good deal of respect from his colleagues. They were furious about his campaign blunders. Why was it that Tony never knew when to hold his tongue, where to draw the line? Where was his judgment? Where was his heart?

The Forgotten Ones:
Parramatta, 8 July 2012

Bronwyn Bishop gets the biggest cheer of all from the party workers assembled in the big dark room on the fourth floor of the leagues club. What an old stager: the hair, the heels, the fox around the neck, the raw enthusiasm for the limelight and the fight. They take her to their hearts like a club act remembered fondly from a long time ago. On this Sunday afternoon in the western suburbs of Sydney, Tony Abbott is introducing his candidates to the men and women who will hand out the leaflets, staff the booths and watch the count for the Liberal Party.

"We are in this position today we could not have dreamed of because of Tony Abbott," declares the warm-up act, Arthur Sinodinos. "He is working his guts out, laser-focused." Applause erupts. These people don't share the doubts and hesitations of so much of Australia. Their eyes are bright. The idea of an Abbott government turns them on. Sinodinos is washed with applause as he lays it on thicker and thicker. Abbott is an action man in the best sense of the word; he is not afraid to stand against the tide; he loves campaigning in factories against the carbon tax; he's not the sort of man who would out his sister as a lesbian on *Q&A*. "He is a flesh-and-blood human being. He's not Mother Teresa in drag."

We've already heard the campaign anthem sung in a drawl that's part Tamworth and part Tennessee: "That's our Australia, let's make it strong." Around the hall hang banners displaying something like a traffic sign: a red circle crossed by a diagonal red line barring entry to the silhouette of an Indonesian fishing boat. The banner reads: SECURE OUR BORDERS. When Abbott walks onstage he is wearing not the blue and white habit of the Missionaries of Charity but his Liberal Party uniform of grey suit, white shirt and blue tie. And he sends the applause off the dial with this: "The fact is, John Howard stopped the boats."

His stump speech is good. Very good. The words are plain, the images sharp and the rhetoric Churchillian as he introduces the candidates:

You will see them at your bus stops, you will see them at your railway stations, you will see them in your shopping centres, you will see them knocking on your doors ... They will be visible, because

Labor is in hiding. Labor is in hiding from the people of Western Sydney. Labor is particularly in hiding from the businesses of Western Sydney, because what Labor has given the businesses and the job providers of Western Sydney is nothing but pain.

Government can be won out here. The Liberals have been working this vast stretch of suburbs for decades. This is talkback territory, the land of Alan Jones. For as long as anyone can remember, it's been in Labor's pocket. But the squalor of the last state government has left the electors of Sydney's west open to the message that everything wrong – from drug crime to traffic jams – can be fixed by a Coalition government in Canberra. The nation might turn against Abbott; polls might show the two-party-preferred vote drawing neck-and-neck; but whatever the nation's mood there are ten unhappy seats in Sydney's west Labor seems set to lose. Ten is enough to decide the outcome. Party tacticians on both sides are saying the national campaign when it comes will be a battle to win the hearts and minds of these few dozen suburbs.

Abbott's message isn't original. Even Menzies wasn't the first to tell disgruntled voters they were neglected, overlooked, forgotten. But Abbott has given Menzies' "forgotten people" a rather DLP twist: they are his "forgotten families" and they have his full attention today in Parramatta:

> I often talk about the forgotten families of Australia, but no families anywhere in this country have been more forgotten than the families of Western Sydney. You have been denied infrastructure, you have been denied attention by a political movement that for too long has taken you for granted. Well, I will never take you for granted. None of my candidates will ever take you for granted.

Family has its own meaning for Abbott. He believes families hold the world together. His sort of families are, of course, heterosexual. He won't have men marrying each other. Ditto women. Nor does he want gay and lesbian couples to bring up children. He strongly disapproves of them being allowed to adopt and of lesbians having access to IVF. He is rigidly hard-line Catholic on all this. He doesn't quite say it would be better if such children were never adopted or never born but he birches the parents for their thoughtless indulgence: "Only the most starry-eyed member of the Woodstock generation would maintain that a parent's self-fulfilment readily justifies depriving children of living with both a mother and a father, especially when the children are young."

Like everyone on earth he would prefer marriages to last. But in *Battlelines* he sketched a plan to bring back fault-based divorce – adultery, cruelty, private detectives etc. – for those who opt for what they call in America a covenant marriage, which Abbott sees as "a type of marriage that approximates to the Christian ideal." The idea seems to have sunk like a stone. More durable has been the policy he sprang on his party soon after becoming leader: a $3.3 billion-a-year paid parental-leave scheme funded by business. For him and the Liberals it was totally left-field. Women who earn more will be paid more while on leave. Eventually, the payments will be taken over by the Commonwealth. After announcing the scheme, Abbott sought with some charm the absolution of his startled party. "Sometimes," he said, "it is better to ask forgiveness rather than permission."

Santamaria raged against working mothers. Abbott is married to one. She runs community-based child care. Abbott credits her with alerting him to the needs of children whose parents work, their care and early education. And he acknowledges with great candour that she, essentially, brought up their three daughters. The inevitable lot of a family-values politician is to spend a great deal of time away from the family. This champion of self-reliance, the man who made the unemployed work for the dole, has no doubt that families like his deserve a great deal of help from government. Twenty years ago he declared "middle-income families with children" to be "Australia's new poor." He doesn't see private health insurance rebates or support for private school education as middle-class welfare. He sees it as backing family aspiration, sound public policy encouraging people to do more for themselves. And help should not be cut off simply because a family is earning a hundred thousand dollars or more a year. It's in the Parramatta stump speech and earns an ovation:

> you are people who want to do the right thing by yourselves and your families and you are not rich. Julia Gillard thinks you are rich. Julia Gillard thinks that a policeman married to a shop assistant is rich. Julia Gillard thinks that two schoolteachers bringing up a family together are rich. Well, I say you aren't rich. You are decent Australians wanting to get ahead and we will always stand by you.

Out by the escalators he gives a brief press conference under a sign offering 50 per cent off the club's live seafood banquet. His answers are perfunctory. Earlier that morning he was on *Insiders*. I was there, watching from the couch as he avoided Barrie Cassidy's questions. It was one of his rare bouts with a tough, experienced political interviewer. He gave a boxer's performance: ducking, weaving and blocking. I found it dispiriting. Abbott must have too, for the transcript never makes it to his website. But those among the faithful at the leagues club who saw the show think he was terrific. Why? Because he gave nothing away. Abbott departs. His followers disperse into the winter afternoon. The background music in the foyer is Creedence Clearwater Revival's "Bad Moon Rising."

Skin in the Game

Abbott had dropped his daughters at the bus stop and was driving back across Roseville Bridge at about 7.30 a.m. when he turned on 2GB and heard Malcolm Turnbull having a set-to with Alan Jones. It was 2 November 2009. Turnbull refused to kowtow to Jones, who became hysterically agitated about the "hoax" of global warming and a secret deal by world leaders to bleed $50 billion from Australia and send it off to South America. Turnbull kept his dignity. He was sharp with Jones once or twice, asking to be heard, reminding him his heroes Margaret Thatcher and John Howard wanted action on global warming: "Don't you think," asked the leader of the Opposition, "you sound like the old lady who says the whole world is mad except for thee and me, and I have my doubts about thee?"

Abbott thought Turnbull's leadership was terminal at that moment. He wasn't hearing a robust exchange but a bar-room brawl between his leader and the guru of a great swathe of the Liberal Party. This was no way to deal with Alan Jones. Turnbull wasn't showing the necessary respect. It would cause immense damage.

Abbott was all over the shop on emissions trading. He feared destruction at the ballot box if the Opposition blocked Rudd. "The government's emissions trading scheme is the perfect political response to the public's fears," he had said in late July 2009. "It's a plausible means to limit carbon emissions that doesn't impose any obvious costs on voters." But behind the scenes he was already questioning the reality of global warming. In late September his tongue got the better of him at a meeting of farmers in Beaufort north of Melbourne. He said: "The argument on climate change is absolute crap." He backtracked afterwards as he always did, but that was the view of the man who now had his ear, the arch-denier Nick Minchin. They had a conversation next day as Abbott drove back from Beaufort that crystallised his thinking: the only way to avoid a catastrophic split inside the Coalition was to reject the ETS. But he was still wavering weeks later when he heard the exchange between Turnbull and Jones. Another three weeks passed before he finally told the party he had moved into the opponents' camp. This was his sixth position on the ETS. In *Shitstorm*, Lenore Taylor and David Uren wrote:

his constant changes of heart were the subject of "ridicule" in shadow cabinet meetings. Abbott had a reputation as a "conviction" politician, but on this issue his position appeared to depend entirely on his reading of the polls and the mood of his party.

Coalition politicians were under intense pressure from the minerals and energy lobby. Tens of thousands of phone calls, emails and letters flooded their offices. Helen Coonan received 8000 emails calling on the Opposition to reject Rudd's ETS. Alan Jones was rampaging across the political landscape, broadcasting the wildest claims of the deniers. Abbott and Minchin were now leading a team of far-right figures on the Coalition back bench, many of them veterans of ACM's campaign against the republic. On 26 November the two men told Turnbull he must delay a vote on the ETS until after the looming Copenhagen conference or lose his job. Turnbull refused. Next day Abbott announced he was challenging. Four days later he was the leader of the Opposition.

Abbott had taken only two years to climb from humiliation to victory. After Howard's defeat he threw his hat in the ring. He didn't expect to win the leadership. He was doing what young politicians do to show they see themselves as contenders one day.

His bid provoked mockery. Annabel Crabb latched onto his claim to have the "people skills" needed for the job. She has never let go. His colleagues had not forgotten Bernie Banton and they, unlike him, wished to put Howard behind them. Loyalty is deep in Abbott's DNA. He wouldn't betray his master. Again he drew the lesson that he must muffle his beliefs:

> this constant message that I got was: "You're too hard-line – you turn people off." So, lest anyone think that the art of success in democratic politics is to have principles and to proclaim them very loudly; lest anyone think that in the words of Scripture we should "set ye up a standard in the land" and "blow the trumpet amongst the nations" (Jeremiah 51:27), we need to know that, if that is done, the result is just as likely to be defeat and failure, as triumphant success.

When he realised he had only five or six support-ers in the party room, he withdrew from the race. Brendan Nelson became leader and demoted him to the junior post of shadow minister for Families, Community Services, Indigenous Affairs and the Voluntary Sector. Nelson said patronisingly: "This will be the making of him." Abbott was a bit player again. He withdrew to a tiny office in a far wing of parliament, hung a picture of the Queen on the wall and wondered what to do next. Only later did he realise what he was going through: bereavement.

Nelson lasted less than a year. These were scrappy months for Abbott. He remained withdrawn, at times not bothering to turn up to shadow cabinet. For days or weeks, colleagues didn't know where to find him. Opposition brought a $90,000-a-year pay cut and financial difficulties for a man who seems hardly to have a materialistic bone in his body. He needed another mortgage. His sister Christine Forster let him know she had left her husband for a woman. The apostle of Catholic family values found himself dealing with human reality very close to home. He coped. He was not entirely out of the public eye. Just as Kevin Rudd had used Seven's *Sunrise* to win himself a wider public, Abbott chose a new ABC television show, *Q&A*. He was the most frequent guest in its first couple of years. Early on he found himself on a panel with the publisher Louise Adler, who persuaded him to write the memoir cum manifesto that became *Battlelines*. Abbott hoped to pay off a chunk of the mortgage and work on softening his image. But such a book always has another purpose: it's a job application.

When Nelson fell in September 2008, Abbott supported Turnbull. A fortnight later the navy stopped a boat near the Ashmore islands carrying a dozen asylum seekers, mostly Afghans. It was only the second to arrive in Rudd's time. There would be six more in 2008. The boats were back. For now the public was not particularly concerned. Rudd appeared untouchable.

Abbott wrote. As he worked on *Battlelines* he churned out dozens of opinion pieces. He was against sentimental attitudes to Aborigines; against Rudd's blather in parliament and twaddle in the *Monthly*; for paying maternity leave even to stay-at-home mothers; for George W. Bush giving John Howard the Congressional Medal of Freedom; for middle-class welfare to build a fair society; against guest workers coming in from the Pacific islands; for Michael Kirby on his retirement from the High Court; against the Rudd government's plans for halving rates of homelessness; for riding bicycles; for the NSW hard-right Christian faction leader David Clarke; against regarding the GFC as "a fundamental crisis in capitalism"; for Canberra being given all power in all fields in order that "the national government calls the shots"; and very much for the visit of "meek, shy, courtly, modest" Pope Benedict and 500 bishops for World Youth Day.

Turnbull shuffled his front bench in February 2009 and gave Abbott nothing new. Abbott would tell Tom Dusevic of the *Australian:*

I was none too pleased, not to put too fine a point on it, about this reshuffle and I told Malcolm in the most extraordinarily blunt terms how disappointed and annoyed I was. He countered by telling me quite plainly that I'd been psychologically AWOL for much of the previous fifteen months, or whatever it was, and after I reflected on that I thought perhaps there was some point to what he said. And I thought, "Yeah, I do need to move on."

Abbott's luck had seemed to run out with the fall of Howard but in the winter of 2009 it began to run in his favour once again. Rudd and Turnbull both stumbled. The prime minister was so keen to exploit division in the Coalition over the ETS that he failed to clinch a deal with the Opposition. And Turnbull went off on one of the great wild-goose chases of Australian politics. Godwin Grech, an Opposition source inside Treasury, persuaded him that Rudd's office had given special consideration to the Ipswich car dealer who lent the prime minister a 1996 Mazda Bravo ute to use in his electorate. Turnbull called for Rudd's resignation. But when the key email that was supposed to prove the prime minister's corruption finally saw the light of day, it turned out to be a fraud. Turnbull's reputation was shattered. Support for the Coalition nosedived. Nielsen put Labor ahead on a two-party-preferred basis 58 per cent to the Coalition's 42 per cent. An election would see the Opposition crushed.

Christopher Pyne was in Jerusalem the day the Coalition had to face the wreckage in parliament. Abbott took his place as manager of Opposition business and performed brilliantly: he placed his body in the line of fire; he rained down points of order; he lobbed Goebbels into the debate; he hounded Rudd over his links to the car dealer; and did what he could to present the wretched Grech as a heroic whistle-blower and his leader as a parliamentary titan: "The Labor Party threw everything at Malcolm and he did not flinch." The party and the Canberra press gallery saw a resurgent Abbott. "After a year and a bit of what has at times looked dangerously like a sulk," wrote Annabel Crabb, "People Skills has got the lead back in his pencil."

Battlelines was launched a few weeks later. This odd, thin book was taken seriously by commentators and its author had a chance in the interviews that followed to be several of his many selves: Values Abbott, Politics Abbott and even Intellectual Abbott. It was big-picture time. *Battlelines* was clearly a calling card for national attention, a reminder to the people of Australia that there was another leader in waiting. He rather slavishly praised Turnbull as he nakedly promoted fresh directions for the party. Crippled by the Godwin Grech affair, Turnbull was losing his struggle to control the backwoodsmen, the sceptics and the friends of energy and minerals industries on the Opposition benches. As his troops began to mutiny, pollsters were searching for a new Liberal leader. They did not pick Abbott. He came last by a long way. Turnbull still had strong support. But in the days before the 1 December challenge, the man most Australians wanted to lead the Liberal Party was Joe Hockey.

Abbott went into the party room with a few scribbled notes of an acceptance speech just in case he won. Until the last minute it had seemed only a remote possibility. Turnbull was supposed to be eliminated in the first round of voting. He wasn't. Hockey went instead. This was sheer luck, not design. The party was left to choose between a man who had come to exasperate them and a fresh contender who was willing to save them from the difficult challenge of emissions trading. One member of the party was absent, sick. Another scrawled "NO" on the ballot paper. Abbott won by a vote. He immediately called for a secret ballot to decide whether to block Rudd's ETS in the Senate. The procedure was impeccable and the result decisive: 54 votes to 29. The bipartisan alliance on global warming was over. A few days later, Rudd went off to the Copenhagen summit empty-handed.

Abbott's election would prove a big win for the forces of climate change denial in Australia. Campaigners once considered ratbags began to be taken seriously by the media. Fronts formed. Alliances were made. Many of the groups clamouring for Abbott's attention over the years that followed believe climate change is a hoax designed to create a world government run by a cabal of fabulously wealthy bankers. Alan Jones is patron of the Galileo Movement that argues just that. But the first fortune obviously in play was Gina Rinehart's, as she footed the bill for Viscount Monckton to campaign in Western Australia. Abbott positioned himself in this mayhem with enough wiggle room to put the science aside and only play the politics. The climate is not warming but changing, he says. Humans and greenhouse gases play a role, but only a role. These lines come straight from the handbooks of the denialists. Abbott is speaking their language.

Young Tony did well in science at Riverview. It's not a blind spot. But his real skill is politics. He hadn't betrayed his deepest self in shifting from support to opposition. What changed was his grasp of how the politics might be played. A mentor had come along to persuade him the world was in the grip of shallow and fashionable ideas. There was a mission here for a brave man to confront the zeitgeist. The Coalition was splintering. A hero was required. It was the republican referendum all over again. At this point the polls were against him: there was still a big majority for change but a passionate minority for blocking change. Abbott would bring to bear what had proved so magnificently effective before: fear, doubt, confusion and scorn. Naturally, he did not put the challenge he faced in quite those words. Three days after his victory he sat down and wrote a postscript for *Battlelines* that came to this rather colourful conclusion:

> When Winston Churchill drove to Buckingham Palace in the dark days of 1940 to accept the king's commission, he felt that his whole life had been but a preparation for this moment, or so he recounts in his memoirs. This is not wartime Britain. And I am certainly not Churchill. Still, I feel well equipped to take on the leadership of the party in what are testing times for the conservative side of politics.

This was the summer of red Speedos. Abbott was seen diving, swimming and scrambling from the surf after yet another ocean swim in his budgie-smugglers. The slang entered the language. Once again he was telling his life story to the press and television to show that he was so much more than a hard-line monarchist Catholic head-kicker. He did not deny his past. "I'm not sure I could truthfully say that I am a vastly different or better man than I was," he told Tom Dusevic. "I hope I am wiser, I'm certainly more experienced. I hope my intuitions are deeper and more subtle than they were." Most urgently Abbott wanted to convince Australia he was female-friendly. That his wife, Margie, was interviewed by the *Women's Weekly* at this time and once or twice went out campaigning emphasised rather than disguised what a lonely political figure Abbott was in that marriage. The political game was not for her. Nor did she share her husband's intense faith: "I'm a Catholic, but I don't go to mass regularly. So I think he is disappointed by that."

Abbott is only human. In government he complained about the Opposition taking too literally the advice of Lord Randolph Churchill: "Oppose everything, suggest nothing, and turf the government out." In Opposition he has taken the advice to heart. Other models were available, particularly for a political leader who claims to worship at the shrine of Bob Menzies. His strategy was to oppose selectively and use Opposition as a time for study and renewal. Menzies rejected advice urged on him during the war to attack the government daily in order to keep his name in the papers:

> It would seem quite picturesque for a few weeks, but before long the electors would begin to say, "Oh, here's Menzies again! He wants us to believe that the Government is *always* wrong." And they would soon weary of my attitude.

Abbott disregarded Menzies in favour of Churchill Sr, John Howard and the strategists of the US Republican Party who discovered, a decade or so ago, that a campaign of absolute opposition can play havoc with an administration. Abbott couldn't quite follow the American recipe: he couldn't fire up the electorate on abortion or paint government itself as the enemy. But he could rail against debt – though we essentially have none – and he could pursue a strategy of continuous scorn. Josh Gordon of the *Sunday Age* saw the parallels early: "Like the Republicans in the US, the Coalition's new strategy appears to be to undermine, block, discredit, confuse, attack and hamper at every opportunity."

He gathered a strong office. Its focus was campaigning, not policy. He had Howard's old press secretary Tony O'Leary running communications strategy for the leader and the Coalition front bench.

His new chief of staff was Peta Credlin, a tall Victorian who had worked with Nelson and, unhappily, with Turnbull. There were ructions when she arrived. She guarded Abbott's door – he still works with his door shut tight – deciphered his handwriting and travelled everywhere with him. It was all close-knit: Credlin is the wife of Brian Loughnane, the federal director of the Liberal Party. She is a one-woman policy and politics machine. Abbott came to trust her absolutely. Credlin calls herself "the Queen of no." He calls her "the *force majeure.*"

Rudd was spooked. Labor strategists believed he would call a double dissolution election in early 2010 to pass the ETS and destroy Abbott. But he baulked. In April he walked away from "the great moral challenge of our time" and Abbott was able to attack him mercilessly for his hypocrisy, indecision and want of courage. Abbott gave Labor no quarter. He exposed the chaos of Labor's free home insulation scheme and attacked Rudd's plans – so similar to his own – to take over the nation's hospitals. He lined up with the miners to attack Rudd's audacious decision to tax their super-profits. But above all, and with the greatest skill, Abbott drove a panic over the boats. He was playing with the old race fears of Australia without a qualm. He was made for the work. Howard gave him his blessing: "Tony has altered the political scene; there's no doubt about that. There's no disrespect to anybody else, but if you don't recognise that, well, you don't recognise anything about Australian politics."

"PHO-NEY!" yelled the government benches as Abbott came to the dispatch box. "PHO-NEY! PHO-NEY!" It was just another Question Time in June 2010. To a wall of howls, groans and snatches of song, Rudd battled to say nothing new about Pink Batts. Two Liberals were thrown out. "On yer boat," yelled Labor backbenchers as the Opposition's immigration spokesman, Scott Morrison, headed for the door. Each question was worse than the last. By number three – government hypocrisy over government advertising – the Opposition was baying for blood, an animal sound I haven't heard since playground brawls at Gordon Public a very long time ago. Bronwyn Bishop, doing what she could to add chaos to disorder, was silenced by the Speaker before she uttered a word. Limp in her hands was a copy of Standing Orders bookmarked like an evangelist's Bible. Her mouth sagged in disbelief.

Abbott was sitting where it matters and where no one but he and his doting family ever expected him to be: down the front in the swivel chair, clear of the rabble behind him, facing the rabble in front. In six months, he had made Rudd and his government look shabby. He's so good at this. Baiting is an old skill. He knows the cruel truth that the baiters are never blamed when their victims lose their cool. His own mask never slips. When he makes the government play his game in the House, they don't look like a government and Rudd didn't look like a prime minister.

Abbott kept the message simple and hostile. The advice of pundits and senior figures in his own party to get positive was ignored. He brought a Tea Party anger to his task, anger sustained week after week. It struck a chord. He kept his tongue in check, but memorable gaffes dogged him. On the *7.30 Report* one night, Kerry O'Brien asked how he squared a pledge made on radio months earlier to raise no new taxes with the policy just announced of charging businesses billions to fund parental leave. "Kerry," he replied, "I know politicians are gonna be judged on everything they say, but sometimes, in the heat of discussion, you go a little bit further than you would if it was an absolutely calm, considered, prepared, scripted remark, which is one of the reasons why the statements that need to be taken absolutely as gospel truth is those carefully prepared scripted remarks."

Abbott shrugged off the ridicule. He was moving beyond the reach of his critics. In six months he had transformed the fortunes of the Coalition. The party he took over in December 2009 faced a rout, but six months later the polls were saying it was in a position to beat the government. The fall in Rudd's personal popularity in that time was the most dramatic a prime minister had suffered in a decade. But for Abbott, the Coalition parties would not be where they were. Yet he remained stubbornly unpopular. His approval rating was falling in lock-step with Rudd's. The question troubling Abbott's Liberal colleagues was whether this unloved leader could eventually take them across the line.

Rudd was sacked on 24 June. It was a fundamental blunder provoked by Abbott's success. Howard rang his protégé: "You have achieved the greatest prize that any Opposition leader can: you have secured the scalp of a prime minister." Julia Gillard's lead in the polls lasted a month. Even her big lead with women evaporated. She called an election for 21 August. Abbott reduced his stump speech to a lethal fifteen words: "End the waste, pay back the debt, stop the new taxes and stop the boats." For the best part of a year, Labor tacticians had been waiting for Abbott to fall apart. They were sure he would finally come undone in the campaign. It didn't happen. There were no Bernie Banton moments. And on election night Abbott thought he had pulled off the first defeat of a first-term government since the Depression. Labor won more votes but the Coalition won more seats. Dissatisfaction with both Abbott and Gillard had led to the election of four Independents and one Green in the House of Representatives. All Abbott had to do was talk a few of them across and the prize was his.

But he couldn't. He had never wanted to look like a prime minister in waiting before and didn't now. Gillard moved swiftly and negotiated strategically. Abbott held back too long and then came in too hard. Tony Windsor was perhaps his best bet. Windsor doesn't think Abbott all bad: a good health minister, fit and hard-working. "But Tony Abbott is still at university in terms of the way he does stuff. I think it's his style. There's a number of them on both sides that live that life. They are still there." Abbott took Windsor and Rob Oakeshott for granted in the early days of the negotiations, but Windsor says the bravado didn't last. "You know he portrays himself as the man of the moment, the man of great strength, physical strength. But during part of that period it was quite pitiful." Windsor thought Abbott would even have agreed to a carbon tax if that would make him prime minister. "I quite believe him when he said, 'I'll do anything to get this job, anything other than sell my arse.' And he said he'd really have to think hard about that. He wasn't joking. He was desperate. That was at the stage where it was quite pitiful."

Gillard was sworn in and so began the life of a parliament that would be poor, nasty and brutish but not, it turned out, short. Abbott was out to wreck the joint. He believed that at any moment death, disgrace or defection could make him prime minister. It didn't happen. Despite the scandals laid on by the Labor Party, the parliament functioned. Gillard survived. Complex legislation was passed. And month in, month out pollsters reported that Australians were loathing it all: minority government, the taxes, the tone of national debate, Gillard and Abbott.

Abbott threw everything he had into whipping up a "people's revolt" against Gillard's carbon tax: the stunts in car yards and at dry-cleaners, the unrestrained hyperbole and the personal endorsements given to dodgy protests outside parliament. In March 2011 the Sydney shock-jock Chris Smith brought a crowd of about a thousand to Canberra. Pauline Hanson was wandering around. There were nutters and conspiracy theorists everywhere. Abbott brought the hard right of his front bench with him to the rally. "I do not see scientific heretics," Abbott told the cheering crowd. "I do not see environmental vandals, I see people who want honest government." Nor, it seems, did he see the placards denouncing Gillard as "Ju-Liar" or hear the chants of "Ditch the bitch." It was all caught on television. His judgment was in question twice in those days: first for addressing that bizarre rally and then for mocking Gillard for going to the royal wedding: "She may not believe in God, the monarchy or marriage but there will be a royal wedding bounce." In a single sentence he managed to abuse the prime minister, all de facto couples, everyone who doesn't believe in God, and republicans, who make up roughly half the country. He wasn't winning the affection of the nation.

This was not for want of friends in the press. News Limited had long taken Abbott to its bosom. He was one of them. He had been publishing opinion pieces in News Limited papers for thirty-five years. Most weeks the leader of the Opposition visited Holt Street in Sydney or the *Herald and Weekly Times* in Melbourne. He had become close to the *Australian*'s editor, Chris Mitchell, who had become one of his constituents. Many Saturday nights were spent eating at the Mitchells' in Manly. On talkback radio he spoke directly to his core supporters, what he called "the base." He shied away from interrogations on *7.30*, preferring to chew the fat with Alan Jones, Andrew Bolt, Ray Hadley and the team on Channel Nine's *Today Show*. But none of this was winning hearts and minds. "Abbott personally is a very unpopular leader," wrote Peter Hartcher in November 2011. "He has offered himself as the human boot to stamp on the face of the Prime Minister. But it seems that Australians don't want to be led by an angry boot. The polls are telling us that as much as Australia would like to be rid of Gillard, it is loath to replace her with Abbott."

In late 2011 his party room was becoming fractious. There were those who believed Abbott's policy of total opposition wasn't working. His economic credentials were coming under sustained attack. For fifteen months he had been driven by the belief that there might be an election any day. But Gillard's government wasn't collapsing. She was unpopular but resilient. Abbott had spooked Rudd, but not her. Wasn't it time, senior Liberals were asking, for the party to change tack? Go positive? Abbott rejected the idea emphatically. He reminded the faint of heart that his strategy had raised the primary vote of the party to a magnificent 48 per cent. Abbott had managed to drag Labor support down to the lowest level in fifteen years. The plan was to stay negative in 2012. In autumn he delivered a series of John Howard-style "headland" speeches – on the economy, the environment, the boats, infrastructure and communities – but he would go on doing what he had been doing until the job was finished. He still hoped to collapse the government. With unabated determination he attacked Labor's legitimacy and competence; fanned fears of boat people; and relentlessly pursued Gillard's "toxic tax based on a lie" even after its introduction in July proved such a fizzer. And then towards the end of winter the polls began to turn against him.

Darkness at Noon:
30 July 2012

I f he opened the blinds of his corner office above
Phillip Street, Abbott might look Liberal Sydney in
the eye. All around him are the towers of the great
law firms and the merchant banks of the city. Down
below is Chifley Square, with its statue of the pipe-
smoking man Abbott jokes was the last DLP prime
minister of Australia. But in the middle of this perfect
winter day, with a blue sky over the city, the blinds are
shut tight. The lights are blazing. It's strange. Abbott
can't see the outside world and no one out there can
catch a glimpse of him. This doesn't have the feel of an
office that's much used: Hansards on the shelves and
standard-issue furniture. No picture of the Queen.
Two gifts are the only personal touch. One is a painting of Coober Pedy. The other, at eye level when he's
sitting at his desk, is an autographed photograph of
Aussie Joe Bugner in the ring with Muhammad Ali.

Abbott is bursting out of his shirt. To be face to
face with him is to be in the presence of one of the

most intriguing contests in Australian politics: Abbott
with his own body. Was there ever an Australian politician for whom the body counted so much, who did
so much to keep his packet of muscle and bone in
trim? Until he was leader of the Opposition he was a
mass-a-day man. He once wrote: "The mass was a
chance to quietly restore one's energies." Getting to
mass isn't always possible now but he works his body
six days a week. He's up before dawn for an hour on
his bike and maybe later – especially after a gruelling
Question Time – he spends some time in the gym. He
doesn't win those ocean swims and the bike rides. He
doesn't see himself as a great competitor. He is in it for
the discipline. His early discipline master, Fr Paul
Mankowski S.J., is regularly in Australia. They meet.
Abbott's regard for him appears undimmed, a priest
who teaches dead languages while fighting "culture
wars on behalf of Catholic positions," an ascetic who
longs for the cloister: "Monks are, or used to be, our
masters at saying no to the self."

For a long time the taming of Tony Abbott has
owed more to his forceful wife than this shadowy,
charismatic priest. Those who know Margie Abbott
credit her steadying hand over twenty-five years for
domesticating the volatile man she married. Time and
children have played their part. So has the prospect of
power. Since that unexpected shift of votes in 2009

delivered him the leadership, Abbott has been curb-
ing his tongue. Words are weapons, he says, and he
deploys them with ruthless energy. But for the most
part he has managed not to turn them on himself.
He has advisers to warn him to take care, to stay on
message. And he has a very Abbott way of turning
ambition into mission. He must not betray by ill discipline those who have placed their trust in him to
destroy Labor. Yet Abbott bears himself like a bully.
The body language of the man is awkward and
threatening. Those who saw his ugly face-off with
Channel Seven reporter Mark Riley in February 2011
– everyone in the country who watched the news that
night – will not soon forget it. Abbott was just back
from Afghanistan, where he had been accused of dis-
missing the deaths of Australian soldiers with the
quip: "Shit happens." He might easily have pointed
out the truth: the claim was baseless. Instead, the
nation watched him struggling in silence not to raise
his fists. That he won was hardly the point. Why was
he struggling?

Those who played football with this man forgive
him so much. Peter FitzSimons, journalist and biographer of our national heroes, has had it out with
Abbott over gays, climate change, abortion, the
republic, asylum seekers and industrial relations.
But the affection remains. FitzSimons watched the

famous punch-up between coach Abbott and player Joe Hockey in the late 1980s: "a blistering array of uppercuts, hay-makers and wild swings." FitzSimons sees in the politician the young man's love of rugby scrums:

Abbo never saw a scrum that he didn't like ... what he most loved, and I mean this, was doing it when the conditions were *appalling*. One night in June, 1989, it all came together. A howling wind, screaming imprecations at the devil. Sheets of rains without end. A whole *quagmire* of mud to work with. Situation perfect ... as we maddened muddy wombats staggered after him. Forty minutes in, as our eyeballs rolled with exhaustion, I dinkum remember looking at his own beatific countenance, all grin and ears, the rain pouring off his uncovered head and having this distinct thought: "I think he's a little bit insane – in a hugely likeable way."

He gave up football in his mid-thirties, about the time he married. A couple of decades later he's still running, swimming and cycling and from time to time pushing himself through a ten-hour triathlon. Few men of that age are pushing themselves through ten hours of triathlon. If he is ever living in Kirribilli House, he won't be taking power walks along the shore in a Vodafone tracksuit. He will be up at 4 a.m. for a fifty-kilometre ride in Lycra. The punishment is necessary. Abbott jokes about this but knows it is true: "If I didn't get regular exercise I'm sure I'd drink more, I might be popping pills, I might be going slightly round the twist."

He is just back from Washington and Beijing, where he delivered a couple of big speeches, both written by himself. The first had the traditional function of reassuring America that the man who is looking every inch the next prime minister is a safe pair of hands. He laid it on thick: "Few Australians would regard America as a foreign country. We are more than allies, we're family." He passed on the thanks of a grateful nation for the chance to fight side by side with America in Vietnam, Iraq and Afghanistan. He acknowledged America as the guardian of the great traditions of the Western world. The scourge of the boats dared quote the "huddled masses" line from the Statue of Liberty. It was all astonishingly banal. Abbott urged his hosts at the Heritage Foundation to bring the nation's debts and deficits under control and not lose faith in themselves: "America needs to believe in itself the way others still believe in it." Yet there was a faint note of reproach in Abbott's flattery:

America's military expeditions may sometimes be mistaken but they're always well-meaning; even if others are tempted to conclude, with Graham Greene of the Quiet American, that he'd never known a man with such good intentions for all the trouble he'd caused!

Abbott had made the same, odd point in *Battlelines* and when welcoming Barack Obama to the Australian parliament in 2011. The Quiet American of Greene's prophetic novel was the naive do-gooder Alden Pyle, the kind of man with the kind of thinking that drew the United States into the bloodbath of Vietnam. Abbott doesn't often lace his rhetoric with literary references. What he was doing here had a purpose: to signal a deeper, perhaps snobbish fondness for Pyle's adversary, a cynical British journalist, a man who understood the ways of the world. When puzzling over these references to Greene's dangerous fool, commentators forgot that Abbott is, in the end, an Australian Anglophile. His old-fashioned rhetoric of the Anglosphere – which doesn't play well in Africa and the Caribbean – embraces American might but honours the nous of Great Britain.

Abbott went up to Manhattan to pay the other call any would-be prime ministers must make in America. Though squads of his executives were under arrest in London and a Lord Justice of Appeal was raking through his newspapers, due deference had still to be paid to Rupert Murdoch. Nothing had changed for Murdoch in Australia. His censure was still feared and his papers were barracking for Tony Abbott. Not since they turned on Gough Whitlam had they shown such a united determination to bring down a government. Once home, Abbott heaped praise on Murdoch in the *Spectator*: "Along with the commander of the First AIF, Sir John Monash, and the penicillin inventor, Lord Florey, he is one of the Australians who have made the most difference in the world."

China feted Abbott. The officials he met were high-powered. His was regarded as a visit of importance. His address was not craven. He did not lay it on thick. How many times must Chinese officials have heard Australian dignitaries try to explain this continent's early wretched relationship with the Chinese? They know the truth. Why not speak the truth? Abbott put about as good a spin on it as he could: early Chinese settlers, early Chinese politicians and Chinese restaurants in country towns were "an early sign of our readiness to absorb foreign ways and make them our own." He even claimed for his party the credit due to Labor for ending the "embarrassment" of White Australia. But there were three tough messages in his breakfast speech to the Australian Chamber of Commerce in Beijing: we will never break with America, China must become free, and Australia is wary of Chinese investment. His real audience at that moment was the National Party back home: "Chinese investment is complicated by the prevalence of state-owned enterprises. It would rarely be in Australia's national interest to allow a foreign government or its agencies to control an Australian business."

Back from the world stage, Abbott is on the road again. That morning he has been in the western suburbs of Sydney complaining about the impact of the carbon tax on Pirtek Fluid Transfer Solutions. Over the next couple of days he is due to do the same at the Tamar Valley Dairy in Tasmania and Hart Marine on the Mornington Peninsula. Sunday will see him up the coast for the Coffs Coast Cycle Challenge. That's his life. But now, after I'd been trailing him for a couple of months, the time had come for the interview. He would be pithy, funny and illuminating. Everything we discussed is somewhere in this essay. I haven't wasted a scrap. But he has allowed me to quote only his response to Barbara Ramjan: "I certainly don't remember – and I think it would be profoundly out of character had it occurred – punching a wall each side of someone's head."

He is so close. Abbott is a patient man but this must be agony. Power is just the other side of the glass. All he has to do, one senior Labor figure told me, is stay vertical. Meanwhile he is so cautious he threatens to become what he has never been before: a bore. "The beauty of being leader is you are freer to be yourself," he said a couple of years ago. That's not true. Leadership has made Abbott less himself. The spark has gone out of his writing. Those vast headland speeches were so dull they made no impact at all. Perhaps that was the point: to look like a big thinker without showing his hand.

The joke goes that Abbott might be the first DLP prime minister of Australia. He wouldn't mind us believing that. He still carries a torch for Santa, and none of the old warrior's disciples has risen as high on the Liberal side of politics as Abbott. Ever since he stepped into parliament he has been invoking God and the Catholic values that drive him. They are his political persona. They are the proof that there is depth and humanity to this attack dog. Yet what impact have they had, in the end, on this man's life in power? How much would they drive Tony Abbott, PM? Which Abbott are we going to get when things are tough, I asked, Values Abbott or Politics Abbott?

I wish I could quote his answer. My sense is we'll get the Abbott he decides to give us at any particular time. He is certainly not stepping back from those lessons he learnt as an eyewitness to the Hewson debacle: politicians need to know how to finesse their principles.

> If you have them so strongly, and so dogmatically, that they cause the public to shrink from you in fear, there is a problem. And I'm not saying that you necessarily surrender your principles; but I am saying that you have got to be conscious of the fact that no matter how right your principles are, if they don't resonate with the general public, and you are living in a democratic polity, you've got a problem.

Values Abbott in power would mean no prospect in this country of gay marriage, drug reform, euthanasia, a republic or a bill of rights. The last on the list he regards as a complete waste of time. Win or lose, nothing will be done to roll back abortion rights because Politics Abbott knows that's simply not possible. Values Abbott would work to cushion families from the realities of economic life. And if the Coalition parties allowed him, Values Abbott would protect working men and women from the full force of the labour market. Values Abbott is not there to help the nation's rich get richer. But he won't put his career on the line for any of this. He won't abandon his old faith-based principles, but he won't be a martyr to them either.

The Abbott that matters is Politics Abbott. That's the one who got him where he is today: an aggressive populist with a sharp tongue; a political animal with lots of charm; a born protégé with ambitions to lead; a big brain but no intellectual; a bluff guy who proved a more than competent minister; a politician with little idea what he might do if he ever got to the top; and a man profoundly wary of change. His values have never stood in his way. The result has been a spectacularly successful term as leader of the Opposition. He isn't there yet but with Labor's help he has brought the Coalition from ruin almost to triumph in less than four years. "There is a crude genius to this," wrote the ABC's Chris Uhlmann:

> But this scorched-earth politics ignores something crucial: how much damage Abbott has done to himself. His approach is consuming the better parts of his nature and defining him politically and personally ... As he wrestles, too late, with the task of convincing a sceptical public that there is more to him than meets the eye, he might reflect on the words of Luke's Gospel: "For what does it profit a man if he gains the whole world and loses himself?"

Invisible Man

I should have seen the punch coming. Weeks of gaffes by Abbott and his men meant that even before my Quarterly Essay – the precursor of this book – appeared in early September 2012, Abbott's problem with women was back on the political agenda. He was thrown from the House for sledging Gillard with sotto voce taunts of "liar, liar." A couple of days later Leigh Sales took him apart on *7.30* and the former Liberal machine man Grahame Morris called her a "real cow." Morris apologised. Gillard lashed out at the "misogynists and the nut jobs" pursuing her on the internet for her supposed crimes in the 1990s when she was the partner of, and solicitor for, the now disgraced Australian Workers' Union official Bruce Wilson. Cataloguing the sexist abuse directed at Gillard on and off the internet, the feminist Anne Summers defended her in the Fairfax press as an abused employee of the nation: "The Prime Minister, like the rest of us, is entitled to be able to do her job without harassment, bullying or sex discrimination." Almost the same day, the Liberal guru Alan Jones named Gillard on a list of women leaders "destroying the joint" and again suggested they all be thrown into the sea in a chaff bag.

On Friday a week later, Abbott was delivered an early copy of the Quarterly Essay. It was not yet in the shops. Next morning, a chunk of the essay covering Abbott's university years would see the light of day in the Fairfax press. At some point on the Friday, he decided he had not punched the wall. Late that afternoon, one of his staff rang the *Sydney Morning Herald* with an urgent one-line statement from the leader of the Opposition: "It never happened." Abbott might have admitted those blows and said truthfully that he has done a lot of growing up since 1977. He might have stuck to the safe ground of not remembering what happened that night. His absolute denial at this late stage would turn an ugly little incident from a long time ago into a big deal in the politics of 2012. Back then the issue was a young man's bad behaviour in chaotic times. Now the issue was a leader's credibility.

The punch became the essay. Labor declared Abbott a misogynist bully. Gillard's front bench spoke as if the leader of the Opposition was still getting about with bloodied knuckles. Abbott went to ground. No one could remember a time when he had been so inaccessible. For days there were no door-stops, no visits to factories crippled by the carbon tax. But Abbott's friends sprang to his defence. None were more fiercely protective than the Santamaria alumni who now command the conservative heights of newspaper commentary. Greg Sheridan raged in the *Australian*. Gerard Henderson sneered in the *Sydney Morning Herald* at Ramjan's account of that night as "the uncorroborated testimony of the aggrieved." This provoked devastating retaliation from the senior Sydney barrister David Patch, who wrote a detailed account in the Fairfax press of finding Ramjan shaken and scared moments after the confrontation with Abbott all those years ago and never doubting her account, then or since.

Abbott broke cover next morning on Nine's *Today* show, still insisting the punch never happened. To hold to that course required him to attack Patch and Ramjan. "There is no doubt," he told Nine's Karl Stefanovic, "that the Labor Party dirt unit is running a serious campaign here and I've been saying to Margie and the kids, Karl, that they can expect a lot more of this between now and polling day." He pointed out that Patch had once been a Labor candidate. A few hours later, on the steps of an IGA supermarket in the Canberra suburbs, he repeated his "dirt unit" line. He offered nothing to back the charge. He attacked me too:

> Question: Mr Abbott, are you suggesting that the Labor dirt unit is feeding this information to David Marr, this specific allegation? Is that what you're saying today?
>
> Tony Abbott: There is a Labor dirt unit and it's feeding information to people left, right and centre.

Ramjan and Patch put out statements that day denying the dirt unit allegation. I was flying up from Melbourne unaware of the tack Abbott had taken that morning and unaware my publishers had also rushed out a statement denying I'd been fed the story by the Labor Party. The fact is I heard about Ramjan and the punch from lawyers at a dinner early in 2012 celebrating the fortieth anniversary of our graduation from Sydney University Law School. In the early afternoon Abbott rang. I took notes. "He said he was not accusing me of being part of any Labor Party dirt unit or operation against him and that he was taking care not to blame me." I thanked him for that. He added that the essay was thoughtful and intelligent. "While I don't by any means accept all your judgments, you did a highly professional job."

Ramjan is a respected figure in Sydney, with connections to the highest levels of the judiciary. But the shoring up of Abbott's denials required the destruction of her credibility. Michael Kroger took on the task armed with a Spartacist League newsletter from the 1970s accusing Ramjan of inventing death threats against her. Though his mortal enemies back then, the Sparts were useful to Kroger now. His first stop was the Andrew Bolt show on Channel Ten, where he accused Ramjan of lying about the punch and lying about the death threats. He also gave the leaflet to the *Australian*, which next day reported on page one:

> Liberal powerbroker Michael Kroger yesterday accused the woman who levelled allegations of physical aggression against Tony Abbott during his student years of being a serial manufacturer of false complaints against her political opponents.

That night Kroger was on Steve Price's radio show in Sydney calling Ramjan "an ex-communist who is now a nobody, a nobody attacking Tony Abbott to get publicity" and "lying and cheating against Tony Abbott in a fairly disgusting way." Next morning he was with Alan Jones calling Ramjan "a nutter from the left" involved in "one of the most sinister, nasty and vicious campaigns I've seen." Their grim exchange was laced with effusive praise for Abbott.

Ramjan and Jones have as a mutual friend the colourful Sydney lawyer Chris Murphy. He spoke to the broadcaster. Next day Jones made an apology on air as complete and elegant as is imaginable: "Now, on this program we try to be fair no matter who is involved. Since that interview yesterday it has been pointed out to me by several people that Barbara Ramjan is indeed a woman of distinction who in whatever she says deserves to be taken seriously ..."

Ramjan sued both Kroger and the *Australian*. As this book goes to press, the defamation case is proceeding to trial in Sydney.

Jones did not apologise so elegantly four days later when he was caught telling the annual dinner of Sydney University Liberal Club that Gillard's lies had killed her father. A young News Limited journalist, Jonathan Marshall, secretly recorded Jones's fifty-minute rant:

> "The old man recently died a few weeks ago of shame ... To think that he had a daughter who told lies every time she stood for parliament. Every person in the caucus of the Labor Party knows that Julia Gillard is a liar ..."

The top-rating radio star went on to say Ms Gillard had enjoyed a recent spike in polls sparked by her tears. He also said she was being given an easy ride by the "brainwashed" Liberal Party who had backed down because she was a woman.

Jones was there that night to spruik for Abbott, the youngster he helped propel into parliament decades earlier: "His overweening weakness is his humility. You will never ever hear this bloke argue his ability, his virtue, or indeed his competence. He is a man of incomparable integrity and conviction."

A wave of disgust swept public life. Jones's apology was a shambles. Abbott's reproaches were tepid at first but after a few days he cranked himself up to condemn Jones's words as "wrong, unacceptable, offensive." At the same time he made it clear he would not boycott the show: "I am not in the business of ignoring a big audience." Jones's sponsors deserted him. His audience grew.

Nothing quite like the politics of the last months of 2012 had been seen before in this country. Abbott was mired in accusations of misogyny. Labor Party polling showed that within a month of the publication of the Quarterly Essay, 60 per cent of Australians had heard of the punch. Not all believed it happened, but they'd heard the story. Ten days after

Jones made things so much more difficult for him, Abbott committed his worst gaffe since becoming leader of the party. True, he had used such words often enough in the past but this was no time to talk of "another day of shame for a government which should have already died of shame." The context was the last hours in office of the humiliated speaker Peter Slipper. Gillard's reply rose above that sordid context:

> I say to the Leader of the Opposition: I will not be lectured about sexism and misogyny by this man. I will not. The government will not be lectured about sexism and misogyny by this man – not now, not ever …

Within a week a million people around the world had watched Gillard's speech on YouTube. Her stocks were rising sharply. Abbott's were falling. He was no longer the preferred prime minister. A Nielsen poll in late October gave her a "net approval rating" of minus one. His was as low as it had ever been for him: minus 23. At least for the time being, her leadership was secure. His was being questioned within his own party. Backbenchers were complaining that Abbott was too rigid, too old-fashioned, too controlling. For the first time in a long time he faced serious questioning across the media. His backers were nervous.

For once, Values Abbott could not ride to the aid of the junkyard dog. The values were the problem. "People see him as a kind of mad Catholic and a bit of a zealot, a bit of an ideologue," Ipsos Australia's director, Rebecca Huntley, told me. She has been listening to voters discuss Abbott for years and saw no change in late 2012 to a verdict formed long ago. Gillard is a polarising figure. He is not. Dislike – often extreme dislike – is the norm. Expressions of admiration are rare. "The women do talk about him as a misogynist. They talk about him having views about society and life that they think are too prescriptive and perhaps not easygoing enough – on a range of issues from gay marriage to the role of women in society, the whole issue around single mothers and around abortion. Even men talk about him as a mad Catholic."

So in the misogyny crisis of 2012, Abbott produced the women in his life – his mother, his formidable wife, Margie, his sisters, his daughters – to vouch for what really wasn't at issue: that he loved women and the women of his family loved him. We learnt from his wife that he loved *Downton Abbey* and from his daughters that he was a kind and supportive father. Early in the new year *Marie Claire* magazine revealed he was happy for his chief of staff, Peta Credlin, to keep IVF drugs in the office fridge. The net effect of this was rather creepy. Those with

long memories were glad, for her sake, that Credlin
was married and heterosexual. In 2000 Abbott backed
Howard's failed attempt to ban IVF for single women
and lesbians. In 2005 he attacked the Victorian Law
Reform Commission for recommending such women
be guaranteed access to IVF. Both times he argued the
pure Vatican line: children must start life with a
mother and father. In 2007 as health minister he held
the line on Medicare funding, saying he was "certainly
not in favour of extending IVF to lesbian couples."
But as the Credlin story broke in January 2013, the
would-be prime minister wrote in the *Sunday Telegraph*: "I have never opposed IVF."

That Abbott is determined to keep these ancient
battles alive has little resonance for most Australians
and makes many women profoundly uneasy. The
young have no sympathy for this stuff at all, pollsters
report. It makes them see Tony Abbott as a figure
from another age, a man who has little to teach them
about life. Ipsos Australia asked 21-year-olds in 2012
about their role models. They thought the question
rather old-fashioned. They showed admirable cyni-
cism about celebrities. They found it easier to say
who they didn't want to be:

Twenty-one-year-olds named a range of public
figures and friends that did not inspire them.

Noteworthy examples were Tony Abbott and Kim Kardashian.

One of the 21-year-olds is quoted in the Ipsos report of December 2012: "I think there are lots of people out there who I think are bad role models. Sometimes I see Tony Abbott and I think 'I'm glad I'm not Tony Abbott.'"

But that young Australian is, more than likely, preparing to vote for him. The momentum towards Gillard petered out over summer. Labor's primary vote fell. Abbott nudged ahead as preferred prime minister. Rudd was again on the prowl. As Canberra reopened for business in February 2013, there was, more than ever, a feeling in the air that Labor was done for. The press gallery was accommodating itself to regime change in September. From Barack Obama, Labor had pinched the bright idea of claiming to speak for "modern families" and "modern Australia" while denouncing the other side for representing an Australia that no longer exists. It did not ring true: on most of the social issues that define modern Australia Gillard's party and Abbott's party see eye to eye. Santamaria's followers have filtered back into both sides of politics. The drift of the world is resisted all over the House. The peculiar conservatism of contemporary Canberra is the late-life triumph of the DLP.

The old Abbott slipped further from view as he pulled back, shut up, left the attacks to his colleagues and began talking up the needs of the nation. Behind the scenes, Liberal strategists spoke of repositioning their leader as the adult in the room. It's another pinch from America. Smearing Gillard over the AWU mess he left mostly to his deputy, Julie Bishop. He was less than ever on the front line attacking refugees, although as Scott Morrison plunged deeper into the sewer of race fear he was there to commend him for doing a fine job. The retreat was done with some skill. Abbott was perfecting the art of remaining highly visible while keeping his head down. A *Crikey* analysis of his media appearances in late 2012 showed him busy dealing with the press while screening himself from scrutiny:

> He prefers to avoid questioning by the press gallery and the ABC, in favour of media doorstops across the country ... it also means he tends to field questions from less-experienced or non-political journalists ... Abbott also avoids the ABC like the plague, gracing it just four times in a six-month period ... Abbott went on Andrew Bolt's TV program (three times) almost as often as he went on the entire ABC (radio and TV).

This is not the old Abbott. Lately he has whinged a little about the "left-of-centre ethos" of the ABC, as if that were a reason for not appearing on *Insiders* or *Q&A*. But the ethos of the national broadcaster never held him back in the past. He was on everything. Nor was Abbott ever much of a warrior in the culture wars against the ABC. His present wariness and recent rhetoric show, more than anything, the influence of his media team led by Tony O'Leary, a formidable veteran of John Howard's office.

"The talk about town is that he'll be run by Pell on one side and Howard on the other," says John Hewson. He's not endorsing the view, only reporting what he hears in Sydney when business men and women gather. The cardinal remains a spiritual adviser but Abbott has shown himself willing to put daylight between himself and Pell's absolute defence of their church. Abbott welcomed the royal commission into child abuse and rejected Pell's argument that the confessions of paedophiles remain under seal. "I think everyone has to obey the law," said Abbott. "The law is no respecter of persons." Including priests? "Indeed."

But as polling day approaches, Abbott is more and more channelling his old political mentor. His tactics are John Howard's and so is much of his rhetoric. One of the old man's most famous lines sprang to his lips when Gillard named the day: "This election will be about trust." He holds Howard up as the model of effective government: "The point I keep making is if you want John Howard-style results, you have to put in John Howard-style policies." None of this should be any surprise. Howard found Abbott, put him into parliament and was the patron of his rise. Abbott never broke with him. He was not one of those who felt the party needed to shift its position fundamentally after the defeat of 2007. He had differences with Howard – particularly over the apology and Work-Choices – but he remained loyal. "*Battlelines* was my attempt to work out a new Liberal conservative agenda for Australia," he told Annabel Crabb in 2010, "to consider how it might be possible to keep faith with the values of the Howard era without being an action replay of it." From the moment he became leader of the Opposition, Abbott pledged to take Australia back to the lost golden time of John Howard. For those about to switch their votes to Abbott, these protestations of loyalty to the past prime minister are oddly reassuring.

"They just want the whole Labor saga to be over," says Rebecca Huntley of the Ipsos discussion groups. They still don't like Abbott and their dislike is often visceral. Extreme. Yet he has won their grudging respect for staying the course and not going to pieces as they once feared he would. They sense he has gone quiet lately and reckon he should stay quiet until a few weeks before the poll. *Downton Abbey* hasn't swung their views: they still think he's pugilistic and weird about women. They don't care about the carbon tax one way or the other. Now that it's here, they think it might as well stay. They want an effective mining tax. They are not talking about voting for independents and third parties, as they did in 2010. Huntley reads their mood as resignation: "The alternative is not supportable, therefore I'm just going to close my eyes and grit my teeth and vote for Abbott." Some of those preparing to change their vote take heart from the thought that he might run more a Howard government than an Abbott government. Others find bleak reassurance in doubting the country's pessimism. They argue: "Everybody says he's going to be absolutely terrible and the end of the world but he can't be that bad. He can't possibly be like that."

Abbott was on the spot when the new ground rules of politics were set by Hewson's defeat in 1993. He isn't going to make the mistake of believing the election is in the bag, and the Coalition's platform will be kept under wraps until polling day is in sight. That's basic. But the deeper lesson of the Hewson debacle was this: Opposition leaders with a tough agenda must play a long game. Winning is everything. Don't let the program stand in the way of victory. Argue for change in office, not in Opposition. Howard understood this: he waited until he was in power before putting a GST on the table. Abbott is following the same strategy. Laura Tingle reported in the *Australian Financial Review* that he is telling those clamouring for him to be tough on trade unions to bide their time:

> The message from Abbott to business is: if you want change, look to our second term. If we are going to do more in the way of radical change, it will be from the platform of government and with the policies clearly announced as second-term agenda items before that election.

We know an Abbott win in 2013 will mean no carbon tax and no mining tax: no reasonable prospect of dealing with global warming and no dividend from this or any other minerals boom. That is a price he is willing to pay for victory. We know an Abbott win will lock in the toxic politics of the boats. When refugees don't stop arriving by sea he will find himself exposed to all the abuse he heaped on Rudd and Gillard. The rule will be: what worked for Abbott will be done to Abbott. So a victory would also confirm his brutally effective style of Opposition. Whether we like it or not – and the polls say we don't – politics promises to be a bare-knuckle sport in this country for a long, long time.

Every morning Abbott saddles up for a long ride in the dark. For an hour or so, he is alone on his bike. Reflection is part of every working day, reflection and discipline. Ask him why he wants to be prime minister and he talks of values that go beyond personal ambition; of a vision he has for a better and more cohesive society where people might be their best selves. Over the years he has spoken of being a conservative prime minister who would bring his values to bear on a changing world: leaving well alone when he can but confronting the zeitgeist where he must. This romantic notion of himself has survived twenty brutal years in Canberra. So much about Abbott makes the kind of prime minister he might become uniquely hard to predict: his fine rhetoric and his brawling ways; his Catholic loyalties and his absolutely secular determination. He speaks as if power would resolve these old contradictions: that the politician who clawed his way to the top might then make way for another self, the one who set out on this quest when he was still a kid at Riverview. He isn't there yet. He knows he might lose. The months ahead are a political eternity. And he knows he might win only to find he is stuck with Politics Abbott after all. He understands the risks politicians run of making too many promises and too many compromises and sacrificing too many principles on the long haul to power. "You will find you are like the dog who catches the car," he wrote. "What do you do when you finally get that great office for which you have striven all these years?"

5 March 2013

Sources

My thanks to Josephine Tovey, who helped me research Rudd's life and career for *Power Trip*. A version of the afterword to *Power Trip* appeared in the *Guardian* on 27 June 2013.

Political Animal is built on the work of dozens of my colleagues over many years. I thank them. I thank Tony Abbott and his staff for the help they gave. I thank the politicians and bureaucrats, named and unnamed, who shared their experiences with me. My particular thanks go to Rebecca Giggs, who was my ferocious researcher and sounding board. And first to last my thanks to Sebastian Tesoriero.

3   "one of the greatest moral": Speech to the Bali conference, 12 December 2007.

6   "Why can't we even mention our own targets": *Guardian*, 23 December 2009, 10.

6   "We prevailed": *Australian,* 21 December 2009, 1.

13   *Griffith Review 21: Hidden Queensland,* 2008, 179, 181.

16   "I was the last" and "Have you made" to Julia Baird, ABC Radio, *Sunday Profile,* 5 March 2006; "When he was" in Robert Macklin, *Kevin Rudd: The Biography*, Viking, Melbourne, 2008, 39; "Is it so hard" in *Sydney Morning Herald,* 27 April 2007, 1; "I always remember in the dim" in address at the launch of *Shell-Shocked: Australia After Armistice*, National Archives of Australia Canberra, 12 November 2008.

17 "I grew up in a Queensland": Address to the sesquicentenary celebrations of Queensland, reported *Sunday Mail*, 7 June 2009, 53.

17 "Mum would bellow out the window": Macklin, 66.

18 "old-style Queensland": *Compass*, ABC TV, 8 May 2005.

18 "Every branch in me that beareth not fruit": John 15: 1–13 is identified as her favourite passage in the program for her funeral.

19 "Rudd told *Sixty Minutes*' Ellen Fanning": as quoted by Piers Akerman in the *Daily Telegraph*, 13 March 2007, 20.

20 *Women's Weekly*, January 2007, 28.

20 All *Sun-Herald* quotes: 11 March 2007, 10.

21 All Alan Ramsey quotes: *Sydney Morning Herald*, 31 March 2007, 39.

23 "a terribly dignifying experience": *Compass*, ABC TV, 8 May 2005.

23 "he told Julia Baird": *Sunday Profile*, ABC Radio, 5 March 2006.

24 *Sydney Morning Herald*, 27 April 2007, 1.

24 "in a dorm with fifty guys": to Cosima Marriner, ibid.

24 "You've always got to be polite": ibid.

25 "It doesn't get much crooker than this": Macklin, 57.

25 "he detested the joint": Marriner, 1.

26 "I watched with wide eyes on the flickering tube": address at the Sir Edward "Weary" Dunlop Asialink Medal presentation to Gough and Margaret Whitlam, University of Melbourne, 6 February 2001.

26 "As a kid growing up in the Queensland country": ibid.

27 "a deep sense of loss of dignity": Baird, 5 March 2006.

29 "in his maiden speech": Hansard, 11 November 1998, 166.

31 *Chronicle*, 25 July 1974, 9.

33 "I held it" and "Consternation broke out": from the Asialink address, 6 February 2001.

35 "Through that process": Baird, 5 March 2006.

36 "I was mopping a floor in the emergency department": to me, 8 April 2010.

36 "To escape": quoted in Nicholas Stuart, *Kevin Rudd: An Unauthorised Political Biography*, Scribe, Melbourne, 2007, 44.

36 *Women's Weekly*, January 2007, 26.

37 "marvellously snotty": Macklin, 70.

37 "I personally committed to Christ": as quoted by Kate Legge in the *Australian*, Weekend Australian Magazine, 18 July 2009, 13.

37 "He told me about growing up in Eumundi": ibid.

37 "He dissected the fledgling Fraser government": ibid.

37 Macklin, 115.

38 Jeremy Paxman, *The Political Animal: An Anatomy*, Michael Joseph, London, 2002, 36.

40 *Australian Financial Review*, 23 February 2007, 44.

42 "As a possibility, yes": to me, 8 April 2010.

47 "I identified the top forty companies in Queensland": *Australian Financial Review*, 23 February 2007, 42.

48 "First, to run a traditional Labor government": *Sydney Morning Herald* & *Age*, Good Weekend, 1 July 1995, 23.

50 Noel Pearson, *Up from the Mission*, Black Inc., Melbourne, 2009, 374.

50 "I recall witnessing a 33-year-old Rudd": Pearson, 375.

52 David Malouf, *12 Edmondstone Street*, Chatto & Windus, London, 1985, 3.

53 "That was all quietly fixed": *Sydney Morning Herald*, 15 October 1994, 39.

54 "On the fateful night in 1989": *Sydney Morning Herald* and *Age*, Good Weekend, 1 July 1995, 27.

57 "You might like to think about that, Kevin": *Australian*, 2 September 1995, 8.

57 "Queenslanders are sitting on their verandas": Pamela Williams, *The Victory*, Allen & Unwin, Sydney, 1997, 327.

60 "When my father was accidentally killed": Hansard, 11 November 1998, 163

61   "Politics is about power": ibid., 162.

66   Mark Latham, *The Latham Diaries*, Melbourne University Press, Melbourne, 2005, 119.

66   "He was a man who": *Australian Financial Review*, 7 February 2003, 10.

70   Reports of the polls: *Australian*, 5 November 2002, 1–2; 15 April 2003, 1.

71   *Age*, 18 April 2003, 3.

72   "more votes in the community than in caucus": *Bulletin*, 2 December 2003 (but published a week earlier), 30.

72   *Sunday Telegraph*, 30 November 2003, 4.

72   Morgan poll finding 3691, published 30 November 2003.

74   Latham, 276.

77   *Sydney Morning Herald*, 25 October 2008, 29.

77   Latham, 365.

78   "Her public support was in the high teens": the polls are Morgan 19–20 January; Newspoll 21–23 January; and Nielsen 21–22 January.

79   "I've got a field marshal's baton": *Courier-Mail*, 25 January 2005, 1.

80   "The terms of reference make it possible": *Australian Financial Review*, 18 January 2006, 4

81   "The prime minister's now routine manipulation": *Monthly*, October 2006, 24, 30.

82   "31 to 27 per cent": *Sydney Morning Herald*, 22 May 2006, 4.

83   "Go for it": *Advertiser*, 17 November 2007, 16.

84   "As a professional of fifteen": *The Howard Years*, Part IV, ABC TV.

84   Traits vis-à-vis Beazley and Howard: Newspoll 10–12 November; *Australian*, 12 December 2006, 1. Two party preferred under Rudd or Beazley: Nielsen 30 November to 2 December; *Sydney Morning Herald*, 4 December 2006, 1. Enthusiasm for Rudd–Gillard team: Newspoll, *Australian*, 4 December 2006, 1.

85 "Compassion is not a dirty word": Hansard, 5 December 2006, 44.

87 "The man caucus had regarded ...": Newspoll 16–18 March 2007; *Australian*, 20 March 2007, 1–2.

87 "A Nielsen poll in June ...": *Sydney Morning Herald*, 18 June 2007, 4.

88 "Absolutely revolting": *Daily Telegraph*, 23 May 2008, 4.

92 *Meet the Press*, Channel 10, 7 November 2004.

93 "Rudd was appealing to a bigger audience ...": 70 per cent: *Sydney Morning Herald*, 9 November 2006, 17. 50 per cent: Nielsen poll reported in *Sydney Morning Herald*, News Review, 9 December 2009, 1.

93 "Look at atheist parents": *Sydney Morning Herald*, 8 July 2005, 15.

94 "One of my Labor Party colleagues said": *Courier-Mail*, 7 November 2001, 17.

94 "When you see people in strife": *Compass*, ABC TV, 8 May 2005.

95 *Sunday Profile*, ABC TV, 5 March 2006.

95 "Surely a family's ability": *Courier-Mail*, 13 December 2004, 13.

96 "The message from Howard to the churches": *Australian*, 8 August 2005, 8.

96 "A Christian perspective on": *Monthly*, October 2006, 27.

96 "I am a Jeffersonian separatist": *Bulletin*, 2 December 2003, 27.

96 "Denominationalism means": Baird, 5 March 2006.

97 "My mother was a Catholic": Hansard, 6 December 2006, 119.

97 "most reluctant supporters": ibid.

98 "I see very little evidence": *Monthly*, October 2006, 26.

98 *Q&A*, ABC TV, 22 May 2008.

99 "What do you do about people": *Sydney Morning Herald*, Good Weekend, 5 November 2005, 24.

101 "Black says the profile": *Australian Financial Review*, 29 February 2008, 88.

102 "Here he was, the winner": *Age*, 26 November 2007, 2.

103 "I'm probably the first bloke for quite a while": to Laurie Oakes, *Sunday*, Channel 9, 10 February 2008.

103 "Anyone who says that it's easy ...": *Compass*, ABC TV, 8 May 2005.

106 "The biblical injunction": *Monthly*, October 2006, 29.

106 "scum of the earth ...": *Australian*, 18 April 2009, 7.

109 <www.acl.org.au/makeitcount/rudd_speech.wmv>

110 "Part of modernising the Labor Party": *7.30 Report*, ABC TV, 29 November 2007.

111 "When ministers arrive": *Australian Financial Review*, 8 March 2010, 1.

113 *Sydney Morning Herald*, 11 April 2009, 9.

115 "You can't go to Kevin": *Australian Financial Review*, 26 September 2008, 52.

117 "I understand that there has been": press conference, 29 May 2008.

118 "Rudd is starting to resemble": *Sydney Morning Herald*, 29 September 2008, 11.

118 "84 per cent of us": *Australian*, 5 March 2008, 6.

119 "before Copenhagen": Essential Report, 7 December 2009.

121 "Fair shake of the sauce bottle, mate": uttered to David Speers, Sky News, 9 June 2009; explained to *Sunrise*, 12 June 2009.

122 "Kevin starts at around six in the morning": *Sydney Morning Herald*, News Review, 18 July 2009, 1.

122 "Prissy, precious prick": *Sydney Morning Herald*, 28 April 2007, 35.

125 "Knowing the dangers that lie ahead": "We Are All in This Together," address at Australia Day citizenship ceremony, Regatta Point, Canberra, 26 January 2009.

128 "His belief in what was good policy": *Australian*, 2 December 1999, 13.

128 Radio 2UE, 7 Dec 2007.

130 "audacious and historic": Gough Whitlam Lecture, University of Sydney, 11 September 2008.

130 "That trip took real political courage": Inaugural Tom Burns Memorial Lecture, Brisbane, 31 July 2008.

131 "… a new era of national reform": NSW Parliament House, 6 November 2008.

131 "Regimes around the world": "Australia and China in the World," 2010 Morrison Lecture, ANU, 23 April 2010.

132 "The planet cannot speak for itself": *Monthly*, October 2006, 28.

133 "There is no public-policy justification": *Age,* 20 December 2008, 21.

149 "God almighty": *Age,* 2 December 2009, p. 1.

150 "I accept at times": *Australian,* 2 December 2009, p. 7. See also p. 1 of the *Age* and p. 4 of the *Sydney Morning Herald* for that day.

151 "These usually": Tony Abbott, *Battlelines*, Melbourne University Press, Melbourne, 2009, p. 7.

152 *"Gallipoli"* etc: *Sunday Age,* 6 December 2009, p. 5.

152 "A Don Quixote": Peter Costello, *The Costello Memoirs,* Melbourne University Press, Melbourne, 2009, p. 55.

153 "We haven't warmed to him": Essential Vision, 14 January 2013, essentialvision.com.au/leader-attributes-%E2%80%93-tony-abbott-2.

153 "About 60 per cent of us have disapproved of his performance": Nielsen polls reported in the *Australian Financial Review,* 17 February 2013, p. 2.

154 "Something we have never been keen to do before: vote out an unpopular prime minister on behalf of an unpopular leader of the Opposition": often cited in rebuttal is Howard in 1996, but he was preferred prime minister and had net positive approval ratings.

156 "He was wild": *Sydney Morning Herald,* Spectrum, 11 March 2000, p. 1.

157 "Most students will be interested": *Democrat,* 22 March 1976.

158 "His mother and I knew pretty early on": *Australian,* 21 August 2010, p. 10.

158 "Even in those days": Channel Nine, *Sunday,* 15 July 2001.

159 "Sir John, this must be frightfully boring": there are many versions of this story. According to Lenore Taylor in the *Australian Financial Review,* 30 April 2004, p. 28, Abbott was suggesting a Labor rally but Abbott in *Battlelines,* p. 8, says it was a Liberal rally.

159 "Fantastic!": *Sydney Morning Herald,* 4 November 1995, p. 26.

160 "I first met him": Channel Nine, *Sunday,* 15 July 2001.

160 "the most important male influence": *Australian,* 2 December 2009, p. 13.

161 "Some instinct whispered": *Age,* 30 January 2007, p. 13.

161 "It was a thrill": *Battlelines,* p. 11.

161 "I have been under the Santamaria spell": *Age,* 30 January 2007, p. 13.

161 "The greatest living Australian": *Hansard,* 3 March 1998, p. 248.

162 "A philosophical star": *Hansard,* 3 March 1998, p. 248.

163 "His real role": *Daily Telegraph,* 26 February 1998, p. 4.

164 "This organisation has a long history": *Honi Soit,* 28 February 1977, p. 4.

164 "As an infrequently practising": *University of Sydney News,* "Election of Student Fellows of Senate," 1976, p. 184.

164 "He came down to the SRC": *Honi Soit,* 28 February 1977, p. 4.

164 "Tony was a warm": Bullock to me.

165 "It was as necessary to break": Patrick Morgan (ed.), *B.A. Santamaria: Running the Show: Selected Documents 1939–1999,* Miegunyah Press, Melbourne, 2008, pp. 373–4.

166 "The present crop": B.A. Santamaria, *Santamaria: A Memoir,* Oxford University Press, Melbourne, 1997, p. 266.

168 "I ACCUSE": *Weekend Australian,* 29 January 1977, p. 21.

169 "She was infatuated": *Bulletin*, 1 March 2005, p. 23.

170 "I loved uni": *Sydney Morning Herald,* Good Weekend, 14 April 2006, p. 22.

171 "I decided" and "I just wasn't ready": *Bulletin*, 1 March 2005, p. 24.

172 "When AUS champions": *Democrat*, 12 May 1977.

173 "Suddenly a flying squad": to me, 20 February 2013. This distinguished academic who wishes to remain anonymous first contacted the *Sydney Morning Herald's* Mark Coultan whose report appeared online, 13 September 2012, www.smh.com.au/opinion/political-news/abbotts-goon-squad-threw-me-against-a-wall-20120913-25ty2.html.

174 "But no": Ramjan to me.

175 "Ramjan found": *Sydney Morning Herald,* 13 September 2012, p. 13.

176 "Comments like": *Honi Soit*, 13 September 1977, p. 2.

176 "I really don't": *Honi Soit*, 27 September 1977, p. 3.

176 "Why don't you smile" and "I jumped back": *Daily Telegraph*, 12 January 1978, p. 4.

176 "She was speaking": *Daily Telegraph,* 13 January 1978, p. 5.

177 "At times it was": *Bulletin*, 4–5 June 1994, p. 10.

178 "The leading light": 7 February 1978, p. 19.

179 "unprovoked and unnecessary": SRC minutes, 27 June 1978.

180 "Tony settled on a plan": *The Costello Memoirs*, pp. 54–5.

182 "senseless, futile and provocative": *Cue*, 3 October 1978, authorised by Jeremy Jones and Paul Brereton.

182 "newly elected president": *Sydney Morning Herald,* 22 September 1978, p. 1.

183 "Luckily, it is lunchtime": *Honi Soit,* 9 April 1979, p. 6.

183 "This is a man's room": *Honi Soit,* 23 July 1979, p. 3.

183 "Marxists realised": *Nationwide*, 20 March 1979, www.youtube.com/watch?v=-CbRpxd3_EH0&feature=player_embedded.

184 "Flames were shooting": *Sydney Morning Herald,* 11 March 2000, Spectrum, p. 1.

185 "All physical objects": *Honi Soit,* 5 March 1979, p. 4.

185 "Tony and I": *Australian,* 24 October 1998, p. 9.

185 "The main point": *Australian,* Media Section, 11 January 2001, p. 6.

186 "The SRC is unnecessary": SRC minutes, 30 May 1978.

186 "the Active Defence": letter of 29 October 1979, reproduced in University of Sydney Senate Minutes, 5 November 1975, pp. 957–8.

187 "Otherwise high-handed": *University of Sydney News,* 2 October 1979, p. 136.

188 "moral force of character": from the terms of Rhodes's will, www.rhodeshouse.ox.ac.uk/page/about.

188 "Second-grade footballer": source to me.

188 "extreme causes": *Sydney Morning Herald,* 22 November 1980, p. 4.

190 "The thing about boxing": *Grandstand,* ABC Radio National, 22 June 2012, partly republished in the *Sun Herald,* 24 June 2012, p. 12.

190 "Within a couple": *Battlelines,* p. 14.

190 "not just": Quarterly Essay 48, *After the Future,* Correspondence, p. 82.

191 "He waded in": Nicholas Stafford-Deitsch in the *Sydney Morning Herald,* 14 August 2010, p. 54.

191 "I loved the rugby": ABC Radio National, 22 June 2012.

191 "Mr Abbott needs to temper": a favourite quote of Abbott's perhaps given first to Paul Kelly, *Australian,* magazine, 18 December 2003, p. 18.

191 "a few of us": Quarterly Essay 48, pp. 82–3.

195 "The RSPCA is one of Australia's": www.liberal.org.au/Latest-News/2012/-06/-26/Tony-Abbott-doorstop-interview.aspx.

196 "I can tell": *Sydney Morning Herald*, 27 June 2012, p. 6.

197 "But I found it difficult": *Bulletin*, 18 August 1987, p. 62.

197 "Meeting Mankowski": *Battlelines*, pp. 14–5.

198 "He wanted to be": ABC *Four Corners*, "The Authentic Mr Abbott," 19 March 2010.

198 "We were all just horrified" and "It's what he's": *Sydney Morning Herald*, Good Weekend, 14 April 2006, p. 22.

198 "He wasn't so much a big fish": *Courier Mail*, 5 April 1997, p. 24.

199 "He didn't strike me as starkly changed": San Miguel to me, 15 February 2013.

199 "As time went by": *Australian*, 13 June 1984, p. 11.

200 "Tony wasn't one": Debien to me.

201 "St Patrick's is a microcosm": *Sydney Morning Herald*, 26 September 1985, p. 64.

202 "Three years' grinding": *Bulletin*, 18 August 1987, p. 58.

202 "serving a local": *Australian*, Magazine, 13 December 2003, p. 18.

203 "Things would be different": *Australian*, 13–14 October 2012, pp. 1–2. Abbott's letter dated 21 April 1987 is among the Santamaria papers in the Victorian State Library.

204 "Very intelligent": ABC *Four Corners*, "The Authentic Mr Abbott," 19 March 2010.

204 "He would make": Kennedy to me.

205 "chatted about": Michael Duffy, *Latham and Abbott*, Random House Australia, Sydney, 2004, p. 79.

205 "He wanted" and all the passages that immediately follow: *Australian*, 13–14 October 2012, pp. 1–2.

208 "philosophical star": *Hansard*, 3 March 1998, p. 248.

208 "prominent member": *Battlelines*, p. 17.

208 "found the Liberals more attractive": Duffy, *Latham and Abbott*, p. 82.

209 "Diversity of opinion" and "I spoke off the cuff": Hewson to me, 19 February 2013.

209 "He had called": *News Weekly,* 20 December 2008, p. 13.

210 "In twenty-five years": *Sydney Morning Herald,* 15 June 1991, p. 21.

211 "who keeps very": *Sydney Morning Herald,* 16 August 1990, p. 26.

211 "In any street": *Age,* 9 September 1992, p. 15.

212 "He was one of the most": ABC *Four Corners,* "The Authentic Mr Abbott," 19 March 2010.

212 "political and communications": *Australian Financial Review,* 11 February 1992, p. 5.

212 "While I always": *Australian Financial Review,* 4 December 2009, p. 62.

212 "How can you sacrifice," "If you don't," "The art of effective" and "Unless you're in": *News Weekly,* 20 December 2008, pp. 12–14.

216 "We have always believed": *Hansard,* 27 June 2012, p. 8222.

216 "This matter turns": *Hansard,* 27 June 2012, p. 8232.

216 "We did try hard today": www.tonyabbott.com.au/LatestNews/ InterviewTranscripts/tabid/85/articleType/ArticleView/arti-cleId/8771/Joint-Press-Conference-Parliament-House-Canberra. aspx.

217 "key Liberal party strategist": *Sydney Morning Herald,* 18 December 2010, p. 6.

219 "He put it on the table": *Sydney Morning Herald,* News Review, 19 February 2011, p. 9.

219 "It works incredibly": *Courier Mail,* 24 February 2011, p. 32.

219 Essential poll, 9 July 2012, asked: "Do you think the current debate over handling of asylum seekers shows that Australian politicians are genuinely concerned about the welfare of asylum seekers or are they just playing politics over the issue?" To which 78 per cent replied "playing politics." The 20 August 2012 polls were titled, "Approval of Recommendations on Asylum Seekers" and "Effectiveness of Recommendations." All can be found at essentialvision.com.au/essential-research.

221 "This very possessed" and "We never looked back": Waddy to me.

222 "incorrigible Anglophile": *Battlelines,* p. 7.

224 "when you haven't got the numbers, be vicious": this is not a quotation but a comment. Is that clear, Gerard? It is my analysis. I am the source.

224 "There is no reason" and "The issue is": *Australian,* 31 May 1990, p. 8.

225 "I had been altogether": *Australian,* Magazine, 13 December 2003, p. 18.

227 "a very good": *Sydney Morning Herald,* 19 February 1994, p. 3.

228 "reclaiming our political": *Battlelines,* p. 20.

228 "who sparked my interest," "the contemporary politician" and "May God": *Hansard,* 31 May 1994, p. 1080.

228 "junkyard dog": *Sydney Morning Herald,* 28 March 1994, p. 4.

229 "political horsepower": *Australian,* Magazine, 13 December 2003, p. 18.

229 "Abbott's concerns": Channel Nine, *Sunday,* 15 July 2001. This allegation was also put by Richard Flanagan and denied by Abbott in the *Age,* 31 March 2001, p. 5.

230 "Tony copped a lot": *Sydney Morning Herald,* 11 March 2000, Spectrum, p. 1.

230 "He's a dangerous": *Sydney Morning Herald,* 17 June 1998, p. 12.

230 "My view was" and "So there was never": *Sydney Morning Herald,* News Review, 30 August 2003, p. 30.

232 "Misleading the ABC": *Sydney Morning Herald,* Spectrum, 11 March 2000, p. 1.

232 "Abbott and Costello": Bob Ellis, *Goodbye Jerusalem: Night Thoughts of a Labor Outsider,* first printing, Random House, Sydney, pp. 472–3.

233 "weak and unreliable": statement of claim quoted in the *Age,* 24 October 1998, p. 1.

233 "Under modern adoption": *Courier Mail,* 5 April 1997, p. 24.

235 "What will you say": www.tonyabbott.com.au/News/tabid/94/ articleType/ArticleView/articleId/8780/Interview-with-David-Speers-Sky-News.aspx.

236 Abbott a coward: *Australian*, 9 July 2012, p. 7.

236 "What you've got": ABC *Four Corners*, "The Authentic Mr Abbott," 19 March 2010.

237 "It's going to be": *Sydney Morning Herald*, 5 June 2012, p. 1.

237 "It will make every job" etc: from various interviews on 1 to 4 July to be found at www.tonyabbott.com.au/LatestNews.aspx.

238 "This is an important local manufacturer": www.tonyabbott.com. au/News/tabid/94/articleType/ArticleView/articleId/8796/Joint-Doorstop-Interview-Central-Coast-New-South-Wales.aspx.

238 Polls: *Sydney Morning Herald*, 30 July 2012, p. 1.

238 "Party polling": *Australian Financial Review*, 16 July 2012, p. 11.

240 "My department": source to me.

241 "On my first day": *Battlelines*, p. 47.

244 "It takes considerable": *Sydney Morning Herald*, 31 December 1999, p. 11.

245 "perilously close": *Sunday Herald Sun*, 10 September 2000, p. 16.

245 "Organisations should not": *Australian*, 15 September 2000, p. 33.

246 "It's okay": Michael Kirby, *A Private Life: Fragments, Memories, Friends*, Allen & Unwin, Sydney, 2011, p. 110.

247 "Tony Abbott wrote": *Michael Kirby, Paradoxes and Principles*. Federation Press, Sydney, 2011, p. 317.

247 "a bit threatened": Channel Nine, *60 Minutes*, 5 March 2010.

247 "challenges orthodox": ABC *Lateline*, 8 March 2010.

247 "intrinsic moral evil": *On the Pastoral Care of Homosexual Persons*, letter to the Congregation for the Doctrine of the Faith, paragraph 3.

248 "ethnic cleansing": *Sydney Morning Herald*, 2 September 1999, p. 7.

248 "telling whoppers": *Age*, 20 October 1999, p. 19.

248 "proxy war": *Australian Financial Review*, 18 January 1999, p. 2.

249 "Clearly explain how": *Sydney Morning Herald*, 16 October 1999, p. 1.

250 "We can't stop": *Sydney Morning Herald*, 10 July 2001, p. 3, quoting ABC *Four Corners*.

251 "This idea that" and "Every Australian needs": *Australian*, Magazine, 13 December 2003, p. 18.

252 "instrument for giving": *Hansard*, 31 May 1994, p. 1080.

252 "You know what": ABC *Lateline*, 14 July 2011.

253 Western civilisation.

"an essential part": *Age*, Opinion, 14 June 2001, p. 17.

"scientific and cultural": address to CIS Consilium "The West and its Challenges," 8 August 2003.

"We don't support": *Australian*, Opinion, 4 August 2003, p. 9.

"the oldest continuing": *Age*, Opinion, 20 October 1999, p. 19.

"to uphold universal": *Battlelines*, p. 158.

"the whole edifice" and "the presumption of": *Australian*, Magazine, 14 June 2008, p. 14.

"fundamental to": *Hansard*, 21 August 2002, p. 5303.

"The question haunting": *Australian*, Magazine, 14 June 2008, p. 14.

255 "He showed a great": Coonan to me.

255 "Ian Hickie": *Sydney Morning Herald*, News Review, 7 August 2010, p. 1.

257 "a perfectly good" and "Power divided": speech to the Young Liberals' National Conference reported in the *Australian*, 25 January 2005, p. 13.

257 "Eventually he was" and "He wasn't ruthless": source to me.

258 "If we hadn't": Peter Hartcher, *To the Bitter End*, Allen & Unwin, Sydney, 2009, p. 52.

259 "The problem with": from "The Ethical Responsibilities of a Christian Politician," 16 March 2004, www.tonyabbott.com.au/

latestnews/speeches/tabid/88/articletype/articleview/articleid/3550/the-ethical-responsibilities-of-a-christian-politician.aspx.

260 "He's just too right-wing": *Courier Mail*, 20 March 2004, p. 37.

262 "Margie and my daughters": *Bulletin*, 1 March 2005, p. 21.

262 "I'm sorry that poor": *Age*, 22 March 2005, p. 1.

262 "Right at the end": Coonan to me.

263 "Never one to be": *The Costello Memoirs*, p. 55.

264 "You have given": *Daily Telegraph*, 22 August 2005, p. 2.

265 "A catastrophic political": *Battlelines*, pp. 25–6.

265 "It was always": *To the Bitter End*, p. 81.

266 "There is no one Catholic": *Australian*, 21 August 1998, p. 1.

266 "moral snobbery" and "Finding fault": *Australian*, 23 April 1998, p. 13.

267 "A political argument": *Age*, 12 October 2007, p. 9.

269 "Political leadership": *Battlelines*, pp. 42–3.

270 "We were in parallel universes": *The Costello Memoirs*, p. 251.

270 "Abbott thought": *The Costello Memoirs*, p. 250.

270 "From the very beginning": ABC *Four Corners*, "The Authentic Mr Abbott," 19 March 2010.

270 "You can't even get here": ABC *Lateline*, 31 October 2007.

271 "Look, it was a stunt": *Sydney Morning Herald*, 31 October 2007.

271 "the very best of good": *Australian*, 26 November 2007, p. 12.

274 "You will see them" and "I often talk" and "you are people": Address to the Western Sydney Seats Launch and the Carbon Tax Rally, Parramatta, Sydney, 8 July 2012, www.tonyabbott.com.au/LatestNews/Speeches/tabid/88/article Type/ArticleView/articleId/8803/Address-to-the-Western-Sydney-Seats-Launch-and-the-Carbon-Tax-Rally-Parramatta-Sydney.aspx.

276 "Only the most" and "a type of marriage": *Battlelines*, p. 177.

277 "Sometimes it is better": *Australian Financial Review*, 10 March 2010, p. 9.

278 "middle-income families": *Hansard,* 31 May 1994, p. 1080.

280 "Don't you think": Radio 2GB, 2 November 2009.

281 "It's a plausible": *Australian,* 24 July 2009, p. 12.

281 "absolute crap": *Pyrenees Advocate,* 2 October 2009, p. 5.

282 "his constant changes": Lenore Taylor & David Uren, *Shitstorm: Inside Labor's Darkest Days,* Melbourne University Press, p. 190.

283 "this constant message": "The Ethical Responsibilities of a Christian Politician," 16 March 2004, www.tonyabbott.com.au/latest-news/speeches/tabid/88/articletype/articleview/articleid/3550/the-ethical-responsibilities-of-a-christian-politician.aspx.

283 "This will be the making of him": ABC *7.30 Report,* 6 December 2007.

285 "a fundamental crisis": *Australian,* 7 February 2009, p. 23.

285 "the national government": *Australian,* 12 November 2008, p. 14.

285 "meek, shy": *Australian,* Magazine, 14 June 2008, p. 14. Abbott was quoting an unnamed writer in the *New York Times.*

286 "I was none": *Australian,* Magazine, 20 March 2010, p. 14.

287 "The Labor Party": *Australian,* 27 June 2009, p. 5.

288 Polling for preferred Liberal leader: Nielsen poll, *Sydney Morning Herald,* 30 November 2009, p. 1. The figures were Hockey 36 per cent, Turnbull 32 per cent and Abbott 20 per cent.

290 "When Winston Churchill": *Battlelines,* p. 187.

291 "I'm not sure": *Australian,* Magazine, 20 March 2010, p. 14.

291 "I'm a Catholic": *Women's Weekly,* February 2010, p. 24.

292 "It would seem": Sir Robert Menzies, *The Measure of the Years,* Coronet Books, London, 1970, p. 22.

292 "Like the Republicans": *Sunday Age,* 28 March 2010, p. 19.

293 "Queen of no" and *"force majeure"*: *Australian,* Magazine, 5 November 2011, p. 12.

293 "Tony has altered": ABC *Four Corners,* "The Authentic Mr Abbott," 15 March 2010.

295 "Kerry, I know politicians": *Herald Sun,* 18 May 2010, p. 2.

296 "You have achieved": *Sunday Age,* 27 June 2010, p. 4.

297 "But Tony Abbott is": Windsor to me.

298 "I do not see": *Age,* 24 March 2011, p. 1.

299 "She may not": *Sydney Morning Herald,* 23 March 2011, p. 4.

299 "Abbott personally": *Sydney Morning Herald,* 26 November 2011, p. 9.

303 "The mass": *Bulletin,* 18 August 1987, p. 59.

303 "culture wars" and "Monks are": Mankowski to the Confraternity of Catholic Clergy, 15 July 2003, www.freerepublic.com/focus/f-religion/1107388/posts.

305 "a blistering array": *Sydney Morning Herald,* 3 November 2001, p. 81.

305 "Abbo never saw": *Sun Herald,* Sport, 22 August 2010, p. 6.

306 "If I didn't": *Sun Herald,* 5 December 2010, p. 30.

306 "Few Australians" and other references to the 18 July 2012 address to the Heritage Foundation: www.tonyabbott.com.au/LatestNews/Speeches/tabid/88/ articleType/ArticleView/articleId/8816/Address-to-the-Heritage-Foundation-Washington-DC.aspx.

308 "Along with": *Spectator Australia,* 28 July 2012, p. ix.

308 "an early sign" and other references to the 24 July 2012 address to the Australian Chamber of Commerce, Beijing: www.tonyabbott.com.au/LatestNews/Speeches/ tabid/88/articleType/ArticleView/articleId/8818/Address-to-AustCham-Beijing-China.aspx.

310 "The beauty of being": *Sydney Morning Herald,* News Review, 10 April 2010, p. 1.

311 "If you have": *News Weekly,* 20 December 2008, p. 13.

312 "There is a crude": Quarterly Essay 48, *After the Future,* pp. 87–8.

312 "For what does it profit a man": Luke 9:25.

313 "real cow": *Sydney Morning Herald,* 29 August 2012, p. 5.

313 "misogynists and the nut jobs": *Canberra Times,* 24 August 2012, p. 1.

313 "The Prime Minister": *Sydney Morning Herald,* 1 September 2012, p. 11.

314 "destroying the joint": *Herald Sun,* 1 September 2012, p. 20.

314 "It never happened": *Sydney Morning Herald,* 8 September 2012, p. 5.

315 "the uncorroborated testimony": *Sydney Morning Herald,* 11 September 2012, p. 11.

315 "There is no doubt": Channel Nine, *Today,* 14 September 2012, www.liberal.org.au/latest-news/2012/09/14/tony-abbott-inter-view-karl-stefanovic-today-show-nine-network.

316 "Mr Abbott, are you suggesting": www.liberal.org.au/latest-news/2012/09/14/tony-abbott-doorstop-interview-canberra.

317 "Liberal powerbroker Michael Kroger": *Australian,* 24 September 2012, p. 1.

317 "an ex-communist who is now a nobody": transcript supplied to me.

318 "Now, on this program": transcript supplied to me.

318 "The old man recently": *Sunday Telegraph,* 30 September 2012, p. 5.

319 "wrong, unacceptable" and "I am not": www.tonyabbott.com.au/LatestNews/InterviewTranscripts/tabid/85/articleType/Article-View/articleId/8904/Doorstop-Interview-Raymond-Terrace.aspx.

320 "another day of shame": *Hansard,* 9 October 2012, p. 11577.

320 "I say to the Leader of the Opposition": *Hansard,* 9 October 2012, p. 11581.

320 Nielsen poll, late October 2012: *Age,* 22 October 2012, p. 1.

322 "certainly not in favour": *Age,* 9 June 2007, p. 11.

322 "I have never opposed IVF": *Sunday Telegraph,* 6 January 2013, p. 85.

322 "Twenty-one-year-olds" and "I think there are lots of people": Ipsos Australia, *Mind & Mood Mini Report: Who inspires 21-year-olds today?* p. 10.

324 "He prefers to avoid": www.crikey.com.au/2013/02/13/myth-busting-on-abbott-and-the-media-but-who-asked-the-questions/?wpmp_switcher=mobile&comments=50.

325 "left-of-centre ethos": *Australian Financial Review*, 21 December 2012, p. 7.

325 "I think everyone": 14 November 2012, www.liberal.org.au/latest-news/2012/11/14/tony-abbott-transcript-joint-doorstop-interview-peter-dutton-brisbane.

326 "This election will be about trust": *Sydney Morning Herald*, 30 January 2013, p. 1.

326 "The point I keep making": *Courier-Mail*, 16 August 2012, p. 9.

326 "*Battlelines* was my attempt": Slow TV, www.themonthly.com.au/battlelines-tony-abbott-talks-annabel-crabb-p2-2519.

328 John Howard's polling figures, 1996: Herald–AGB McNair polls, *Sydney Morning Herald*, 29 January 1996, p. 2; 12 February, p. 7; 19 February p. 1 and 26 February p. 1.

328 "The message from Abbott": *Australian Financial Review* Magazine, 28 September 2012, p. 40.

330 "You will find": *News Weekly*, 20 December 2008, p. 13.